SPIRITUAL SONNETS

THE OTHER VOICE IN EARLY MODERN EUROPE

A Series Edited by Margaret L. King and Albert Rabil Jr.

RECENT BOOKS IN THE SERIES

Gabrielle de Coignard

SPIRITUAL SONNETS

A Bilingual Edition

ॐ

Edited and Translated
by
Melanie E. Gregg

THE UNIVERSITY OF CHICAGO PRESS
Chicago & London

Gabrielle de Coignard, ca. 1550 − 86

Melanie E. Gregg is assistant professor of French at Wilson College.

The University of Chicago Press, Chicago 60637
The University of Chicago Press, Ltd., London
© 2004 by The University of Chicago
All rights reserved. Published 2004
Printed in the United States of America
13 12 11 10 09 08 07 06 05 04   1 2 3 4 5

ISBN: 0-226-13983-2 (cloth)
ISBN: 0-226-13984-0 (paper)

Library of Congress Cataloging-in-Publication Data

Coignard, Gabrielle de, d. 1586.
  [Sonnets spirituels. English & French]
  Spiritual sonnets : a bilingual edition / Gabrielle de Coignard ; translated and edited
by Melanie E. Gregg. — 1st ed.
      p. cm. — (The other voice in early modern Europe)
Includes bibliographical references and index.
  ISBN 0-226-13983-2 (cloth : alk. paper) — ISBN 0-226-13984-0 (pbk. : alk. paper)
  I. Gregg, Melanie E.   II. Title.   III. Series.
PQ1607.C56A7613 2004
841'.3—dc22

                                                                              2003012759

To Colette H. Winn

CONTENTS

ACKNOWLEDGMENTS

I would like to express my gratitude to those who have helped me bring this project to completion. First, I am greatly indebted to Sandra G. Connolly for her tireless labor and assistance with the Biblical references included in the notes to this translation. I thank her, too, for the time she so willingly devoted to reading (and rereading) my translation and introduction. Her critique and suggestions were crucial to my revisions for the final draft. I would also like to thank Sylvia S. Johnson for her diligent and thorough reading of both the introduction and the translation. I am grateful in particular for her sensitive ear: several of her recommendations served to improve the quality and flow of the verse in translation. Melinda W. Schlitt's assistance with this project has also been invaluable. Her critical reading of the introduction and the translation, as well as our numerous discussions about possible renderings in English of the more convoluted lines of the original, facilitated and vastly improved the final draft. I thank her, above all, for her untiring support, encouragement, and availability throughout the entire process of this project. The comments, questions, and suggestions I received from my anonymous reader were most helpful to the final revisions of the manuscript and sparked some ideas for future projects as well. Finally, I would like to thank Albert Rabil and Margaret King for including my translation in their series. It has been a privilege to work with such a fine team. I am particularly grateful to Albert Rabil for his kind and generous guidance throughout the various stages of this project.

Melanie E. Gregg

THE OTHER VOICE IN
EARLY MODERN EUROPE:
INTRODUCTION TO THE SERIES

Margaret L. King and Albert Rabil Jr.

THE OLD VOICE AND THE OTHER VOICE

In western Europe and the United States, women are nearing equality in the professions, in business, and in politics. Most enjoy access to education, reproductive rights, and autonomy in financial affairs. Issues vital to women are on the public agenda: equal pay, child care, domestic abuse, breast cancer research, and curricular revision with an eye to the inclusion of women.

These recent achievements have their origins in things women (and some male supporters) said for the first time about six hundred years ago. Theirs is the "other voice," in contradistinction to the "first voice," the voice of the educated men who created Western culture. Coincident with a general reshaping of European culture in the period 1300–1700 (called the Renaissance or early modern period), questions of female equality and opportunity were raised that still resound and are still unresolved.

The other voice emerged against the backdrop of a three thousand—year history of the derogation of women rooted in the civilizations related to Western culture: Hebrew, Greek, Roman, and Christian. Negative attitudes toward women inherited from these traditions pervaded the intellectual, medical, legal, religious, and social systems that developed during the European Middle Ages.

The following pages describe the traditional, overwhelmingly male views of women's nature inherited by early modern Europeans and the new tradition that the "other voice" called into being to begin to challenge reigning assumptions. This review should serve as a framework for understanding the texts published in the series "The Other Voice in Early Modern Europe." Introductions specific to each text and author follow this essay in all the volumes of the series.

TRADITIONAL VIEWS OF WOMEN, 500 B.C.E.–1500 C.E.

Embedded in the philosophical and medical theories of the ancient Greeks were perceptions of the female as inferior to the male in both mind and body. Similarly, the structure of civil legislation inherited from the ancient Romans was biased against women, and the views on women developed by Christian thinkers out of the Hebrew Bible and the Christian New Testament were negative and disabling. Literary works composed in the vernacular of ordinary people, and widely recited or read, conveyed these negative assumptions. The social networks within which most women lived—those of the family and the institutions of the Roman Catholic Church—were shaped by this negative tradition and sharply limited the areas in which women might act in and upon the world.

GREEK PHILOSOPHY AND FEMALE NATURE. Greek biology assumed that women were inferior to men and defined them as merely child bearers and housekeepers. This view was authoritatively expressed in the works of the philosopher Aristotle.

Aristotle thought in dualities. He considered action superior to inaction, form (the inner design or structure of any object) superior to matter, completion to incompletion, possession to deprivation. In each of these dualities, he associated the male principle with the superior quality and the female with the inferior. "The male principle in nature," he argued, "is associated with active, formative and perfected characteristics, while the female is passive, material and deprived, desiring the male in order to become complete."[1] Men are always identified with virile qualities, such as judgment, courage, and stamina, and women with their opposites—irrationality, cowardice, and weakness.

The masculine principle was considered superior even in the womb. The man's semen, Aristotle believed, created the form of a new human creature, while the female body contributed only matter. (The existence of the ovum, and with it the other facts of human embryology, was not established until the seventeenth century.) Although the later Greek physician Galen believed there was a female component in generation, contributed by "female semen," the followers of both Aristotle and Galen saw the male role in human generation as more active and more important.

In the Aristotelian view, the male principle sought always to reproduce itself. The creation of a female was always a mistake, therefore, resulting

---

1. Aristotle, *Physics* 1.9.192a20–24, in *The Complete Works of Aristotle,* ed. Jonathan Barnes, rev. Oxford trans., 2 vols. (Princeton, 1984), 1:328.

from an imperfect act of generation. Every female born was considered a "defective" or "mutilated" male (as Aristotle's terminology has variously been translated), a "monstrosity" of nature.[2]

For Greek theorists, the biology of males and females was the key to their psychology. The female was softer and more docile, more apt to be despondent, querulous, and deceitful. Being incomplete, moreover, she craved sexual fulfillment in intercourse with a male. The male was intellectual, active, and in control of his passions.

These psychological polarities derived from the theory that the universe consisted of four elements (earth, fire, air, and water), expressed in human bodies as four "humors" (black bile, yellow bile, blood, and phlegm) considered, respectively, dry, hot, damp, and cold and corresponding to mental states ("melancholic," "choleric," "sanguine," "phlegmatic"). In this scheme the male, sharing the principles of earth and fire, was dry and hot; the female, sharing the principles of air and water, was cold and damp.

Female psychology was further affected by her dominant organ, the uterus (womb), *hystera* in Greek. The passions generated by the womb made women lustful, deceitful, talkative, irrational, indeed—when these affects were in excess—"hysterical."

Aristotle's biology also had social and political consequences. If the male principle was superior and the female inferior, then in the household, as in the state, men should rule and women must be subordinate. That hierarchy did not rule out the companionship of husband and wife, whose cooperation was necessary for the welfare of children and the preservation of property. Such mutuality supported male preeminence.

Aristotle's teacher Plato suggested a different possibility: that men and women might possess the same virtues. The setting for this proposal is the imaginary and ideal Republic that Plato sketches in a dialogue of that name. Here, for a privileged elite capable of leading wisely, all distinctions of class and wealth dissolve, as, consequently, do those of gender. Without households or property, as Plato constructs his ideal society, there is no need for the subordination of women. Women may therefore be educated to the same level as men to assume leadership. Plato's Republic remained imaginary, however. In real societies, the subordination of women remained the norm and the prescription.

The views of women inherited from the Greek philosophical tradition became the basis for medieval thought. In the thirteenth century, the supreme Scholastic philosopher Thomas Aquinas, among others, still echoed

---

2. Aristotle, *Generation of Animals* 2.3.737a27–28, in *The Complete Works*, 1:1144.

Aristotle's views of human reproduction, of male and female personalities, and of the preeminent male role in the social hierarchy.

ROMAN LAW AND THE FEMALE CONDITION. Roman law, like Greek philosophy, underlay medieval thought and shaped medieval society. The ancient belief that adult property-owning men should administer households and make decisions affecting the community at large is the very fulcrum of Roman law.

About 450 B.C.E., during Rome's republican era, the community's customary law was recorded (legendarily) on twelve tablets erected in the city's central forum. It was later elaborated by professional jurists whose activity increased in the imperial era, when much new legislation was passed, especially on issues affecting family and inheritance. This growing, changing body of laws was eventually codified in the *Corpus of Civil Law* under the direction of the emperor Justinian, generations after the empire ceased to be ruled from Rome. That *Corpus*, read and commented on by medieval scholars from the eleventh century on, inspired the legal systems of most of the cities and kingdoms of Europe.

Laws regarding dowries, divorce, and inheritance pertain primarily to women. Since those laws aimed to maintain and preserve property, the women concerned were those from the property-owning minority. Their subordination to male family members points to the even greater subordination of lower-class and slave women, about whom the laws speak little.

In the early republic, the *paterfamilias*, or "father of the family," possessed *patria potestas*, "paternal power." The term *pater*, "father," in both these cases does not necessarily mean biological father but denotes the head of a household. The father was the person who owned the household's property and, indeed, its human members. The *paterfamilias* had absolute power—including the power, rarely exercised, of life or death—over his wife, his children, and his slaves, as much as over his cattle.

Male children could be "emancipated," an act that granted legal autonomy and the right to own property. Those over fourteen could be emancipated by a special grant from the father or automatically by their father's death. But females could never be emancipated; instead, they passed from the authority of their father to that of a husband or, if widowed or orphaned while still unmarried, to a guardian or tutor.

Marriage in its traditional form placed the woman under her husband's authority, or *manus*. He could divorce her on grounds of adultery, drinking wine, or stealing from the household, but she could not divorce him. She could neither possess property in her own right nor bequeath any to her children upon her death. When her husband died, the household property passed not to her but to his male heirs. And when her father died, she had no claim to any family inheritance, which was directed to her brothers or more remote male relatives. The effect of these laws was to exclude women from civil society, itself based on property ownership.

In the later republican and imperial periods, these rules were significantly modified. Women rarely married according to the traditional form. The practice of "free" marriage allowed a woman to remain under her father's authority, to possess property given her by her father (most frequently the "dowry," recoverable from the husband's household on his death), and to inherit from her father. She could also bequeath property to her own children and divorce her husband, just as he could divorce her.

Despite this greater freedom, women still suffered enormous disability under Roman law. Heirs could belong only to the father's side, never the mother's. Moreover, although she could bequeath her property to her children, she could not establish a line of succession in doing so. A woman was "the beginning and end of her own family," said the jurist Ulpian. Moreover, women could play no public role. They could not hold public office, represent anyone in a legal case, or even witness a will. Women had only a private existence and no public personality.

The dowry system, the guardian, women's limited ability to transmit wealth, and total political disability are all features of Roman law adopted by the medieval communities of western Europe, although modified according to local customary laws..

CHRISTIAN DOCTRINE AND WOMEN'S PLACE. The Hebrew Bible and the Christian New Testament authorized later writers to limit women to the realm of the family and to burden them with the guilt of original sin. The passages most fruitful for this purpose were the creation narratives in Genesis and sentences from the Epistles defining women's role within the Christian family and community.

Each of the first two chapters of Genesis contains a creation narrative. In the first "God created man in his own image, in the image of God he created him; male and female he created them" (Gn 1:27). In the second, God created Eve from Adam's rib (2:21–23). Christian theologians relied principally on Genesis 2 for their understanding of the relation between man and woman, interpreting the creation of Eve from Adam as proof of her subordination to him.

The creation story in Genesis 2 leads to that of the temptations in Genesis 3: of Eve by the wily serpent and of Adam by Eve. As read by Christian theologians from Tertullian to Thomas Aquinas, the narrative made Eve responsible for the Fall and its consequences. She instigated the act; she deceived her husband; she suffered the greater punishment. Her disobedience made it necessary for Jesus to be incarnated and to die on the cross. From the pulpit, moralists and preachers for centuries conveyed to women the guilt that they bore for original sin.

The Epistles offered advice to early Christians on building communities of the faithful. Among the matters to be regulated was the place of women. Paul offered views favorable to women in Galatians 3:28: "There is neither Jew nor Greek, there is neither slave nor free, there is neither male nor female; for you are all one in Christ Jesus." Paul also referred to women as his coworkers and placed them on a par with himself and his male coworkers (Phlm 4:2–3; Rom 16:1–3; 1 Cor 16:19). Elsewhere, Paul limited women's possibilities: "But I want you to understand that the head of every man is Christ, the head of a woman is her husband, and the head of Christ is God" (1 Cor 11:3).

Biblical passages by later writers (although attributed to Paul) enjoined women to forgo jewels, expensive clothes, and elaborate coiffures; and they forbade women to "teach or have authority over men," telling them to "learn in silence with all submissiveness" as is proper for one responsible for sin, consoling them, however, with the thought that they will be saved through childbearing (1 Tm 2:9–15). Other texts among the later Epistles defined women as the weaker sex and emphasized their subordination to their husbands (1 Pt 3:7; Col 3:18; Eph 5:22–23).

These passages from the New Testament became the arsenal employed by theologians of the early church to transmit negative attitudes toward women to medieval Christian culture—above all, Tertullian (*On the Apparel of Women*), Jerome (*Against Jovinian*), and Augustine (*The Literal Meaning of Genesis*).

THE IMAGE OF WOMEN IN MEDIEVAL LITERATURE. The philosophical, legal, and religious traditions born in antiquity formed the basis of the medieval intellectual synthesis wrought by trained thinkers, mostly clerics, writing in Latin and based largely in universities. The vernacular literary tradition that developed alongside the learned tradition also spoke about female nature and women's roles. Medieval stories, poems, and epics also portrayed women negatively—as lustful and deceitful—while praising good housekeepers and loyal wives as replicas of the Virgin Mary or the female saints and martyrs.

There is an exception in the movement of "courtly love" that evolved in southern France from the twelfth century. Courtly love was the erotic love between a nobleman and noblewoman, the latter usually superior in social rank. It was always adulterous. From the conventions of courtly love derive modern Western notions of romantic love. The tradition has had an impact disproportionate to its size, for it affected only a tiny elite, and very few women. The exaltation of the female lover probably does not reflect a higher evaluation of women or a step toward their sexual liberation. More likely it gives expression to the social and sexual tensions besetting the knightly class at a specific historical juncture.

The literary fashion of courtly love was on the wane by the thirteenth century, when the widely read *Romance of the Rose* was composed in French by two authors of significantly different dispositions. Guillaume de Lorris composed the initial four thousand verses about 1235, and Jean de Meun added about seventeen thousand verses—more than four times the original—about 1265.

The fragment composed by Guillaume de Lorris stands squarely in the tradition of courtly love. Here the poet, in a dream, is admitted into a walled garden where he finds a magic fountain in which a rosebush is reflected. He longs to pick one rose, but the thorns prevent his doing so, even as he is wounded by arrows from the god of love, whose commands he agrees to obey. The rest of this part of the poem recounts the poet's unsuccessful efforts to pluck the rose.

The longer part of the *Romance* by Jean de Meun also describes a dream. But here allegorical characters give long didactic speeches, providing a social satire on a variety of themes, some pertaining to women. Love is an anxious and tormented state, the poem explains: women are greedy and manipulative, marriage is miserable, beautiful women are lustful, ugly ones cease to please, and a chaste woman is as rare as a black swan.

Shortly after Jean de Meun completed *The Romance of the Rose*, Mathéolus penned his *Lamentations*, a long Latin diatribe against marriage translated into French about a century later. The *Lamentations* sum up medieval attitudes toward women and provoked the important response by Christine de Pizan in her *Book of the City of Ladies*.

In 1355, Giovanni Boccaccio wrote *Il Corbaccio*, another antifeminist manifesto, although ironically by an author whose other works pioneered new directions in Renaissance thought. The former husband of his lover appears to Boccaccio, condemning his unmoderated lust and detailing the defects of women. Boccaccio concedes at the end "how much men naturally surpass women in nobility" and is cured of his desires.[3]

---

3. Giovanni Boccaccio, *The Corbaccio, or The Labyrinth of Love*, trans. and ed. Anthony K. Cassell, rev. ed. (Binghamton, N.Y., 1993), 71.

WOMEN'S ROLES: THE FAMILY. The negative perceptions of women expressed in the intellectual tradition are also implicit in the actual roles that women played in European society. Assigned to subordinate positions in the household and the church, they were barred from significant participation in public life.

Medieval European households, like those in antiquity and in non-Western civilizations, were headed by males. It was the male serf (or peasant), feudal lord, town merchant, or citizen who was polled or taxed or succeeded to an inheritance or had any acknowledged public role, although his wife or widow could stand as a temporary surrogate. From about 1100, the position of property-holding males was further enhanced: inheritance was confined to the male, or agnate, line—with depressing consequences for women.

A wife never fully belonged to her husband's family, nor was she a daughter to her father's family. She left her father's house young to marry whomever her parents chose. Her dowry was managed by her husband, and at her death it normally passed to her children by him.

A married woman's life was occupied nearly constantly with cycles of pregnancy, childbearing, and lactation. Women bore children through all the years of their fertility, and many died in childbirth. They were also responsible for raising young children up to six or seven. In the propertied classes that responsibility was shared, since it was common for a wet nurse to take over breast-feeding and for servants to perform other chores.

Women trained their daughters in the household duties appropriate to their status, nearly always tasks associated with textiles: spinning, weaving, sewing, embroidering. Their sons were sent out of the house as apprentices or students, or their training was assumed by fathers in later childhood and adolescence. On the death of her husband, a woman's children became the responsibility of his family. She generally did not take "his" children with her to a new marriage or back to her father's house, except sometimes in the artisan classes.

Women also worked. Rural peasants performed farm chores, merchant wives often practiced their husbands' trades, the unmarried daughters of the urban poor worked as servants or prostitutes. All wives produced or embellished textiles and did the housekeeping, while wealthy ones managed servants. These labors were unpaid or poorly paid but often contributed substantially to family wealth.

WOMEN'S ROLES: THE CHURCH. Membership in a household, whether a father's or a husband's, meant for women a lifelong subordination to others. In western Europe, the Roman Catholic Church offered an alternative to the career of wife and mother. A woman could enter a convent, parallel in function to the monasteries for men that evolved in the early Christian centuries.

In the convent, a woman pledged herself to a celibate life, lived according to strict community rules, and worshiped daily. Often the convent offered training in Latin, allowing some women to become considerable scholars and authors as well as scribes, artists, and musicians. For women who chose the conventual life, the benefits could be enormous, but for numerous others placed in convents by paternal choice, the life could be restrictive and burdensome.

The conventual life declined as an alternative for women as the modern age approached. Reformed monastic institutions resisted responsibility for related female orders. The church increasingly restricted female institutional life by insisting on closer male supervision.

Women often sought other options. Some joined the communities of laywomen that sprang up spontaneously in the thirteenth century in the urban zones of western Europe, especially in Flanders and Italy. Some joined the heretical movements that flourished in late medieval Christendom, whose anticlerical and often antifamily positions particularly appealed to women. In these communities, some women were acclaimed as "holy women" or "saints," whereas others often were condemned as frauds or heretics.

In all, although the options offered to women by the church were sometimes less than satisfactory, they were sometimes richly rewarding. After 1520, the convent remained an option only in Roman Catholic territories. Protestantism engendered an ideal of marriage as a heroic endeavor and appeared to place husband and wife on a more equal footing. Sermons and treatises, however, still called for female subordination and obedience.

THE OTHER VOICE, 1300–1700

When the modern era opened, European culture was so firmly structured by a framework of negative attitudes toward women that to dismantle it was a monumental labor. The process began as part of a larger cultural movement that entailed the critical reexamination of ideas inherited from the ancient and medieval past. The humanists launched that critical reexamination.

THE HUMANIST FOUNDATION. Originating in Italy in the fourteenth century, humanism quickly became the dominant intellectual movement in Europe. Spreading in the sixteenth century from Italy to the rest of Europe, it fueled the literary, scientific, and philosophical movements of the era and laid the basis for the eighteenth-century Enlightenment.

Series Editors' Introduction

Humanists regarded the Scholastic philosophy of medieval universities as out of touch with the realities of urban life. They found in the rhetorical discourse of classical Rome a language adapted to civic life and public speech. They learned to read, speak, and write classical Latin and, eventually, classical Greek. They founded schools to teach others to do so, establishing the pattern for elementary and secondary education for the next three hundred years.

In the service of complex government bureaucracies, humanists employed their skills to write eloquent letters, deliver public orations, and formulate public policy. They developed new scripts for copying manuscripts and used the new printing press to disseminate texts, for which they created methods of critical editing.

Humanism was a movement led by males who accepted the evaluation of women in ancient texts and generally shared the misogynist perceptions of their culture. (Female humanists, as we will see, did not.) Yet humanism also opened the door to a reevaluation of the nature and capacity of women. By calling authors, texts, and ideas into question, it made possible the fundamental rereading of the whole intellectual tradition that was required in order to free women from cultural prejudice and social subordination.

A DIFFERENT CITY. The other voice first appeared when, after so many centuries, the accumulation of misogynist concepts evoked a response from a capable female defender: Christine de Pizan (1365–1431). Introducing her *Book of the City of Ladies* (1405), she described how she was affected by reading Mathéolus's *Lamentations:* "Just the sight of this book . . . made me wonder how it happened that so many different men . . . are so inclined to express both in speaking and in their treatises and writings so many wicked insults about women and their behavior."[4] These statements impelled her to detest herself "and the entire feminine sex, as though we were monstrosities in nature."[5]

The rest of *The Book of the City of Ladies* presents a justification of the female sex and a vision of an ideal community of women. A pioneer, she has received the message of female inferiority and rejected it. From the fourteenth to the seventeenth century, a huge body of literature accumulated that responded to the dominant tradition.

The result was a literary explosion consisting of works by both men and women, in Latin and in the vernaculars: works enumerating the achievements of notable women; works rebutting the main accusations made against women;

---

4. Christine de Pizan, *The Book of the City of Ladies,* trans. Earl Jeffrey Richards, foreword by Marina Warner (New York, 1982), 1.1.1, pp. 3–4.
5. Ibid., 1.1.1–2, p. 5.

works arguing for the equal education of men and women; works defining and redefining women's proper role in the family, at court, in public; works describing women's lives and experiences. Recent monographs and articles have begun to hint at the great range of this movement, involving probably several thousand titles. The protofeminism of these "other voices" constitutes a significant fraction of the literary product of the early modern era.

THE CATALOGS. About 1365, the same Boccaccio whose *Corbaccio* rehearses the usual charges against female nature wrote another work, *Concerning Famous Women*. A humanist treatise drawing on classical texts, it praised 106 notable women: ninety-eight of them from pagan Greek and Roman antiquity, one (Eve) from the Bible, and seven from the medieval religious and cultural tradition; his book helped make all readers aware of a sex normally condemned or forgotten. Boccaccio's outlook nevertheless was unfriendly to women, for it singled out for praise those women who possessed the traditional virtues of chastity, silence, and obedience. Women who were active in the public realm—for example, rulers and warriors—were depicted as usually being lascivious and as suffering terrible punishments for entering the masculine sphere. Women were his subject, but Boccaccio's standard remained male.

Christine de Pizan's *Book of the City of Ladies* contains a second catalog, one responding specifically to Boccaccio's. Whereas Boccaccio portrays female virtue as exceptional, she depicts it as universal. Many women in history were leaders, or remained chaste despite the lascivious approaches of men, or were visionaries and brave martyrs.

The work of Boccaccio inspired a series of catalogs of illustrious women of the biblical, classical, Christian, and local pasts, among them Filippo da Bergamo's *Of Illustrious Women*, Pierre de Brantôme's *Lives of Illustrious Women*, Pierre Le Moyne's *Gallerie of Heroic Women*, and Pietro Paolo de Ribera's *Immortal Triumphs and Heroic Enterprises of 845 Women*. Whatever their embedded prejudices, these works drove home to the public the possibility of female excellence.

THE DEBATE. At the same time, many questions remained: Could a woman be virtuous? Could she perform noteworthy deeds? Was she even, strictly speaking, of the same human species as men? These questions were debated over four centuries, in French, German, Italian, Spanish, and English, by authors male and female, among Catholics, Protestants, and Jews, in ponderous volumes and breezy pamphlets. The whole literary genre has been called the *querelle des femmes*, the "woman question."

The opening volley of this battle occurred in the first years of the fifteenth century, in a literary debate sparked by Christine de Pizan. She exchanged letters critical of Jean de Meun's contribution to *The Romance of the Rose* with two French royal secretaries, Jean de Montreuil and Gontier Col. When the matter became public, Jean Gerson, one of Europe's leading theologians, supported de Pizan's arguments against de Meun, for the moment silencing the opposition.

The debate resurfaced repeatedly over the next two hundred years. *The Triumph of Women* (1438) by Juan Rodríguez de la Camara (or Juan Rodríguez del Padron) struck a new note by presenting arguments for the superiority of women to men. *The Champion of Women* (1440–42) by Martin Le Franc addresses once again the negative views of women presented in *The Romance of the Rose* and offers counterevidence of female virtue and achievement.

A cameo of the debate on women is included in *The Courtier,* one of the most widely read books of the era, published by the Italian Baldassare Castiglione in 1528 and immediately translated into other European vernaculars. *The Courtier* depicts a series of evenings at the court of the duke of Urbino in which many men and some women of the highest social stratum amuse themselves by discussing a range of literary and social issues. The "woman question" is a pervasive theme throughout, and the third of its four books is devoted entirely to that issue.

In a verbal duel, Gasparo Pallavicino and Giuliano de' Medici present the main claims of the two traditions. Gasparo argues the innate inferiority of women and their inclination to vice. Only in bearing children do they profit the world. Giuliano counters that women share the same spiritual and mental capacities as men and may excel in wisdom and action. Men and women are of the same essence: just as no stone can be more perfectly a stone than another, so no human being can be more perfectly human than others, whether male or female. It was an astonishing assertion, boldly made to an audience as large as all Europe.

THE TREATISES. Humanism provided the materials for a positive counterconcept to the misogyny embedded in Scholastic philosophy and law and inherited from the Greek, Roman, and Christian pasts. A series of humanist treatises on marriage and family, on education and deportment, and on the nature of women helped construct these new perspectives.

The works by Francesco Barbaro and Leon Battista Alberti—*On Marriage* (1415) and *On the Family* (1434–37)—far from defending female equality, reasserted women's responsibility for rearing children and managing the housekeeping while being obedient, chaste, and silent. Nevertheless, they served the cause of reexamining the issue of women's nature by placing domestic issues at the center of scholarly concern and reopening the pertinent classical texts. In addition, Barbaro emphasized the companionate nature of marriage and the importance of a wife's spiritual and mental qualities for the well-being of the family.

These themes reappear in later humanist works on marriage and the education of women by Juan Luis Vives and Erasmus. Both were moderately sympathetic to the condition of women without reaching beyond the usual masculine prescriptions for female behavior.

An outlook more favorable to women characterizes the nearly unknown work *In Praise of Women* (ca. 1487) by the Italian humanist Bartolommeo Goggio. In addition to providing a catalog of illustrious women, Goggio argued that male and female are the same in essence, but that women (reworking the Adam and Eve narrative from quite a new angle) are actually superior. In the same vein, the Italian humanist Maria Equicola asserted the spiritual equality of men and women in *On Women* (1501). In 1525, Galeazzo Flavio Capra (or Capella) published his work *On the Excellence and Dignity of Women*. This humanist tradition of treatises defending the worthiness of women culminates in the work of Henricus Cornelius Agrippa *On the Nobility and Preeminence of the Female Sex*. No work by a male humanist more succinctly or explicitly presents the case for female dignity.

THE WITCH BOOKS. While humanists grappled with the issues pertaining to women and family, other learned men turned their attention to what they perceived as a very great problem: witches. Witch-hunting manuals, explorations of the witch phenomenon, and even defenses of witches are not at first glance pertinent to the tradition of the other voice. But they do relate in this way: most accused witches were women. The hostility aroused by supposed witch activity is comparable to the hostility aroused by women. The evil deeds the victims of the hunt were charged with were exaggerations of the vices to which, many believed, all women were prone.

The connection between the witch accusation and the hatred of women is explicit in the notorious witch-hunting manual *The Hammer of Witches* (1486) by two Dominican inquisitors, Heinrich Krämer and Jacob Sprenger. Here the inconstancy, deceitfulness, and lustfulness traditionally associated with women are depicted in exaggerated form as the core features of witch behavior. These traits inclined women to make a bargain with the devil—sealed by sexual intercourse—by which they acquired unholy powers. Such bizarre claims, far from being rejected by rational men, were broadcast by intellectuals. The German Ulrich Molitur, the Frenchman Nicolas Rémy, and the Italian Stefano Guazzo all coolly informed the public of sinister orgies and midnight pacts with the devil. The celebrated French jurist, historian, and political philosopher Jean Bodin argued that because women were especially prone to diabolism, regular legal procedures could properly be suspended in order to try those accused of this "exceptional crime."

A few experts such as the physician Johann Weyer, a student of Agrippa's, raised their voices in protest. In 1563, he explained the witch phenomenon thus, without discarding belief in diabolism: the devil deluded foolish old women afflicted by melancholia, causing them to believe they had magical powers. Weyer's rational skepticism, which had good credibility in the community of the learned, worked to revise the conventional views of women and witchcraft.

WOMEN'S WORKS. To the many categories of works produced on the question of women's worth must be added nearly all works written by women. A woman writing was in herself a statement of women's claim to dignity.

Only a few women wrote anything before the dawn of the modern era, for three reasons. First, they rarely received the education that would enable them to write. Second, they were not admitted to the public roles—as administrator, bureaucrat, lawyer or notary, or university professor—in which they might gain knowledge of the kinds of things the literate public thought worth writing about. Third, the culture imposed silence on women, considering speaking out a form of unchastity. Given these conditions, it is remarkable that any women wrote. Those who did before the fourteenth century were almost always nuns or religious women whose isolation made their pronouncements more acceptable.

From the fourteenth century on, the volume of women's writings increased. Women continued to write devotional literature, although not always as cloistered nuns. They also wrote diaries, often intended as keepsakes for their children; books of advice to their sons and daughters; letters to family members and friends; and family memoirs, in a few cases elaborate enough to be considered histories.

A few women wrote works directly concerning the "woman question," and some of these, such as the humanists Isotta Nogarola, Cassandra Fedele, Laura Cereta, and Olympia Morata, were highly trained. A few were professional writers, living by the income of their pens; the very first among them was Christine de Pizan, noteworthy in this context as in so many others. In addition to *The Book of the City of Ladies* and her critiques of *The Romance of the Rose*, she wrote *The Treasure of the City of Ladies* (a guide to social decorum for women), an advice book for her son, much courtly verse, and a full-scale history of the reign of King Charles V of France.

WOMEN PATRONS. Women who did not themselves write but encouraged others to do so boosted the development of an alternative tradition. Highly placed women patrons supported authors, artists, musicians, poets, and learned men. Such patrons, drawn mostly from the Italian elites and the courts of northern Europe, figure disproportionately as the dedicatees of the important works of early feminism.

For a start, it might be noted that the catalogs of Boccaccio and Alvaro de Luna were dedicated to the Florentine noblewoman Andrea Acciaiuoli and to Doña María, first wife of King Juan II of Castile, while the French translation of Boccaccio's work was commissioned by Anne of Brittany, wife of King Charles VIII of France. The humanist treatises of Goggio, Equicola, Vives, and Agrippa were dedicated, respectively, to Eleanora of Aragon, wife of Ercole I d'Este, duke of Ferrara; to Margherita Cantelma of Mantua; to Catherine of Aragon, wife of King Henry VIII of England; and to Margaret, duchess of Austria and regent of the Netherlands. As late as 1696, Mary Astell's *Serious Proposal to the Ladies, for the Advancement of Their True and Greatest Interest* was dedicated to Princess Anne of Denmark.

These authors presumed that their efforts would be welcome to female patrons, or they may have written at the bidding of those patrons. Silent themselves, perhaps even unresponsive, these loftily placed women helped shape the tradition of the other voice.

THE ISSUES. The literary forms and patterns in which the tradition of the other voice presented itself have now been sketched. It remains to highlight the major issues around which this tradition crystallizes. In brief, there are four problems to which our authors return again and again, in plays and catalogs, in verse and letters, in treatises and dialogues, in every language: the problem of chastity, the problem of power, the problem of speech, and the problem of knowledge. Of these the greatest, preconditioning the others, is the problem of chastity.

THE PROBLEM OF CHASTITY. In traditional European culture, as in those of antiquity and others around the globe, chastity was perceived as woman's quintessential virtue—in contrast to courage, generosity, leadership, or rationality, which were seen as virtues characteristic of men. Opponents of women charged them with insatiable lust. Women themselves and their defenders—without disputing the validity of the standard—responded that women were capable of chastity.

The requirement of chastity kept women at home, silenced them, isolated them, left them in ignorance. It was the source of all other impediments. Why was it so important to the society of men, of whom chastity was not required, and who more often than not considered it their right to violate the chastity of any woman they encountered?

Female chastity ensured the continuity of the male-headed household. If a man's wife was not chaste, he could not be sure of the legitimacy of his offspring. If they were not his and they acquired his property, it was not his household, but some other man's, that had endured. If his daughter was not chaste, she could not be transferred to another man's household as his wife, and he was dishonored.

The whole system of the integrity of the household and the transmission of property was bound up in female chastity. Such a requirement pertained only to property-owning classes, of course. Poor women could not expect to maintain their chastity, least of all if they were in contact with high-status men to whom all women but those of their own household were prey.

In Catholic Europe, the requirement of chastity was further buttressed by moral and religious imperatives. Original sin was inextricably linked with the sexual act. Virginity was seen as a heroic virtue, far more impressive than, say, the avoidance of idleness or greed. Monasticism, the cultural institution that dominated medieval Europe for centuries, was grounded in the renunciation of the flesh. The Catholic reform of the eleventh century imposed a similar standard on all the clergy and a heightened awareness of sexual requirements on all the laity. Although men were asked to be chaste, female unchastity was much worse: it led to the devil, as Eve had led mankind to sin.

To such requirements, women and their defenders protested their innocence. Furthermore, following the example of holy women who had escaped the requirements of family and sought the religious life, some women began to conceive of female communities as alternatives both to family and to the cloister. Christine de Pizan's city of ladies was such a community. Moderata Fonte and Mary Astell envisioned others. The luxurious salons of the French précieuses of the seventeenth century, or the comfortable English drawing rooms of the next century, may have been born of the same impulse. Here women not only might escape, if briefly, the subordinate position that life in the family entailed, but might also make claims to power, exercise their capacity for speech, and display their knowledge.

THE PROBLEM OF POWER. Women were excluded from power: the whole cultural tradition insisted on it. Only men were citizens, only men bore arms, only men could be chiefs or lords or kings. There were exceptions that did not disprove the rule, when wives or widows or mothers took the place of men, awaiting their return or the maturation of a male heir. A woman who attempted to rule in her own right was perceived as an anomaly, a monster, at once a deformed woman and an insufficient male, sexually confused and consequently unsafe.

The association of such images with women who held or sought power explains some otherwise odd features of early modern culture. Queen Elizabeth I of England, one of the few women to hold full regal authority in European history, played with such male/female images—positive ones, of course—in representing herself to her subjects. She was a prince, and manly, even though she was female. She was also (she claimed) virginal, a condition absolutely essential if she was to avoid the attacks of her opponents. Catherine de' Medici, who ruled France as widow and regent for her sons, also adopted such imagery in defining her position. She chose as one symbol the figure of Artemisia, an androgynous ancient warrior-heroine who combined a female persona with masculine powers.

Power in a woman, without such sexual imagery, seems to have been indigestible by the culture. A rare note was struck by the Englishman Sir Thomas Elyot in his *Defence of Good Women* (1540), justifying both women's participation in civic life and their prowess in arms. The old tune was sung by the Scots reformer John Knox in his *First Blast of the Trumpet against the Monstrous Regiment of Women* (1558); for him rule by women, defects in nature, was a hideous contradiction in terms.

The confused sexuality of the imagery of female potency was not reserved for rulers. Any woman who excelled was likely to be called an Amazon, recalling the self-mutilated warrior women of antiquity who repudiated all men, gave up their sons, and raised only their daughters. She was often said to have "exceeded her sex" or to have possessed "masculine virtue"—as the very fact of conspicuous excellence conferred masculinity even on the female subject. The catalogs of notable women often showed those female heroes dressed in armor, armed to the teeth, like men. Amazonian heroines romp through the epics of the age—Ariosto's *Orlando Furioso* (1532) and Spenser's *Faerie Queene* (1590–1609). Excellence in a woman was perceived as a claim for power, and power was reserved for the masculine realm. A woman who possessed either one was masculinized and lost title to her own female identity.

THE PROBLEM OF SPEECH. Just as power had a sexual dimension when it was claimed by women, so did speech. A good woman spoke little. Excessive speech was an indication of unchastity. By speech, women seduced men. Eve had lured Adam into sin by her speech. Accused witches were commonly accused of having spoken abusively, or irrationally, or simply too much. As enlightened a figure as Francesco Barbaro insisted on silence in a woman, which he linked to her perfect unanimity with her husband's will and her unblemished virtue (her chastity). Another Italian humanist, Leonardo Bruni, in advising a noblewoman on her studies, barred her not from speech but from public speaking. That was reserved for men.

Related to the problem of speech was that of costume—another, if silent, form of self-expression. Assigned the task of pleasing men as their primary occupation, elite women often tended toward elaborate costume, hairdressing, and the use of cosmetics. Clergy and secular moralists alike condemned these practices. The appropriate function of costume and adornment was to announce the status of a woman's husband or father. Any further indulgence in adornment was akin to unchastity.

THE PROBLEM OF KNOWLEDGE. When the Italian noblewoman Isotta Nogarola had begun to attain a reputation as a humanist, she was accused of incest—a telling instance of the association of learning in women with unchastity. That chilling association inclined any woman who was educated to deny that she was or to make exaggerated claims of heroic chastity.

If educated women were pursued with suspicions of sexual misconduct, women seeking an education faced an even more daunting obstacle: the assumption that women were by nature incapable of learning, that reasoning was a particularly masculine ability. Just as they proclaimed their chastity, women and their defenders insisted on their capacity for learning. The major work by a male writer on female education—that by Juan Luis Vives, *On the Education of a Christian Woman* (1523)—granted female capacity for intellection but still argued that a woman's whole education was to be shaped around the requirement of chastity and a future within the household. Female writers of the following generations—Marie de Gournay in France, Anna Maria van Schurman in Holland, and Mary Astell in England—began to envision other possibilities.

The pioneers of female education were the Italian women humanists who managed to attain a literacy in Latin and a knowledge of classical and Christian literature equivalent to that of prominent men. Their works implicitly and explicitly raise questions about women's social roles, defining problems that beset women attempting to break out of the cultural limits that had bound them. Like Christine de Pizan, who achieved an advanced education through her father's tutoring and her own devices, their bold questioning makes clear the importance of training. Only when women were educated to the same standard as male leaders would they be able to raise that other voice and insist on their dignity as human beings morally, intellectually, and legally equal to men.

THE OTHER VOICE. The other voice, a voice of protest, was mostly female, but it was also male. It spoke in the vernaculars and in Latin, in treatises and dialogues, in plays and poetry, in letters and diaries, and in pamphlets. It battered at the wall of prejudice that encircled women and raised a banner announcing its claims. The female was equal (or even superior) to the male in essential nature—moral, spiritual, and intellectual. Women were capable of higher education, of holding positions of power and influence in the public realm, and of speaking and writing persuasively. The last bastion of masculine supremacy, centered on the notions of a woman's primary domestic responsibility and the requirement of female chastity, was not as yet assaulted—although visions of productive female communities as alternatives to the family indicated an awareness of the problem.

During the period 1300–1700, the other voice remained only a voice, and one only dimly heard. It did not result—yet—in an alteration of social patterns. Indeed, to this day they have not entirely been altered. Yet the call for justice issued as long as six centuries ago by those writing in the tradition of the other voice must be recognized as the source and origin of the mature feminist tradition and of the realignment of social institutions accomplished in the modern age.

We thank the volume editors in this series, who responded with many suggestions to an earlier draft of this introduction, making it a collaborative enterprise. Many of their suggestions and criticisms have resulted in revisions of this introduction, although we remain responsible for the final product.

PROJECTED TITLES IN THE SERIES

Isabella Andreini, *Mirtilla*, edited and translated by Laura Stortoni

Tullia d'Aragona, *Complete Poems and Letters*, edited and translated by Julia Hairston

Tullia d'Aragona, *The Wretch, Otherwise Known as Guerrino*, edited and translated by Julia Hairston and John McLucas

Giuseppa Eleonora Barbapiccola and Diamante Medaglia Faini, *The Education of Women*, edited and translated by Rebecca Messbarger

Francesco Barbaro et al., *On Marriage and the Family*, edited and translated by Margaret L. King

Laura Battiferra, *Selected Poetry, Prose, and Letters*, edited and translated by Victoria Kirkham

Giulia Bigolina, *"Urania" and "Giulia,"* edited and translated by Valeria Finucci

Francesco Buoninsegni and Arcangela Tarabotti, *Menippean Satire: "Against Feminine Extravagance" and "Antisatire,"* edited and translated by Elissa Weaver

Maddalena Campiglia, *Flori, a Pastoral Drama: A Bilingual Edition*, edited and translated by Virginia Cox with Lisa Sampson

Rosalba Carriera, *Letters, Diaries, and Art*, edited and translated by Shearer West

Madame du Chatelet, *Selected Works*, edited by Judith Zinsser

Vittoria Colonna, *Sonnets for Michelangelo*, edited and translated by Abigail Brundin

Vittoria Colonna, Chiara Matraini, and Lucrezia Marinella, *Marian Writings*, edited and translated by Susan Haskins

Marie Dentière, *Epistle to Marguerite de Navarre and Preface to a Sermon by John Calvin*, edited and translated by Mary B. McKinley

Princess Elizabeth of Bohemia, *Correspondence with Descartes*, edited and translated by Lisa Shapiro

Isabella d'Este, *Selected Letters*, edited and translated by Deanna Shemek

Fairy-Tales by Seventeenth-Century French Women Writers, edited and translated by Lewis Seifert and Domna C. Stanton

Moderata Fonte, *Floridoro*, edited and translated by Valeria Finucci

Moderata Fonte and Lucrezia Marinella, *Religious Narratives*, edited and translated by Virginia Cox

Francisca de los Apostoles, *Visions on Trial: The Inquisitional Trial of Francisca de los Apostoles*, edited and translated by Gillian T. W. Ahlgren

Catharina Regina von Greiffenberg, *Meditations on the Life of Christ*, edited and translated by Lynne Tatlock

In Praise of Women: Italian Fifteenth-Century Defenses of Women, edited and translated by Daniel Bornstein

Louise Labé, *Complete Works*, edited and translated by Annie Finch and Deborah Baker

Madame de Maintenon, *Dialogues and Addresses*, edited and translated by John Conley, S.J.

Lucrezia Marinella, *L'Enrico, or Byzantium Conquered*, edited and translated by Virginia Cox

Lucrezia Marinella, *Happy Arcadia*, edited and translated by Susan Haskins and Letizia Panizza

Chiara Matraini, *Selected Poetry and Prose*, edited and translated by Elaine MacLachlan

Eleonora Petersen von Merlau, *Autobiography (1718)*, edited and translated by Barbara Becker-Cantarino

Alessandro Piccolomini, *Rethinking Marriage in Sixteenth-Century Italy*, edited and translated by Letizia Panizza

Christine de Pizan et al., *Debate over the "Romance of the Rose,"* edited and translated by Tom Conley with Elisabeth Hodges

Christine de Pizan, *Life of Charles V*, edited and translated by Charity Cannon Willard

Christine de Pizan, *The Long Road of Learning*, edited and translated by Andrea Tarnowski

Madeleine and Catherine des Roches, *Selected Letters, Dialogues, and Poems*, edited and translated by Anne Larsen

Oliva Sabuco, *The New Philosophy: True Medicine*, edited and translated by Gianna Pomata

Margherita Sarrocchi, *La Scanderbeide*, edited and translated by Rinaldina Russell

Madeleine de Scudéry, *Selected Letters, Orations, and Rhetorical Dialogues*, edited and translated by Jane Donawerth with Julie Strongson

Justine Siegemund, *The Court Midwife of the Electorate of Brandenburg* (1690), edited and translated by Lynne Tatlock

Gabrielle Suchon, *"On Philosophy" and "On Morality,"* edited and translated by Domna Stanton with Rebecca Wilkin

Sara Copio Sullam, *Sara Copio Sullam: Jewish Poet and Intellectual in Early Seventeenth-Century Venice*, edited and translated by Don Harrán

Laura Terracina, *Works*, edited and translated by Michael Sherberg

Madame de Villedieu (Marie-Catherine Desjardins), *Memoirs of the Life of Henriette-Sylvie de Molière: A Novel*, edited and translated by Donna Kuizenga

Katharina Schütz Zell, *Selected Writings*, edited and translated by Elsie McKee

VOLUME EDITOR'S
INTRODUCTION

THE OTHER VOICE

In her monumental anthology of women's poetry in France, Jeanine Moulin maintains that Gabrielle de Coignard (ca. 1550–86) was "one of the most important feminine personalities of her century."[1,2] Despite this distinction, she has not drawn the scholarly attention that other more well-known French women poets of the sixteenth century, such as Louise Labé,[3] Pernette du Guillet,[4] and Les Dames des Roches,[5] have garnered in the last several

---

1. I have relied on three sources for much of my information concerning the life and work of Coignard: (1) Colette Winn's introduction in her annotated critical edition of Coignard's *Oeuvres chrétiennes* (Geneva: Droz, 1995); (2) Huguette Renée Kaiser's dissertation *Gabrielle de Coignard: Poétesse dévote* (Atlanta: Emory University, 1975); and (3) Marianne Fizet's Master's degree project at the University of Waterloo, an annotated edition of Coignard's *Sonnetz spirituels* (Ontario, Canada: U. of Waterloo, 1992). I am indebted to these scholars whose extensive research has greatly facilitated my work on this translation.

2. Moulin, *La Poésie féminine de Marie de France à Marie Noël*, 155.

3. Louise Labé (ca. 1520–66) was an active participant in the literary circles of Lyon. Her widely read *Euvres de Louise Labé Lionnoize*, published in 1555, contained a dedicatory epistle, a mythological dialogue written in prose entitled *Le debat de Folie et d'Amour*, twenty-four sonnets (the first one composed in Italian), and three elegies. The work concluded with twenty-four poems, written anonymously by Labé's friends, in praise of the splendors of her literary genius. The complete works of Labé will be published in The Other Voice series.

4. The poems of Pernette du Guillet (ca. 1520–45) were gathered by her husband after her death and published under the title *Rimes*, a collection made up of sixty epigrams, ten songs, five elegies, and two epistles. Du Guillet was a student of Maurice Scève's and is believed to be the primary inspiration for his collection of poems entitled *La Délie*. Du Guillet's complete poems will be published in The Other Voice series.

5. The work of Les Dames des Roches, Madeleine Neveu (1520–87) and her daughter Catherine Fradonnet (1542–87), was greatly respected within humanist circles of their time and in the last decade, thanks to Anne Larsen's critical editions of *Les oeuvres* (1578; Geneva: Droz, 1993) and *Les secondes oeuvres* (1583; Geneva: Droz, 1998), it has received increasing regard from literary scholars and historians. Selected works of the des Roches will be published in The Other Voice series and edited by Anne Larsen.

decades. Aside from a very small number of studies in the latter half of the twentieth century, it has only been in the most recent years, since Colette Winn's publication of an annotated edition of Coignard's work in 1995, that she has captured any modern critical interest at all.[6] And, despite the recent surge of scholarship on women's literature of the Renaissance, Coignard has attracted only a handful of scholars.

This critical disregard within scholarly literature has much to do with Coignard's literary legacy. Historically, scholars have not been drawn to religious women poets of the sixteenth century. The voice of women devotional poets, even more marginal than that of secular women poets of the sixteenth century, has, for the most part, gone unheard. Even the religious lyric poetry of Marguerite de Navarre,[7] one of the great matriarchs of women's poetry in France, is frequently overlooked in favor of her more well-known work *The Heptameron* (1559).[8] Sister Anne de Marquets[9] is another religious woman poet contemporary with Coignard whose *Sonets spirituels* (1605) and other

6. An important study of Coignard's poetry that predates Winn's edition can be found in Terence Cave, *Devotional Poetry in France, c. 1570–1630* (Cambridge: Cambridge University Press, 1969). Cave is among the first contemporary scholars to give Coignard's work the attention it deserves. He examines Coignard's *Oeuvres chrétiennes* in light of the religious and cultural developments of the latter half of the sixteenth century. Other contemporary scholars who have contributed to criticism devoted to Coignard's poetry include Madeleine Lazard, Evelyne Berriot-Salvadore, and Barbara Marczuk-Szwed. See further, translation, note 298.

7. Queen of Navarre, sister to King Francis I, mother of Henri IV, Marguerite de Navarre (1492–1549) was a prolific poet and playwright. *Le miroir de l'âme pécheresse* (1531), *Le dialogue en forme de vision nocturne* (1533), and *La navire* (1547) are among the most notable of her devotional compositions.

8. Marguerite de Navarre's *Heptameron* is a collection of tales inspired by Boccaccio's *Decameron*. I would like to note that although *The Heptameron* is considered by many scholars to be the most important of her works, there have been a few major scholarly studies of Marguerite de Navarre's religious poetry, including Robert Cottrell's *The Grammar of Silence: A Reading of Marguerite de Navarre's Poetry* (Washington, D.C.: Catholic University of America Press, 1986); Paula Sommer's *Celestial Ladders: Readings in Marguerite de Navarre's Poetry of Spiritual Ascent* (Geneva: Droz, 1989); and Gary Ferguson's *Mirroring Belief: Marguerite de Navarre's Devotional Poetry* (Edinburgh: Edinburgh University Press for the University of Durham, 1992), all of which are outstanding contributions to the criticism devoted to her oeuvre.

9. Having spent most of her youth and all of her adult life at the Dominican Priory of Saint Louis at Poissy, Sister Anne de Marquets (ca. 1533–88) enjoyed educational privileges to which only an elite number of women in sixteenth-century France had access. Within her community, she led a rich and fruitful intellectual life, publishing successful collections of poetry that were admired by her contemporaries, such as Dorat, Ronsard, and Scévole de Sainte-Marthe. Her works include *Sonets, prières et devises en forme de pasquins* (1562), *Les divines poesies de Marc Antoine Flaminius* (1568), and her most significant collection of verse, *Sonets spirituels*, which was published posthumously in 1605. Ferguson's recent critical edition of the *Sonets spirituels* (Geneva: Droz, 1997) has made the poetry of Marquets available to modern readers and so, as the study of women religious poets develops in the coming years, her collections will surely be included among the major works of the period.

works have also inexplicably failed to gain much attention, despite their literary merit.

One possible explanation for this neglect of the poetry of religious women authors may lie in the individuality of the devotional voice itself. Secular poets like Labé, Du Guillet, and the des Roches often wrote in the company and support of others. They polished their skills through the guidance and encouragement of friends, lovers, and family, and they shared the influences, inspirations, and interests of their male contemporaries. Their work, therefore, enables modern critics to establish a broader and more enriched view of literary trends in sixteenth-century France. The secular poetry of most women writing during this period fits into particular movements of literary history. Women authors of religious literature, on the other hand, tended to write in isolation, creating poetry of a much more individual and private nature,[10] although their compositions also reflect, in less obvious ways, the cultural moods and literary inclinations of the time. The lack of knowledge regarding the lives of many women devotional poets, combined with the purported less than superior quality of their verse (for lack of formal instruction in most cases), may have also dissuaded critics from developing any serious interest in their work.

Perhaps the literary value of the works of these women poets is underestimated, but, from a number of points of view, this critical perspective is justified. Indeed, the skills of a poet such as Coignard could not compete with the masters of her time, poets such as Pierre de Ronsard and Joachim du Bellay, for example.[11] This does not mean, however, that her work does not have merit. The worth of her poetry lies in the story it imparts to the modern

10. Marquets would be the exception in this case. She composed her verse in the supportive religious community of her convent. Her poems also have a more specifically didactic purpose than those compositions by other religious women poets of the period. Marquets wrote with the hope that others would read and be spiritually inspired by her poems. See Kirk Read's article, "Women of the French Renaissance in Search of Literary Community: A Prolegomenon to Early Modern Women's Participation in Letters," *Romance Languages Annual* (1993): 95–102. The notion of women writing in seclusion is based on what we can deduce from the works of religious authors such as Gabrielle de Bourbon, de Navarre, Jeanne d'Albret, Catherine de Bourbon, and Coignard (regarding their writing habits). Other women religious authors of this period include Georgette de Montenay, Marie Dentière, and Jeanne de Jussie. The works of Dentière and de Jussie will appear in The Other Voice series.

11. Pierre de Ronsard (1524–85), the "Prince of Poets," author of such works as *Odes* (1550), *Amours de Cassandre* (1552), and *Hymnes* (1555), is considered by many to be the most important poet of his century. He, along with Joachim du Bellay (1522–60), the author of *La défense et illustration de la langue françoyse* (1549), was a chief member of the highly influential group known as *La Pléiade*, a circle of seven humanist poets whose primary mission was to bring the French language to its prime through the enrichment of its vocabulary, renewal of form, and perfection of style through imitation of the ancients.

reader and in the picture it paints of a woman of the Renaissance, however fragmented it might be. At the same time, Coignard's oeuvre has a great deal more to offer than many critics might expect.

BIOGRAPHY

Coignard is as elusive today as she was when her *Oeuvres chrétiennes* first resurfaced in the late nineteenth century. Because her life is so poorly documented, many biographical details have not been available to the few scholars who have attempted to reconstruct her identity. Information does exist, however, about the primary male figures in her life. Some of what we know about her father, her husband, and her father-in-law has helped elucidate a few key details regarding such matters as her education, social status, and marriage.

While it is impossible to establish the precise date of her birth, calculations based on Pierre Salies's assertion that she died at the age of 36 on Saturday, November 29, 1586, indicate that she was most likely born in 1550.[12] Born into a prosperous and respected family in Toulouse, France, one of the major cultural centers of the period, Coignard enjoyed access to numerous social and intellectual opportunities.

Upon reading *Les oeuvres chrétiennes*, it is evident that she was well educated and certainly well schooled in Catholicism. Her father, Jean de Coignard, an affluent counselor at the Parlement of Toulouse, was also *maître ès Jeux Floraux*,[13] a position he held for twenty years (1535–55).[14] Because of her father's position in the Parlement and at the Academy of the *Jeux Floraux*, Coignard frequented the more cultivated circles of Toulouse, a privilege that undoubtedly contributed to and enhanced her education.

In 1570, at the age of 20, Coignard married Pierre de Mansencal, seigneur de Miramont, who was the son of the first *président* at the Parlement of Toulouse, Jean de Mansencal, and Jeanne de Vidal-Miremont.[15] According to Winn, this alliance resulted in a significant social promotion for Coig-

---

12. Pierre Salies, "Gabrielle de Coignard: poétesse toulousaine du XVIe siècle," *Archistra* 79 (March–April 1987): 33–43.

13. *Les Jeux Floraux* was a poetic competition held annually in Toulouse that dated back to 1323.

14. He was then elected *mainteneur*, a dignitary of the *Jeux Floraux*, at the *Collège des Art et Science de Rhétorique*, where he served until 1569, resigning one year before his death.

15. As was customary, Coignard kept her maiden name when she married Mansencal. See Natalie Zemon Davis, "City Women and Religious Change," in *Society and Culture in Early Modern France* (Stanford: Stanford University Press, 1975), 65–95. Coignard's father died soon after she was married.

nard.[16] Her husband had a notable career as a statesman.[17] Soon after they were married, he became *président* of the Parlement of Toulouse, a position he occupied from March 1572 until his death in November 1573. The couple had two daughters, Catherine and Jeanne de Mansencal, born in 1571 and 1573, respectively. A widow at the age of twenty-three, Coignard focused her concerns on her children and was very attentive to their needs and education. Although there are no known historical documents or archival material that would indicate otherwise, it is assumed that Coignard and her daughters remained in Toulouse with her husband's family until her death in 1586.

LES OEUVRES CHRÉTIENNES

In 1594, almost a decade after Coignard's death, Jeanne and Catherine published the first edition of their mother's work: *Oeuvres chrestiennes de feu Dame Gabrielle de Coignard. Vefve a feu Monsieur de Mansencal, Sieur de Miremont, President en la Cour de Parlement de Tolose.*[18] The *Oeuvres* is divided into two parts, the first comprised of 129 sonnets, *Les sonnets spirituels*, and the second of twenty-one poetic meditations of greater length on a variety of Biblical themes, *Les vers chrestiens.*[19] The book opens with a dedication that her daughters address to "devout ladies," in which they praise their mother's literary merits and moral

---

16. Upon marrying her husband, the seigneur de Miramont, Coignard gained the title "dame de Miramont," but the source of this title is unknown. Fizet discovered that there did exist a quarter in Toulouse called Miremont, but was unable to locate it or establish a link between this location and the family (*Sonnetz spirituels*, 9). Coignard and her husband resided at 11, place Saint-Etienne, in the mansion of Jean Coignard.

17. In 1561, he was counselor at the *Grand Conseil*; in 1568 he became Advocate General at the Parlement of Toulouse.

18. Published by Pierre Jagourt and Bernard Carles. A copy of this edition is located at the Bibliothèque Municipale de Toulouse. The second edition appeared in 1595, published by Jacques Faure, a bookseller in Avignon. Copies are located at the Bibliothèque Nationale, the Bibliothèque Municipale d'Avignon, and at Harvard University. A reprint of this second edition was made in 1613 in Lyon by Abraham Cloquemin. Following the reprint, three centuries passed before Coignard's work was rediscovered by Hugues Vaganay, who published the first part of the collection (based on the 1594 edition), *Les sonnets spirituels*, in 1900 at Mâcon, chez Protat frères, in the collection *Le thrésor du sonnet (XVI et XVIIe siècles)*, an edition Slatkine reprinted in 1969. In his anthology entitled *Poètes chrétiens du XVIe siècle* (Paris: Bloud et Cie, 1908), Henry La Maynardière included ten of Coignard's sonnets: sonnets 3, 12, 13, 17, 23, 34, 72, 73, 80, and 122. Then, in 1992, Fizet, a graduate student in Canada at the University of Waterloo, produced an edition of the *Sonnets Spirituels* for her M.A. thesis. Finally, Winn published an annotated critical edition of the *Oeuvres chrétiennes* in 1995 (based on the edition of 1594).

19. This translation contains only the first part of *Les oeuvres chrétiennes*, entitled *Les sonnets spirituels*. Coignard's poems in *Les vers chrétiens*, the second part of *Les oeuvres chrétiennes*, take on a variety of

integrity, insisting at the same time on her poetic and devotional humility.[20] This initial general address is followed by a more specific dedication of the *Oeuvres chrestiennes* to two women whom Jeanne and Catherine believe share their mother's virtues.

The first addressee is easily recognized as Marguerite de Valois ("ceste illustre et si devotieuse Princesse enfermée dans son Usson") [this illustrious and devout Princess banished to her château in Usson]).[21] Valois, daughter of Catherine de Medici and Henri II and first wife of Henri IV, was esteemed by the people, who were unaware of her immoral tendencies. Considered an example of piety and moral rectitude, she was revered for her religious fervor and loyalty to the Catholic faith. Renée Kaiser argues that it is entirely natural that the author of such pious poems as *Les oeuvres chrestiennes* would feel a certain affinity for Valois, in whom she saw a heroine persecuted for her faith and who united within herself two values to which many women of this period aspired: erudition and devotion.[22]

The second addressee ("ceste venerable Dame mere de nos Prelatz et Gouverneurs, l'exemple et le vray miroir de toute devotion et vertu") [this venerable lady, mother of our prelates and governors, the example and true mirror of every devotion and virtue] of the dedication cannot be identified with absolute certainty, although Winn suggests Clémence Isaure as a possible candidate. The mythical *Toulousaine*, to whom the foundation of the *Jeux Floraux* has been attributed, became a local heroine for the city of Toulouse and was admired for her legendary generosity.[23]

Coignard's daughters conclude the dedication with a reference to an episode in the Acts of the Apostles (9:36–41), a passage their mother mentions in the "Hymne sur la louange de la charité" (*Les vers chrétiens*, 599). This passage concerns the death of Dorcas, a widow reputed for her generosity and charitable works. Just as Dorcas was resurrected by Peter, Coignard's

---

forms: *stances, hymnes, complaintes, noëls, discours,* and even a miniature epic. Kaiser points out that Coignard's preferences for such genres, and her lack of interest in the older genres (*virelais, rondeaux, ballades,* etc.) place her among those who supported and developed the poetics of the Pléiade. "In this ultra-conservative circle (i.e., *Les Jeux Floraux*), Gabrielle becomes an innovator in matters of poetic genres" (*Poétesse dévote*, 24).

20. The epithet "dame dévote" (devout lady) had a much more precise meaning in the sixteenth century than today. This expression designated any woman, regardless of her status, who intimately allied her religious life with her social obligations (Kaiser, *Poétesse dévote*, 171).

21. Coignard may have met Marguerite de Valois during her stay with Catherine de Medici in Toulouse in 1565 (Winn, *Oeuvres*, 24).

22. Kaiser, *Poétesse dévote*, 9.

23. Winn, *Oeuvres*, 24.

daughters hope to give their mother a second and more beautiful life, one of greater renown through the publication of her poetry.

The dedication is followed by a note to the reader that attributes any errors in the text to the printer, emphasizing that such mistakes are not the responsibility of the poet, whose work, the anonymous editor proclaims, is of such tremendous moral virtue that it will spiritually nourish and console all who read it. Finally, as was customary during this period, the editor includes two prefatory sonnets in which he extols the virtues and the writings of the author of *Les Oeuvres chrestiennes* and commemorates *la muse Toulousaine*.

ORGANIZATION AND MAJOR THEMES OF
LES SONNETS SPIRITUELS

While Coignard may have composed her *Spiritual Sonnets* and *Christian Verses* simultaneously, she did not leave any clues concerning their proper order, or, for that matter, if she even intended for her poems to be organized at all.[24] Nonetheless, the fact that her poems are divided into two parts inevitably invites some sort of thematic arrangement. No certain chronological order can be established, but the poems could be loosely grouped into categories based on subject matter. Although very aware of forcing the issue, Kaiser proposes a system of classification for the sonnets.[25] She groups them in *grappes* (clusters) based on theme and genre. Sonnets 1 and 2 are inaugural pieces, which are the profession of the Christian poetess who places her work beneath the invocation of the crucified Jesus. The two opening sonnets set the tone for the rest of the collection, which will be, above all, lyrical and composed "in the shadow of [the] Cross." Grace is the central theme that unites sonnets 3–17, except for sonnet 16, which is on the Garonne River. Sonnets 18–20 are ethical considerations and meditations. Sonnets 21–22 are contemplations of the Cross. Sonnets 23–49 consist of a long series of colloquies with Jesus and the saints, accompanied by several earnest examinations of conscience. Sonnets 50–51 focus on Psalm 51, one of the seven penitential psalms. Death is the theme of sonnets 52–56. Sonnets 57–66 are devoted primarily to religious celebrations and extolments of God's grace and mercy. Psalm 51 returns to inspire sonnets 67–68. Sonnets 69–75 consist of seven more pieces on the Cross and the death of Jesus Christ. Sonnets

24. Fizet suggests that there are several sections of the sonnets that could be organized according to the liturgical year, but recognizes that it would be a more sound approach simply to link certain groups of poems to specific and individual periods of the liturgical year, such as Christmas and Easter (*Sonnetz spirituels*, 14).

25. For the outline that follows, see Kaiser, *Poétesse dévote*, 51–54.

76–111 treat a variety of subjects: religious festivals, moral considerations, elegiac complaints, anguish, and death, among others. Sonnets 113–118 are devoted to the last seven words of Jesus on the Cross. Sonnets 119–128 are not united by any particular theme, although there is a pair of sonnets within this section (122 and 123) on the theme of the distaff. The final poem in this section, sonnet 129 on the death of Ronsard, stands alone.[26]

Generally speaking, the collection of sonnets is comprised of penitential lyric, Passion poetry, nativity poetry, addresses to the saints, death poetry, prayer poetry, nature poetry, and other lesser genres. The sonnets are not organized by any one central principle. In one way or another, however, each poem is an expression of Coignard's faith. The Cross is perhaps the dominant symbol at the heart of her verse, as she indicates in sonnet 2, already cited above, where she claims to sacrifice everything (her body, her writings, her soul) to "the shadow of [the] Cross."[27] In sonnet 69, she maintains that she "would not know how to write about anything else / But the Cross."

It was during her years of widowhood, when she remained faithful to her husband's memory and refused to yield to social expectations that she remarry, that Coignard embarked upon her solitary spiritual journey. Her sonnets are rich with profound emotion, anguished moments of loneliness, ecstatic moments of mystical union, and heart-wrenching struggles between desiring death as an end to her suffering and needing to live to fulfill her role as a mother.

Coignard turned to poetry as a means of recording her struggles, both those encountered in her relationship with God and those endured during the emotional upheavals of her life. *Les Oeuvres chrétiennes* constitute, as Winn aptly remarks, "a long autobiographical elegy."[28] A general overview of the collection reveals that Coignard's poetry provided her the inviolable space and freedom she needed to transcribe her most private confessions, prayers, and spiritual meditations. Barbara Marczuk-Szwed describes Coignard's work as the intimate journal of a deeply religious soul that longs to express the multitude of sentiments endured in the relationship between person and

---

26. Fizet divides the sonnets into thematic groups as well, with the collection encompassing four main topics: penitence, Passion poetry, the nativity, and the saints. She also discerns subcategories within the frame of penitence and Passion. Individual poems treating sickness, death, or civil war, for example, fall under these two central themes. Fizet implies that no matter what the topic, Coignard is steadfast in her inspiration; she develops each of her themes—be it a lamentation, a contemplation of nature, or a study of the concept of poetry itself—within a spiritual context (*Sonnetz spirituels*, 15).

27. Cf. sonnets 21, 22, 26, 69, 75.

28. Winn, *Oeuvres*, 26.

God.[29] It is easy to recognize in the two parts of *Les oeuvres chrétiennes* what Kaiser refers to as the different stages of "an ascending itinerary"[30] and Winn describes as the successive steps of "a spiritual evolution."[31] *The Spiritual Sonnets* delineates the earlier stages of this process and depicts the many ups and downs that Coignard encounters in the examination of her faith.

The sonnets are full of optimism and pious meditations marked, in Winn's terms, by "an intense aspiration to moral purity."[32] At the same time, the sonnets reveal Coignard's anguish and despair as she struggles to make her way through the trials of her daily life. She must repeatedly confront her own inability to achieve the spiritual perfection to which she aspires. Thus, the sonnets capture the constant fluctuation of her emotional and spiritual states, as she moves from ecstatic rushes of joy to melancholic episodes of somber reflection.

The remarkable presence of the first-person singular in her poems reveals the self-absorption she requires in the early stages of her spiritual development.[33] Coignard's first-person poetic voice also indicates from the opening sonnet the introspection she undertakes in her poems.[34] The use of the personal pronoun "je" ("I") is part of what animates these poems. Through her lyrical confessions and contemplations, we learn a few details about who Coignard was and about some of the struggles she faced.[35]

The "I" of *The Spiritual Sonnets* exists miserably in the present while focus-

---

29. Marczuk-Szwed, "Le thème du péché et son expression poétique dans *Les oeuvres chrestiennes de Gabrielle de Coignard et dans Le mespris de la vie et consolation contre la mort* de J. B. Chassignet," in Zeszyty Naukowe Uniwersteru Jagiellónskiego MLIV (1992), 52.

30. Kaiser, *Poétesse dévote*, 47.

31. Winn, *Oeuvres*, 26.

32. Winn, *Oeuvres*, 27.

33. In *Les vers chrétiens*, on the other hand, Coignard abandons her internal conflicts, reaching a new level of self-detachment and ridding herself of worldly concerns in order to contemplate the divine. She succeeds in letting go of herself and renounces, as Winn maintains, the hope for glory that motivates the literary enterprise, the ideal of formal perfection, and the aesthetic pleasure that the sonnet procures (*Oeuvres*, 28). The subject pronoun "I" rather significantly yields its place to "He." The self-centered sonnet fades out, making way for longer poems of freer form in which the author focuses her creative efforts on capturing the greatness of God.

34. We can safely assume that the "I" of the poems is the "I" of the author. As far as we know, the sonnets contain the revelations of Coignard, not of some fictionalized self or literary persona.

35. Ferguson has also commented on Coignard's use of the first person: "The lyric 'je' [I] of Coignard's verse maintains a strong presence, reflecting many of the particularities of the poet's own situation—'je' is a woman, a widow, a mother; she describes numerous aspects of her life, such as her ill health, her grief at the loss of her husband, her unwillingness to remarry, and the problem of bringing up her daughters alone" (Ferguson, "The Feminisation of Devotion: Gabrielle de Coignard, Anne de Marquets, and François de Sales," in *Women's Writing in the French Renaissance* [Cambridge: Cambridge French Colloquia, 1999], 195).

ing her vision on her future salvation. Her desperate avoidance of present reality leads her to seek escape in a variety of ways. Escape, in fact, rapidly reveals itself as one of the dominant themes of the sonnets. Coignard longs to flee from the city,[36] to find retreat in nature,[37] to free herself from sin and suffering,[38] to relieve herself of parental responsibility,[39] to renounce this life in hope of rebirth in an afterlife.[40]

Many of Coignard's sonnets involve refusal in one form or another.[41] She rejects the notion of remarriage;[42] she shuns worldly vanity and glory;[43] she forbids classical, pagan inspiration and high style;[44] she sees no value in worldly knowledge and rejects it as a symbol of human presumption; she even repudiates her own work.[45] She refuses all of these things in favor of God.

The themes of escape and refusal naturally lead Coignard to the theme of death. Ultimately, Coignard desires the peace that can come only with death.[46] Death, however, has many facets. Coignard also fears death and the divine judgment that will accompany it.[47] It is clear that although she expresses profound faith in God's mercy,[48] she fears His justice.[49] Through her reading and interpretation of the Scriptures, however, Coignard convinces herself of God's benevolence[50] and takes comfort in the promise of forgiveness. This optimism outweighs the moments of despair in the sonnets.

36. Cf. sonnets 11 and 79.

37. Cf. sonnet 11.

38. Cf. sonnets 24, 30, 71, and 119.

39. Cf. sonnets 11 and 119.

40. Cf. sonnets 3, 52, 81, and 119. Coignard's aspirations for death reflect not only the difficult circumstances of her personal life but also her faith and belief that death represents a blissful repose after what has been an excruciating life on earth.

41. Winn discusses the theme of refusal at length in her introduction. See the section entitled "La poésie du refus" (*Oeuvres*, 29–43).

42. Cf. sonnet 105.

43. Cf. sonnets 6, 14, 18, and 42.

44. Cf. sonnets 1, 2, and 8. While Coignard rejects high style, she also desires it. See sonnet 16.

45. Cf. sonnets 14 and 86. Coignard rejects her work for a number of reasons. She fears that she is not learned enough to compose poems of any value. She is afraid that through her compositions she seeks worldly glory. She also fears that she might use writing as a means to alleviate her suffering. See sonnet 83.

46. Cf. sonnets 52 and 76.

47. Cf. sonnets 50 and 55.

48. Cf. sonnet 70.

49. Cf. sonnets 17, 56, 72, 67, and 88. Coignard worries that she has not repented or suffered enough to deserve God's mercy.

50. Cf. sonnet 127.

In many of her poems, Coignard laments the woes of human existence, as well as the intrinsic depravity and weakness of human nature,[51] all fundamentally linked to the body, which becomes the primary agent in the channeling of existential, penitential, and ecstatic experiences.[52] In the face of temptation, Coignard draws strength from her faith. God helps her to resist her sinful tendencies.[53] Nonetheless, there are a few occasions when God seems beyond her reach, unwilling to hear her; these are harrowing moments that leave her feeling utterly alone and dejected.[54]

As I have already suggested above, the presence of the author in her sonnets is one of the many elements that contribute to their poignancy. Unlike many male poets of the period, Coignard is willing to bare her more private struggles and examine more personal concerns, thus giving modern readers a much sought after glimpse into the mind of a Renaissance woman. She distinguishes herself from the devotional poets of her time by her proclivity for introspection, which, as Evelyne Berriot-Salvadore argues, makes her individual experience the true "object" of her poetry.[55]

VERSIFICATION, STYLE, AND LANGUAGE

In my efforts to remain as faithful as possible to the language and imagery of the sonnets, I have made no attempt in this translation to reproduce the rhyme schemes and rhythmic patterns Coignard observes. Nonetheless, it is important to situate the versification, style, and various techniques Coignard uses in her sonnets in relation to her contemporaries and poetic trends of the period. With regard to meter and rhyme disposition in her sonnets, Coignard remains true to tradition. As is the case with her contemporaries Philippe Desportes (*Quelques prieres et meditations chrestiennes,* 1603), J.-B. Chassignet (*Mespris de la vie et consolation contre la mort,* 1594), Antoine Favre (*Centurie premiere,* 1594), and J. de La Ceppède (*Les theoremes,* 1613), Coignard shows an overwhelming preference for alexandrine meter.[56] In fact, 101 out of the 129 sonnets are composed in alexandrine, while the remaining twenty-eight are written in decasyllables. Her respect for the twelve-syllable line is in compli-

---

51. Cf. sonnets 12, 68, 120, and 121.

52. Cf. sonnets 4, 24, 27, 31, 95, 29, and 32.

53. Cf. sonnet 41.

54. Cf. sonnets 4 and 5.

55. Berriot-Salvadore, *Les femmes dans la société française de la Renaissance* (Geneva: Droz, 1990), 438.

56. In French poetry, alexandrine verse consists of twelve-syllable lines. The classic alexandrine line is structured so that the caesura falls after the sixth syllable. (On caesura, see below, note 61.)

ance with Pierre de Ronsard's urging of his contemporaries to write in alexandrine.[57]

For 127 of her sonnets, Coignard chooses a traditional *marotique*[58] rhyme scheme: abba, abba, ccd, eed. Sonnet 7 is the first to vary from the others in that the quatrains follow an unusual pattern of abab, baab. In sonnet 8, Coignard arranges her tercets in accordance with the disposition that Jacques Peletier du Mans adopted in his *Art poétique* (1555): ccd, ede. She regularly observes the alternation of masculine and feminine rhyme,[59] although she strays from the rule in nine sonnets, creating a majority of feminine rhymes. She demonstrates a partiality for *rimes riches*, also consistent with the preferences of the times.[60] Sometimes her use of *rimes riches* leads her to awkward or banal combinations that would have been unacceptable in light of Pléiade standards. Despite the occasional lapse, Coignard proves to be attentive to her rhymes; her use of assonance and of internal rhymes, in particular, lends a certain musical quality to her verse.

One of Ronsard's recommendations Coignard struggles to meet, on the other hand, is that of placing the caesura[61] at the sixth syllable of the alexandrine and at the fourth syllable of the decasyllable, arranging them so that the first hemistich contains full and complete meaning without depending on the words that follow it. While a certain flexibility was allowed in this endeavor, Coignard repeatedly fails to achieve this division of meter—much to

57. Ronsard, *Abrégé de l'art poétique. Traités de poétique et de rhétorique de la Renaissance* (Paris: Librairie Générale Française, 1990): 480–81. Ronsard's *Abrégé de l'art poétique français* (1565) was one among several of the treatises on the art of poetic composition and rhetoric that appeared midcentury. Thomas Sébillet's *Art poétique françois* (1548) and Jacques Peletier du Mans's *Art poétique* (1555) are earlier examples of this type of instructive manual for aspiring poets.

58. Innovative poet at the court of Francis I, protégé of Marguerite de Navarre, Clément Marot (1496–1544) is credited with introducing the elegy into the French language, as well as renewing a number of medieval poetic forms, such as the *rondeau* and the *chanson*. The *marotique* rhyme scheme of the sonnet is a variation on the Petrarchan sonnet, which begins with two quatrains, or an octet, with the rhyme scheme abbaabba, followed by two tercets, or a sestet, based on a variety of rhyme combinations, cdecde, cdccdc, cdedce, and cdcdcd among the most common.

59. In French poetry, a rhyme is considered "feminine" when the final word of the line ends in an unaccented or mute "e." All other rhymes, that is, those that do not end in "e," are considered masculine. Alternation between masculine and feminine rhymes was the standard in classic versification.

60. In French poetry, rhymes can be qualified as "pauvres," "suffisantes," or "riches." Simply defined, the first of the three, "poor rhymes," consists of only one shared phoneme (most often the repetition of an accented vowel). The second, "sufficient rhymes," shares two final phonemes. Rich rhymes are made up of three or more homophonous phonemes.

61. The caesura marks the rhythmic division or accentual pause of a line of verse. In alexandrine verse, the caesura divides a line into two equal hemistiches, six syllables each. A hemistich is a half line of verse.

the annoyance of her critics. Kaiser reminds us, however, that these over-sights on her part are judged according to norms established by a very small number of poets and theorists who imposed them on poetry because they corresponded both to their aesthetic and to their period.[62] Although clearly aware of the rules, Coignard simply does not always force her compositions to fit convention.[63] She has her own unique motivation and purpose as a poet. In those instances where she chooses not to observe certain rules, she opts for a more unrestricted and expressive style better suited to the intimate, emotional nature of her verse.[64]

Another area where Coignard dissatisfies her critics is in the weakness of the final line of her sonnets (*le trait final*).[65] For sixteenth-century rhetoricians, the last line of a sonnet is what gives it its poignancy and power. Coignard's weak conclusions do reveal a certain lack of skill.[66] There are a few excep-tions,[67] but, for the most part, Coignard does not exploit the potential of the final tercet.

Coignard experiments with a few literary strategies and rhetorical fig-ures, although it is not her use of these devices, nor her emulation of others, that gives value to her verse. The success of her sonnets is found in their sub-tlety, her word choice, and her concern for poetic harmony. Nonetheless, she does translate her emotion through poetic techniques that support and reinforce their intensity. She reveals, for example, a strong predilection for the anaphora, a device appropriate to her emphatic intent.[68] She also fre-quently employs vocative interjections and apostrophes that heighten the

62. Kaiser, *Poétesse dévote*, 59.

63. As Kaiser has noted, Coignard, who is always attentive to the harmony of her verse, rather surprisingly shows no concern for the proper position of the hiatus (*Poétesse dévote*, 70). Winn ex-plains that Coignard does not always observe the appropriate division ("la coupe médiane") be-cause this division does not fit the "spoken style" of many of her poems that are prayers, dialogues with God, lamentations, or confessions (*Oeuvres*, 114).

64. For example, her successful use of enjambment, a technique disfavored by the Pléiade poets, serves to communicate the intensity of her inspiration. (Enjambment is the continuation of a sentence or phrase from one poetic line or stanza to the next with little or no pause or syntacti-cal break.)

65. See Raymond Lebègue, *La poésie française de 1560 à 1630* (Paris: Société d'Édition d'Enseigne-ment Supérieur, 1951), 38.

66. Kaiser argues that Coignard's failure to refine the final line of her sonnets might be ex-plained by her greater concern for the message contained in her verse (*Poétesse dévote*, 66). It is important to keep in mind that Coignard did not compose her poems with the intention of pub-lishing them; she simply did not labor to perfect them as others with greater literary ambition might have done.

67. Cf. sonnets 39, 50, 87, and 126.

68. Anaphora is the repetition of a word or group of words at the beginning of successive lines of verse.

fervor and immediacy of her poetic supplications. Her use of the oxymoron captures the ambiguity of many of the emotions and sensations she endures and, at the same time, recalls the Petrarchan poetics of the Lyonnais poets.[69] *Les poètes lyonnais* borrowed some of the themes, images, and rhetorical devices used by the fourteenth-century Italian poet Petrarch. Favored among these poets are rhetorical figures such as the oxymoron and antithesis, images of the cold and merciless beloved, and expressions of the tortured desires and willful suffering of the repudiated lover, all of which Coignard effectively adapts to her religious verse. In fact, Coignard frequently makes use of these devices, casting Petrarchan tropes not to capture the exaggerated sensual and emotional tortures of terrestrial passions, such as those that figure in love poetry of Petrarchan inspiration, but rather to communicate the suffering she endures as a sinner in her relationship with Christ. She trembles in penitential terror of divine wrath at the same time that she delights in the sensual and ecstatic mysticism she experiences in her quest for union with her Savior— contradictions that are successfully conveyed through Petrarchan poetic devices. Coignard's use of the sonnet as her poetic form also clearly indicates her debt to Petrarch, who first introduced the genre.

While Coignard does employ some rhetorical devices, she does not diligently pursue any sort of technical virtuosity—a fact that clearly separates her from the poets of the Pléiade. Sincere emotion, the feeling that her poems are based on real-life experience, and the authenticity of her piety and convictions are the qualities that give to this woman what Winn deems "her admirable and poignant particularity."[70] Coignard's sonnets do not reveal originality or a colorful imagination. Her style is for the most part simple and bare, in accordance with her prescribed humility as well as with her poetic purpose. She successfully sought clarity of expression and did not seriously pursue the mastery that would have earned her immediate glory. Coignard's poetic discourse is endowed with a certain naïveté, a simplicity that nonetheless captures the subtleties of religious experience. Kaiser explains that Coignard did not bring to the composition of her sonnets all the care that a poet conscious of her reputation would have brought. What was important to her was the inspiration of her verse, the sincerity of her expression, and the value of her message. One senses that for Coignard writing was a refuge, a dialogue with herself and, above all, with a God of love and hope.[71] She con-

---

69. The circle of poets living in Lyon, France, writing during the middle of the sixteenth century (1540–60) is referred to as the Lyonnais poets (*les poètes lyonnais*). Maurice Scève, Du Guillet, and Labé are among the most notable members. See notes 3 and 4.

70. Winn, *Oeuvres*, 117.

71. Kaiser, *Poétesse dévote*, 100. Coignard expresses the most profound belief in God's justice and

sidered herself a Christian before all else; her life as a poet was secondary. Her poetry, in effect, was a practice of devotion.

The simplicity of Coignard's language, along with the other aberrations mentioned above, distinguishes her from many of her contemporaries and, in many respects, places her outside Ronsard's campaign to develop and enrich the French language. Her prosaic, and sometimes antiquated, vocabulary, appropriate to her spiritual, physical, and domestic life, is representative of the daily existence of an average upper-class woman of the period. Ironically, as others have already suggested, Coignard's use of the language is almost more forward looking than the progressive techniques prescribed by Ronsard (the creation of neologisms, syntactical shifts, grammatical innovations, etc.). The clarity and plainness of her language anticipate the austerity of early seventeenth-century verse.

Indeed, a number of her early critics, beginning in the seventeenth century, have praised Coignard's purity of language. Guillaume Colletet and Léon Feugère have both noted how her poems recall the thought and language of François de Malherbe, a major figure among poets in the early part of the seventeenth century in France. Colletet, Feugère records in *Les femmes poètes au seizième siècle* (1861), praises her compositions as "well-imagined, full of pathos, remarkable by the sweetness and the beauty of their language."[72] Feugère himself lauds their "wholesome, naturally elevated style."[73] Armand Müller writes in *La poésie religieuse catholique de Marot à Malherbe* (1950) that he is struck by "the penetrating accent" and "the solid language" of Coignard's poems and notes their occasional "veritable eloquence."[74] Henry La Maynardière, who includes ten of her sonnets in his anthology *Poètes chrétiens du XVIe siècle* (1908), praises Coignard's eloquence, concision, inspiration, and charm.[75]

---

clemency. She has faith that her penitence will lead to her salvation. The hardships and emotional struggles she endures are simply a part of the journey. The moments of insecurity and uncertainty that she experiences are not nearly as dire or devastating as those expressed in the works of many male poets, such as Chassignet or Sponde.

72. Feugère, *Les femmes poètes au seizième siècle*, 1861 (Geneva: Slatkine Reprints, 1969), 37. Colletet, according to Feugère, mentions Coignard in *La vie des poètes françois*, a manuscript that was partially burned in a fire at the La Bibliothèque du Louvre in 1871 (*Les femmes poètes au seizième siècle*, 37). The leaflets devoted to Coignard were among those that were lost. See Paul Bonnefon, "Essai de restitution du manuscrit de Guillaume Colletet." *Revue d'histoire littéraire de la France* (1895): 72–73. This reference is provided in Winn's introduction (*Oeuvres*, 13, n. 1). Feugère also mentions that Father Hilarion de Coste and Father Jacob, two other seventeenth-century historians interested in Coignard's work, counted her among their "femmes illustres" [illustrious women] (*Les femmes poètes au seizième siècle*, 38).

73. Feugère, *Les femmes poètes au seizième siècle*, 38.

74. Müller, *La poésie religieuse catholique de Marot à Malherbe* (Paris: Imprimerie R. Foulon, 1950), 205.

75. La Maynardière, *Poètes chrétiens du XVIe siècle*, 132.

As is often the case when scholars evaluate the writings of an author, there are a variety of opinions and perspectives. Coignard's poetic skills are both criticized and admired. While Coignard is faithful to tradition in some respects, she distances herself from sixteenth-century poetic trends. As Kaiser observes, Coignard's inspiration prevails over conventional prescriptions, a condition that distinguishes the poet from a mere *versificateur*.[76]

LES SONNETS SPIRITUELS: SOURCES

The variety of themes she explores in the sonnets reflects the various sources that Coignard drew upon in her literary endeavor. Obviously, for a collection of Christian spiritual sonnets, the Bible is the primary source of inspiration. Indeed, the Bible does provide Coignard a foundation for many of her references and allusions, but she also draws on a number of other sources including hymns, prayers, liturgy, oratorical chants, and any religious literature she would have been exposed to in her regular attendance at mass.

Coignard's work is representative of the spiritual revival of the latter half of the sixteenth century. The religious and political unrest of the period provided fertile ground for the exploration and development of new devotional practices. Henri III, crowned king of France in 1574, promoted this evolution within the spiritual disciplines, purposefully cultivating "the penitential atmosphere" of his reign.[77] The Jesuits eagerly assumed a position of leadership for Catholics and sought, in reaction to the progress of the Protestants, to provide devout followers with practical means to exercise their faith. In response to the Protestants' rejection of penitence as a sacrament, there was a renewed interest among Catholics in reviving the practice and, consequently, a more individualized, emotive spirituality.[78] Devotional handbooks and treatises on methods of penance circulated among Catholics in Latin and in the vernacular, in an effort to reach as many of the devout as possible.

In the midst of this endeavor appeared two important Spanish figures whose works gained tremendous popularity upon their arrival in France:

---

76. Kaiser, *Poétesse dévote*, 72.

77. See Cave, *Devotional Poetry in France*, 110.

78. One of the newer elements of emotive spirituality found in spiritual guides of the Renaissance was an amplification of what had already been promoted by Saint Gregory the Great in the sixth century: meditation and lamentation on the suffering of Christ. Devotional handbooks, such as those by Ignatius of Loyola and Louis of Granada, insisted on the internalization of Christ's experience as a means to be moved to compunction. Christ's Passion was the result of human sin; deliberate recognition of this was intended to stir a genuine, internal response. Coignard devotes several of her sonnets to this kind of emotive, penitential meditation.

Ignatius of Loyola's *Exercitia Spirituali,* published in 1548, and Louis of Granada's *Libro de la oración y meditatión,* published in 1566, translated into French in 1575 by François de Belleforest under the title *Le vray chemin (The True Path).* These two texts succeeded in popularizing Catholic devotional practice all over Europe.[79]

Although we cannot know for certain whether Coignard read Granada's treatise or Loyola's *Spiritual Exercises,* it is evident that she demonstrates what Berriot-Salvadore terms a "volunteerism of devotion" that is faithful to the methods of these two Spanish mystics.[80] It is most likely the influence of their writings that encouraged the introspective nature of her poetry. The numerous ethical contemplations, self-evaluations, accusations, and chastisements also indicate the influence of Granada and Loyola.[81]

Although religious texts were certainly the primary sources that influenced Coignard in her composition of *The Spiritual Sonnets,* she also had some familiarity with classical literature. Her allusions to such mythological figures as Pegasus, Apollo, Athena, Eros, Circe, Ceres, Arachne, and Pallas and to the wind of Aquilon clearly indicate some knowledge of the Greek world, which, as Fizet notes, would not be surprising in a family respected for its

79. The purpose of the spiritual exercises as outlined by Loyola and Granada is to encourage the penitent to turn inward for a thorough self-analysis to achieve the highest level of self-awareness. An examination of one's behavior and emotions would eventually lead a devotee to shed himself of mundane concerns in order to move into a closer relationship with God. In the evening meditations of *The True Path,* Granada encourages emotive reflections on existence in this world: remembrance of personal iniquities and meditations on the misery of life. Ignatius of Loyola insists more, in *The Spiritual Exercises,* on the necessity of remorse for sins, which are the cause of suffering. Dramatic penitential suffering is supposed to culminate in an experience of divine consolation, inciting the soul to love God. The union that results from this devotion is the aim of every penitent. *The Spiritual Exercises* and *The True Path* exemplify a new tendency in devotional literature of the period, a trend that might be referred to as the "feminization" of the spiritual experience. Devotional authors of the sixteenth century sought to develop a more affectionate relationship with God, one that is associated with the emotive nature traditionally accorded to women. This "feminine, emotional mysticism," as Cave refers to it in *Devotional Poetry in France* (1969, 6), flourished among religious thinkers and was promoted in their writings. According to Ferguson, in his essay "The Feminisation of Devotion: Gabrielle de Coignard, Anne de Marquets, and François de Sales," Coignard and Marquets "are often seen as precursors of a feminization of devotion developing towards the end of the sixteenth and throughout the early part of the seventeenth centuries" (187). Chilton argues that this movement can be traced back to Marguerite de Navarre. See Paul Chilton, "Devout Humanism," in *A New History of French Literature* (Cambridge: Harvard University Press, 1994), 256.

80. Berriot-Salvadore, *Les femmes dans la société française de la Renaissance,* 436. Kaiser, Winn, and Cave have all examined this question of Loyola's and Granada's influence on Coignard.

81. The self-accusations that repeatedly emerge throughout the sonnets reflect the lessons of the spiritual guidebooks of Loyola and Granada, but they also indicate the strong influence of the psalmist, a figure with whom many sixteenth-century religious poets identify in their verse. Psalm 51 is particularly important to Coignard, as three of her sonnets are based on its verses.

support of the humanities.[82] Although her rejection of paganism is evident, Coignard demonstrates a certain facility in her allusions to the pagan world, a world absolutely critical to the Renaissance imagination. Her vehement opposition to non-Christian influences reflects her belief and the belief of many of her contemporaries, both Catholic and Protestant, that poetry must be worthy of its celestial origins.[83] Yet her rejection of secular non-Christian inspiration separates her from her contemporaries as well as the entire humanist movement of the period. She does support Ronsard and the poets of the Pléiade for their poetic skills and techniques, but she opposes their conception of poetry, preferring instead that of the group of Christian poets, represented by Guillaume de Salluste du Bartas (1544–90).

Coignard's Christian conception of poetry separates her from the values supported by many writers of the Renaissance. She opposes glory and pride in favor of humility and patience. She rejects encyclopedic knowledge, regarding self-knowledge as the better means to serve God. She repudiates the classical authors admired by her contemporaries, granting primacy to the Bible instead.[84] The few mythological references she does make, images common to the arsenal of many poets of the period, serve simply to enrich her verse or to elucidate some ethical consideration.[85] Although the contradiction is troubling—for how could someone with her religious credence believe or say anything ethical outside a Christian context—Coignard, at times, did work within a humanist framework. Her mythological references are so minor that they hardly conflict with her stated objective as a Christian poet and actually serve as an instrument of moral instruction.

It is impossible to know for certain how well-read Coignard really was or how acquainted she was with the poetry of her contemporaries. Based on references she makes in her work, it is evident that she was familiar with the works of Ronsard and Du Bellay, but any suggestions beyond that would be mere speculation. She could have made all sorts of contacts at the *Jeux Floraux,* and certainly her exposure to and participation in the activities there must have influenced her tremendously. What is apparent are her efforts to find a place for herself amid these influences. Fizet maintains that the "constant struggle to find her own voice, linked to her particular experience, accompanies us every step of the way in the reading of *The Spiritual Sonnets.*"[86]

---

82. Fizet, *Sonnetz spirituels,* 18.

83. Kaiser, *Poétesse dévote,* 84.

84. See Kaiser, *Poétesse dévote,* 176.

85. See Winn, *Oeuvres,* 38.

86. See Fizet, *Sonnetz spirituels,* 19.

While Coignard admires the art of the Pléiade poets, she reproves the inspiration at the heart of their verse. She establishes her literary identity by situating herself in relation and opposition to the discourse of the masters.[87] She strives to purify the poetic techniques of the Pléiade by filtering them through divine inspiration.

CONFLICTING ASPIRATIONS IN *LES SONNETS SPIRITUELS*

Despite Coignard's efforts to emulate the great poets of her century while, at the same time, paying careful attention to maintaining the pure and proper inspiration of her own writing, an insurmountable and fascinating conflict emerges at various points throughout the sonnets. Coignard fears that her use of poetry as a devotional practice is unconsciously concealing some other ambition. She has trouble justifying her literary endeavor. Coignard is a woman author who consistently holds her writing in contempt. The emotional and spiritual conflicts that rise to the surface of her urgent, yet paradoxically reluctant, *prise de parole* endow her verse with an intriguing uneasiness.[88] The colliding impulses at the root of Coignard's inspiration result in compelling introspective debates on writing and literary creation. Her work provides a complex example of the dilemma voiced by many religious women of the Renaissance: writing by its very nature requires a certain egocentricity that opposes selfless, holy contemplation. Hence, where Coignard expresses an intense need and desire to write, she also voices a distinct rejection of that writing.

Coignard defines herself as a Christian writer who disapproves of worldly poetic aspirations but who nonetheless delights in the pleasures of writing. She denounces the imperfections of human language, incapable of justly honoring God, but then offers her writing to God as a gift of reverence. With humility, she professes an inability to write, all the while yearning to prove herself, through her writings, worthy of esteem. The anxious contemplative presence of Coignard in her work mirrors the obstacles she encounters in the duality of her ambition. The longing to assume the role of subject/

---

87. This is a strategy that François Rigolot has examined in his article on feminine writing in the Renaissance, "Ecrire au féminin à la Renaissance: Problèmes et perspectives," *Esprit Créateur* 30, no. 4 (winter 1990): 3–10.

88. Whether Coignard is unusual in the extent to which, as a religious writer, she rejects her writing or whether other religious writers of the time, such as those of the group of Christian poets represented by Du Bartas, similarly voice anxiety with regard to their writing are questions worthy of further inquiry, something that I or others may pursue in the future.

writer clashes with the desired renunciation of self, putting into question the compatibility of godly devotion and literary will.[89]

A NOTE ON THE TEXT

My translation is based on Winn's edition of the *Oeuvres chrétiennes* (Geneva: Droz, 1995), which is based on the 1594 edition (Toulouse: Pierre Jagourt et Bernard Carles), which is located at the Bibliothèque Municipale de Toulouse. I have imported a great number of Winn's notes, as well as some information from Fizet's Master's thesis,[90] into the notes that accompany this translation. With regard to Biblical references, however, I have expanded them in some cases, corrected them in others, and, after some inquiry and reflection, omitted those I judged unsuitable for my own interpretation of the text. There are numerous Biblical references in the notes that are provided in most cases without further explanation. These references are included as possible sources for the imagery and language Coignard uses in her sonnets and to invite readers to compare the sonnets and corresponding Biblical passages for themselves.[91] I have also added explanatory notes where I thought necessary.

I have made every effort in this translation to be as loyal as possible to the original text, striving above all to maintain sound meaning in English. I have not, however, attempted to reproduce or capture the original poetic form beyond adhering to the fourteen lines of the sonnet. The rigid requirements of the alexandrine line and rhyme scheme of the French sonnet proved unfeasible to preserve in translation. I preferred to focus my attention instead on conveying the content of Coignard's poems.

The musical quality of Coignard's sonnets is lost in the line-by-line literal translation, as is the significance of some of her syntactical choices. At the same time, the rendering of the text into English accentuates the frequent

---

89. Berriot-Salvadore touches briefly on this conflict in Coignard's work and seems to question the sincerity of her disinterest in recognition, as well as her claim that God is the sole addressee of her poems: "In her general confession, we have seen Gabrielle de Coignard admit to two faults, which, in reality, endow her poetry with a captivating originality. She considers herself 'singular in her condition': isn't this what engages her to examine herself with such passionate interest? She likes praise and desires to be admired for her 'discours': isn't this what motivates literary creation? Gabrielle de Coignard is in fact well aware of composing an *oeuvre*, even if she insists that she only wants to speak to the 'Eternal one' " (*Les femmes dans la société française de la Renaissance*, 440). See sonnet 14.

90. Ontario, Canada: University of Waterloo, 1992.

91. I have used *The New Oxford Annotated Bible with the Apocryphal/Deuterocanonical Books*, ed. Bruce M. Metzger and Roland E. Murphy (New York: Oxford University Press, 1994), which uses the *New Revised Standard Version* translation, for all Biblical references in the notes.

awkwardness of Coignard's word choice and word order in her effort to conform to the twelve-syllable line and traditional rhyme scheme. With the intention of strengthening some of these weaker verses, although without sacrificing meaning, I have in some cases modified verb tenses. For example, I wanted to avoid Coignard's frequent use of the present participle and opted instead for the present indicative, a strategy that effectively generates a more energetic line in English.

In many of the sonnets I have found it necessary to reorganize the syntax to clarify meaning, which has resulted in a shift of a few words from one line to the next or, in a few cases, the reordering of entire lines within a stanza. I have indicated these instances by an asterisk (*) at the end of the first line requiring a shift with the line or lines that follow it. Finally, I have modified punctuation in order to allow for a more natural flow in English, as well as to improve readability.

VOLUME EDITOR'S
BIBLIOGRAPHY

PRIMARY SOURCES

Agrippa of Nettesheim, Henry Cornelius. *Declamation on the Nobility and Preeminence of the Female Sex*. Edited and translated by Albert Rabil, Jr. Chicago: University of Chicago Press, 1996.

Boccaccio, Giovanni. *Concerning Famous Women*. Translated by Guido Guarino. New Brunswick, N.J.: Rutgers University Press, 1963.

————. *Decameron*. Edited by Vittorio Branca. Turni: Einaudi, 1987.

Bourbon, Catherine de. *Lettres et poésies de Catherine de Bourbon, 1570–1605*. Edited by Raymond Ritter. Paris: Champion, 1927.

Bourbon, Gabrielle de. *Oeuvres spirituelles, 1510–1516*. Edited by Evelyne Berriot-Salvadore. Paris: Champion, 1999.

Bruni, Leonardo. "On the Study of Literature to Lady Battista Malatesta of Montefeltro (1405)." In *The Humanism of Leonardo Bruni: Selected Texts*, translated by Gordon Griffiths, James Hankins, and David Thompson, 240–51. Binghamton, N.Y.: Medieval and Renaissance Texts and Studies, 1987.

Castiglione, Baldassare. *The Book of the Courtier*. Translated by George Bull. New York: Viking Penguin, 1967.

Catherine of Genoa. *Purgation and Purgatory. The Spiritual Dialogue*. Translated by Serge Hughes. New York: Paulist Press, 1979.

Catherine of Siena. *The Dialogue*. Translated by Suzanne Noffke, O. P. New York: Paulist Press, 1980.

Chassignet, Jean-Baptiste. *Le mespris de la vie et consolation contre la mort*. Edited by A. Müller. Geneva: Droz, 1953.

Christine de Pizan. *The Book of the City of Ladies*. Translated by Earl Richards. New York: Persea Books, 1982.

————. *Oeuvres poétiques de Christine de Pisan*. Edited by Maurice Roy. Paris: Librairie de Firmin Didot et Cie, 1886.

————. *The Treasure of the City of Ladies*. Translated by Sarah Lawson. New York: Viking Penguin, 1985.

Coignard, Gabrielle de. *Une édition annotée des Sonnetz spirituels de Gabrielle de Coignard*. Edited by Marianne Ebba Ursula Fizet. M.A. Thesis. Ontario, Canada: University of Waterloo, 1992.

————. *Les oeuvres chrétiennes*. Edited by Colette Winn. Geneva: Droz, 1995.

————. *Sonnets spirituels.* In *Le thresor du sonet, XVIe-XVIIe siècles. III.* Edited by Hugues Vaganay. Macon: Protat Frères, 1900.

Colonna, Vittoria. *Rime.* Edited by Alan Bullock. Bari: Laterza, 1982.

Deming, Lynne, ed. *The Feminine Mystic: Readings from Early Spiritual Writers.* Cleveland, Ohio: The Pilgrim Press, 1997.

Desportes, Philippe. *Prieres et autres oeuvres chrestiennes.* In *Oeuvres.* Edited by Alfred Michiels. Paris: Adolphe Delahays, 1858.

Des Roches, Madeleine et Catherine. *Les oeuvres.* Edited by Anne Larsen. Geneva: Droz, 1993.

————. *Les secondes oeuvres.* Edited by Anne Larsen. Geneva: Droz, 1998.

Du Bellay, Joachim. *Oeuvres poétiques.* Edited by Daniel Aris and Françoise Joukovsky. Paris: Bordas, 1993.

————. *La deffence et illustration de la langue françoyse.* Edited by Henri Chamard. Paris: Didier, 1948.

Du Guillet, Pernette. *Rymes.* In *Oeuvres poétiques.* Edited by Françoise Charpentier. Paris: Gallimard, 1983.

D'Urfé, Anne. *Oeuvres morales et spirituelles.* Edited by Yves le Hir. Geneva: Droz, 1977.

Elyot, Thomas. *Defence of Good Women: The Feminist Controversy of the Renaissance.* Facsimile Reproductions. Edited by Diane Bornstein. New York: Delmar, 1980.

Erasmus, Desiderius. *Erasmus on Women.* Edited by Erika Rummel. Toronto: University of Toronto Press, 1996.

Ferrazzi, Cecilia. *Autobiography of an Aspiring Saint.* Edited and translated by Anne Jacobson Schutte. Chicago: University of Chicago Press, 1996.

Fonte, Moderata. *The Worth of Women Wherein Is Clearly Revealed Their Nobility and Their Superiority to Men.* Edited and translated by Virginia Cox. Chicago: University of Chicago Press, 1997.

Franco, Veronica. *Poems and Selected Letters.* Edited and translated by Ann Rosalind Jones and Margaret F. Rosenthal. Chicago: University of Chicago Press, 1998.

————. *Rime.* Edited by Stefano Bianchi. Milan: Mursia, 1995.

Granada, Luis de. *Libro de la oracíon y meditatíon.* Edited by Alvaro Huerga. Madrid: Fundación Universitaria Española, 1994.

————. *Of Prayer and Meditation Contayning Foureteene Meditations, for the Seaven Dayes of the Weeke, Both for Mornings and Evenings: Treating the Principal Matters and Holy Mysteries of Our Faith.* Translated by Richard Hopkins. London: W. I., 1611.

————. *Le vray chemin et adresse pour acquerir et parvenir à la grace de Dieu, et se maintenir en icelle, par le moyen et compagnie de l'oraison et contemplation en la loy et amour de Dieu.* Translated by François de Belleforest. Paris: Guillaume de la Noue, 1579.

Greimas, Algirdas, and Teresa Keane. *Dictionnaire du moyen français.* Paris: Larousse, 1992.

Henderson, Katherine, and Barbara McManus, eds. *Half Humankind: Contexts and Texts of the Controversy about Women in England, 1540–1640.* Urbana, Ill.: University of Illinois Press, 1985.

Hesiod. *Theogony. Works and Days. Shield.* Edited by Apostolos N. Athanassakis. Baltimore: Johns Hopkins University Press, 1983.

Huguet, Edmond. *Dictionnaire de la langue française du seizième siècle.* 7 vols. Paris: Didier, 1846.

————. *Mots disparus ou vieillis depuis le XVIe siècle.* Geneva: Droz, 1967.

Jones, Ann Rosalind. "Pernette du Guillet: The Lyonnais Neoplatonist." In *Women Writers of the Renaissance and Reformation.* Edited by Katharina Wilson, 219–31. Athens: University of Georgia Press, 1987.

Julian of Norwich. *Showings.* Translated by Edmund Colledge and James Walsh. New York: Paulist Press, 1978.

Kempe, Margery. *The Book of Margery Kempe.* Translated by B. A. Windeatt. New York: Penguin Books, 1986.

King, Margaret L., and Albert Rabil, Jr., eds. *Her Immaculate Hand: Selected Works by and about the Women Humanists of Quattrocento Italy.* Binghamton, N.Y.: Medieval and Renaissance Texts and Studies, 1983.

Klein, Joan Larsen, ed. *Daughters, Wives, and Widows: Writings by Men about Women and Marriage in England, 1500–1640.* Urbana, Ill.: University of Illinois Press, 1992.

Knox, John. *The Political Writings of John Knox. The First Blast of the Trumpet against the Monstrous Regiment of Women and Other Selected Works.* Edited by Marvin Breslow. Washington, D.C.: Folger Shakespeare Library, 1985.

Labé, Louise. *Oeuvres complètes.* Edited by François Rigolot. Paris: Flammarion, 1986.

La Ceppède, Jean de. *Les théorèmes sur le sacré mystère de nostre redemption: premier livre.* Edited by Yvette Quenot. Paris: Librairie Nizet, 1988.

———. *Les théorèmes sur le sacré mystère de nostre redemption: livres II et III.* Edited by Yvette Quenot. Paris: Librairie Nizet, 1989.

Larsen, Anne. "Les Dames Des Roches: The French Humanist Scholars." In *Women Writers of the Renaissance and Reformation.* Edited by Katharina Wilson. Athens: University of Georgia Press, 1987.

Larsen, Anne, and Colette H. Winn, eds. *Renaissance Women Writers: French Texts/American Contexts.* Detroit: Wayne State University Press, 1994.

———. *Writings by Pre-Revolutionary French Women: From Marie de France to Elizabeth Vigée-Le Brun.* New York: Garland, 2000.

Lebègue, Raymond. *La poésie française de 1560 à 1630. Première Partie.* Paris: Société d'Édition d'Enseignement Supérieur, 1951.

Lorris, William de, and Jean de Meun. *The Romance of the Rose.* Translated by Charles Dahlbert. Princeton: Princeton University Press, 1971.

Loyola, Ignace de. *Les exercices spirituels.* Translated by Jean-Claude Guy. Paris: Editions du Seuil, 1982.

Malherbe, François de. *Oeuvres poétiques.* Edited by René Fromilhague and Raymond Lebègue. Paris: Belles Lettres, 1968.

Marinella, Lucrezia. *The Nobility and Excellence of Women and the Defects and Vices of Men.* Edited and translated by Anne Dunhill. Introduction by Letizia Panizza. Chicago: University of Chicago Press, 1999.

Marot, Clément. *Oeuvres poétiques.* Edited by Gérard Defaux. Paris: Bordas, 1990.

Marquets, Anne de. *Sonets spirituels.* Edited by Gary Ferguson. Geneva: Droz, 1997.

Montenay, Georgette de. *Poésies de Georgette de Montenay, fille d'honneur de Jeanne d'Albret, 1571.* Paris: Agence Centrale de la société, 1864.

Moulin, Jeanine. *La poésie féminine de Marie de France à Marie Noël.* Paris: Seghers, 1966.

Navarre, Marguerite de. *Chansons spirituelles.* Edited by Georges Dottin. Geneva: Droz, 1970.

———. *Dialogue en forme de vision nocturne.* Edited by Pierre Jourda. In volume 13 of *Revue du seizième siècle,* 1–49, 1926.

————. *L'Heptaméron*. Edited by Renja Salminen. Geneva: Droz, 1999.

————. *Le miroir de l'ame pecheresse*. Edited by Renja Salminen. Suomalaisen Tiedeaka-
temian Toimituksia Annales Academiae Scientiarum Fennicae. Helsinki: Suoma-
lainen Tiedeakatemia, 1979.

————. *La navire*. Edited by Robert Marichal. In volume 306 of *Bibliothèque de l'école pra-
tique des hautes études. Sciences philologiques et historiques*, 235–303. Paris: Champion,
1956.

————. *Poésies chrétiennes*. Edited by Nicole Cazauran. Paris: Les Editions du Cerf,
1996.

————. *Les prisons*. Edited by Simone Glasson. Geneva: Droz, 1978.

The New Oxford Annotated Bible with the Apocryphal/Deuterocanonical Books. Edited by Bruce
M. Metzger and Roland E. Murphy. New Revised Standard Version. New York:
Oxford University Press, 1994.

Ovid. *Metamorphoses*. Translated by A. D. Melville. Oxford: Oxford University Press,
1986.

Peletier du Mans, Jacques. *Art poétique* (1555). In *Traités de poétique et de rhétorique de la Re-
naissance*. Edited by Francis Goyet. Paris: College Le Livre de Poche Classique,
1990.

Petrarch, Francesco. *Rime, trionfi e poesie latine*. Edited by Raffaele Mattioli, Pietro Pan-
crazi, and Alfredo Schieffini. La letteratura italiana, 6. Milano: R. Ricciardi, 1951.

————. *Petrarch's Lyric Poems: The* Rime sparse *and Other Lyrics*. Edited and translated by
Robert M. Durling. Cambridge, Mass.: Harvard University Press, 1976.

Pindar. *Olympian Odes. Pythian Odes*. Edited and translated by William H. Race. Cam-
bridge: Harvard University Press, 1997.

Romieu, Marie de. *Les premières oeuvres poétiques* (1581). Edited by André Winandy.
Geneva: Droz, 1972.

Ronsard, Pierre de. *Oeuvres complètes*. Edited by Gustave Cohen. Paris: Editions Galli-
mard, 1950.

Rousselot, Paul, ed. *La pédagogie féminine extraite des principaux écrivains qui ont traité de l'édu-
cation des femmes depuis le XVIe siècle*. Paris: Ch. Delagrave, 1881.

de Sales, Francis. *Introduction to a Devout Life*. Translated by Rev. J. M. Lelen. New York:
Catholic Book Publishing, 1946.

Scève, Maurice. *La Délie*. In *Poètes du XVIe siècle*. Edited by Albert Marie Schmidt, 69–
224. Paris: Editions Gallimard, 1953.

Schmidt, Albert Marie, ed. *Poètes du XVIe siècle*. Paris: Editions Gallimard, 1953.

Sébillet, Thomas. *Art poétique françoys* (1548). In *Traités de poétique et de rhétorique de la Re-
naissance*. Edited by Francis Goyet. Paris: College Le Livre de Poche Classique,
1990.

Sponde, Jean. *Oeuvres littéraires*. Edited by Alan Boase. Geneva: Droz, 1978.

Teresa of Avila, Saint. *The Interior Castle*. Translated by Kieran Kavanaugh and Otilio
Rodriguez. New York: Paulist Press, 1979.

————. *The Life of Saint Teresa of Avila by Herself*. Translated by J. M. Cohen. New York:
Penguin Books, 1957.

————. *Teresa of Avila: Mystical Writings*. Edited by Tessa Bielecki. New York: Cross-
road, 1994.

Theocritus. *The Idylls of Theocritus: A Verse Translation*. Translated by Thelma Sargent.
New York: W. W. Norton and Company, 1982.

Traités de poétique et de rhétorique de la Renaissance. Edited by Francis Goyet. Paris: Librairie Générale Française, 1990.

Travitsky, Betty, ed. *The Paradise of Women: Writings by Englishwomen of the Renaissance.* New York: Columbia University Press, 1989.

Van Schurman, Anna Maria. *Whether a Christian Woman Should Be Educated and Other Writings from Her Intellectual Circle.* Edited and translated by Joyce Irwin. Chicago: University of Chicago Press, 1998.

Vives, Juan Luis. *De insitutione feminae christianae: Liber Secundus and Liber Tertius.* Edited by C. Fantazzi and C. Matheeussen. Vol. 7 of *Selected Works of J. L. Vives.* Leiden: Brill, 1998.

Wilson, Katharina, ed. *Women Writers of the Renaissance and Reformation.* Athens: University of Georgia Press, 1987.

SECONDARY SOURCES

Aubaud, Camille. *Lire les femmes de lettres.* Paris: Dunod, 1993.

Baker, Deborah. *The Subject of Desire: Petrarchan Poetics and the Female Voice in Louise Labé.* West Lafayette, Ind.: Purdue University Press, 1996.

Baumgartner, Frederic. *France in the Sixteenth Century.* New York: St. Martin's Press, 1995.

Bauschatz, Cathleen. "To Choose Ink and Pen: French Renaissance and Women's Writing." In *A History of Women's Writing in France,* edited by Sonya Stephens, 41–63. Cambridge: Cambridge University Press, 2000..

Beilin, Elaine V. *Redeeming Eve: Women Writers of the English Renaissance.* Princeton: Princeton University Press, 1987.

Bennett, Judith, and Amy Froide, eds. *Singlewomen in the European Past, 1250–1800.* Philadelphia: University of Pennsylvania Press, 1999.

Benson, Pamela. *The Invention of the Renaissance Woman: The Challenge of Female Independence in the Literature and Thought of Italy and England.* University Park, Penn.: Pennsylvania State University Press, 1992.

Berriot-Salvadore, Evelyne. *Les femmes dans la société française de la Renaissance.* Geneva: Droz, 1990.

———. "Les héritières de Louise Labé." In *Louise Labé: Les voix du lyrisme,* edited by Guy Demerson, 93–106. Saint-Etienne: Publications de l'Université de Saint-Etienne, Éditions du CNRS, 1990.

Blum, Claude. *La représentation de la mort dans la littérature française de la Renaissance.* Paris: Champion, 1989.

Bothe, Catherine. "Ecriture féminine de la Réformation: Témoignage de Marie Dentière." *Romance Languages Annual* 4 (1992): 15–19.

Brée, Germaine. *Women Writers in France: Variations on a Theme.* New Brunswick: Rutgers University Press, 1973.

Bridenthal, R., C. Koonz, and S. Stuard, eds. *Becoming Visible: Women in European History.* 3d ed. Boston: Houghton Mifflin Company, 1998.

Britnell, Jennifer. "Gabrielle de Bourbon and the Not-So-Sinful Soul." In *Women's Writing in the French Renaissance,* edited by Philip Ford, 1–26. Cambridge: Cambridge French Colloquia, 1999.

Bryson, David. *Queen Jeanne and the Promised Land: Dynasty, Homeland, Religion, and Violence in Sixteenth-Century France.* Leiden, Boston, and Koln: Brill, 1999.

Castor, Grahame. *Pléiade Poetics: A Study in Sixteenth-Century Thought and Terminology.* Cambridge: Cambridge University Press, 1964.

Cave, Terence. *Devotional Poetry in France, c. 1570–1613.* Cambridge: Cambridge University Press, 1969.

Cave, Terence, and Michel Jeanneret. *Métamorphoses spirituelles.* Paris: Corti, 1972.

Chamard, Henri. *Histoire de la Pléiade.* 4 vols. Paris: Didier, 1939–40.

Champion, Pierre. "Henri III et les écrivains de son temps." *Bibliothèque de la Renaissance* 1 (1941): 43–72.

Chilton, Paul. "Devout Humanism." *A New History of French Literature.* Edited by Denis Hollier, 253–58. Cambridge: Harvard University Press, 1994.

Clark, Elizabeth. *Ascetic Piety and Women's Faith: Essays on Late Ancient Christianity.* Lewiston, N.Y.: Edwin Mellen Press, 1986.

Clark-Evans, Christine. "On the Communion of Women: Reading and Writing in the Poetry of Pernette Du Guillet and Louise Labé." *Proceedings of the PMR Conference* 12–13 (1987–88): 67–80.

Clements, Robert J. *Critical Theory and Practice of the Pléiade.* New York: Octagon Books: 1970.

Cottrell, Robert. *The Grammar of Silence: A Reading of Marguerite de Navarre's Poetry.* Washington, D.C.: The Catholic University of America Press, 1986.

Davis, Natalie Zemon. *Society and Culture in Early Modern France.* Stanford: Stanford University Press, 1975.

Davis, Natalie Zemon, and Arlette Farge. *Renaissance and Enlightenment Paradoxes.* Vol. 3 of *A History of Women in the West..* Cambridge, Mass.: Harvard University Press, 1993.

Dejean, Joan, and Nancy K. Miller, eds. *The Politics of Tradition: Placing Women in French Literature.* Yale French Studies, 75. New Haven: Yale University Press, 1988.

Delumeau, Jean. *Le péché et la peur.* Paris: Fayard, 1983.

———. *L'aveu et le pardon.* Paris: Fayard, 1990.

———. *La religion de la mère: Le rôle des femmes dans la transmission de la foi.* Paris: Cerf, 1992.

Demerson, Guy. *Louise Labé: Les voix du lyrisme.* Paris: Centre National de la Recherche Scientifique, 1990.

Elwert, W. Theodor. *Traité de versification française des origines à nos jours.* Paris: Klincksieck, 1965.

Ferguson, Gary. "Biblical Exegesis and Social and Theological Commentary in the *Sonets spirituels* of Anne de Marquets." *Oeuvres et critiques* 20, no. 2 (1995): 111–22.

———. "The Feminisation of Devotion: Gabrielle de Coignard, Anne de Marquets, and François de Sales." In *Women's Writing in the French Renaissance,* edited by Philip Ford and Gillian Jondorf. Cambridge: Cambridge French Colloquia, 1999.

———. *Mirroring Belief: Marguerite de Navarre's Devotional Poetry.* Edinburgh: Edinburgh University Press for the University of Durham, 1992.

Ferguson, Margaret, Maureen Quilligan, and Nancy Vickers, eds. *Rewriting the Renaissance: The Discourses of Sexual Difference in Early Modern Europe.* Chicago: University of Chicago Press, 1986.

Fessard, Georges. *La dialectique des "Exercices spirituels" de saint Ignace de Loyola.* Paris: Aubier, 1956.

Feugère, Léon. *Les femmes poètes au seizième siècle, 1861.* Geneva: Slatkine Reprints, 1969.

Flinders, Carol Lee, ed. *Enduring Grace: Living Portraits of Seven Women Mystics.* San Francisco: Harper, 1993.

Fournier, Hannah. "La voix textuelle des *Sonets spirituels* d'Anne de Marquets." *Etudes lit-téraires* 20, no. 2 (fall 1987): 77–92.

Fumaroli, Marc. *L'âge de l'éloquence: Rhetorique et "res literaria" de la Renaissance au seuil de l'époque classique.* Geneva: Droz, 1980.

Furlong, Monica. *Visions and Longings: Medieval Women Mystics.* Boston: Shambhala, 1997.

de Gelis, François. *Histoire critique des Jeux Floraux: Depuis leur origine jusqu'à leur transforma-tion en Académie, 1323–1694.* Geneva: Slatkine, 1981.

Gosset, Thierry. *Femmes mystiques: époque moderne, XVe–XVIIIe siècles.* Paris: La Table Ronde, 1996.

Grammont, Maurice. *Petit traité de versification française.* Paris: Armand Colin, 1965.

Grieco, Sara. "Georgette de Montenay: A Different Voice in Sixteenth-Century Em-blematics." *Renaissance Quarterly* 47, no. 4 (winter 1994): 793–871.

Guillerm, Luce. *Le miroir des femmes: Moraliste et polémistes au XVIe siècle.* Lille: Presses Uni-versitaires de Lille, 1983.

—————. *Le miroir des femmes: roman, conte, théâtre, poésie au XVIe siècle.* Lille: Presses Univer-sitaires de Lille, 1984.

Head, Thomas. "Marie Dentière: Propagandist for the Reform." In *Women Writers of the Renaissance and Reformation,* edited by Katharina Wilson. Athens: University of Georgia Press, 1987.

Hollier, Denis, ed. *A New History of French Literature.* Cambridge, Mass.: Harvard Uni-versity Press, 1994.

Hufton, Olwen. *The Prospect before Her: A History of Women in Western Europe.* New York: Alfred A. Knopf, 1996.

Hull, Suzanne W. *Chaste, Silent, and Obedient: English Books for Women, 1475–1640.* San Marino, Calif.: Huntington Library, 1982.

Jasinksi, Max. *Histoire du sonnet en France.* Paris: Imprimerie H. Brugère, A. Dalsheimer et Cie, 1903.

Jones, Ann Rosalind. *The Currency of Eros: Women's Love Lyric in Europe, 1540–1620.* Bloom-ington, Ind.: Indiana University Press, 1990.

—————. "Surprising Fame: Renaissance Gender Ideologies and Women's Lyric." In *The Poetics of Gender,* edited by Nancy K. Miller. New York: Columbia University Press, 1986.

Jordan, Constance. *Renaissance Feminism: Literary Texts and Political Models.* Ithaca: Cornell University Press, 1990.

Joukovsky, Françoise, ed. *Images de la Femme au XVIe siècle.* Paris: Éditions de la Table Ronde, 1995.

Jourda, Pierre. *Marguerite d'Angoulême, duchesse d'Alençon, reine de Navarre, 1492–1549: Étude biographique et littéraire.* Geneva: Slatkine, 1978.

Kaiser, Huguette-Renée. "Gabrielle de Coignard: Poétesse dévote." Ph.D. thesis. At-lanta: Emory University, 1975.

Kelly, Joan. "Did Women Have a Renaissance?" In *Women, History, and Theory.* Chicago: University of Chicago Press, 1984. Also in Renate Bridenthal, Claudia Koonz, and Susan M. Stuard, eds., *Becoming Visible: Women in European History.* 3d ed.. Boston: Houghton Mifflin, 1998.

Kelso, Ruth. *Doctrine for the Lady of the Renaissance.* Urbana, Ill.: University of Illinois Press, 1978.

Kermina, Françoise. *Jeanne d'Albret: La mère passionnée d'Henri IV.* Paris: Perrin, 1998.

King, Margaret L. *Women of the Renaissance.* Chicago: University of Chicago Press, 1991.

Kritzman, Lawrence D. *The Rhetoric of Sexuality and the Literature of the French Renaissance.* New York: Columbia University Press, 1991.

Labalme, Patricia, ed. *Beyond Their Sex: Learned Women of the European Past.* New York: New York University Press, 1984.

La Maynardière, Henry. *Poètes chrétiens du XVIe siècle.* Paris: Bloud et Cie, 1908.

Laqueur, Thomas. *Making Sex: Body and Gender from the Greeks to Freud.* Cambridge, Mass.: Harvard University Press, 1990.

Larnac, Jean. *Histoire de la littérature féminine en France.* Paris: Éditions Kra, 1929.

Larsen, Anne. "French Women and the Early Modern Canon: Recent Conferences, Editions, Monographs, and Translations." *Renaissance Quarterly* 53, no. 4 (winter 2000): 1183–97.

———. "'Un honneste passetems': Strategies of Legitimation in French Renaissance Women's Prefaces." *L'Esprit Créateur* 30 (1990): 11–22.

Lazard, Madeleine. "Les Dames Des Roches: Une dévotion reciproque et passionnée." In *Autour de Mme de Sevigné,* edited by Roger Duchêne, 9–18. Paris: Papers on French Seventeenth-Century Literature, 1997.

Lerner, Gerda. *The Creation of Patriarchy* and *Creation of Feminist Consciousness, 1000–1870.* 2 vols. New York: Oxford University Press, 1986, 1994.

Levin, Carole, and Jeanie Watson, eds. *Ambiguous Realities: Women in the Middle Ages and Renaissance.* Detroit: Wayne State University Press, 1987.

Loga, Marie-Rose, and Peter Rudnytsky, eds. *Contending Kingdoms: Historical, Psychological, and Feminist Approaches to the Literature of Sixteenth-Century England and France.* Detroit: Wayne State University Press, 1991.

Maclean, Ian. *The Renaissance Notion of Woman: A Study in the Fortunes of Scholasticism and Medical Science in European Intellectual Life.* Cambridge: Cambridge University Press, 1980.

Marczuk-Szwed, Barbara. "Le thème du péché et son expression poétique dans *Les oeuvres chrestiennes* de Gabrielle de Coignard et dans *Le mespris de la vie et consolation de contre la mort* de J. B. Chassignet." *Zeszyty Naukowe Uniwersyteru Jagiellónskiego* MLIV (1992): 51–71.

Mariéjol, Jean H. *La vie de Marguerite de Valois, reine de Navarre et de France, 1553–1615.* Paris: Hachette, 1928.

Marshall, Sherrin, ed. *Women in Reformation and Counter-Reformation Europe: Private and Public Worlds.* Bloomington, Ind.: Indiana University Press, 1989.

Martineau-Génieys, Christine. *Le thème de la mort dans la poésie française de 1450 à 1550.* Paris: Champion, 1978.

Mathieu-Catellani, Gisèle. "La Poétique de la Renaissance." In *Histoire des poétiques,* edited by Jean Bessière, Eva Kushner, Roland Mortier, and Jean Weisgerber. Paris: Presses Universitaires de France, 1997.

———. *La quenouille et la lyre.* Paris: Librairie José Corti, 1998.

Matter, E. Ann, and John Coakley, eds. *Creative Women in Medieval and Early Modern Italy.* Philadelphia: University of Pennsylvania Press, 1994.

Matthews-Grieco, Sara F. *Ange ou diablesse: La représentation de la femme au XVIe siècle.* Paris: Flammarion, 1991.

de Maulde-La Clavière, R. *The Women of the Renaissance: A Study of Feminism.* Translated by George Herbert Ely. Folcroft, Penn.: Folcroft Library Editions, 1978.

Meerhoff, Kees. *Rhétorique et poétique au XVIe siècle en France: Du Bellay, Ramus et les autres.* Leiden: Brill, 1986.

Melchior-Bonnet, Sabine, and Dominique Missika. *Catherine de Bourbon, l'insoumise.* Paris: Nil Éditions, 1999.

Miller, Nancy K. *Subject to Change: Reading Feminist Writing.* New York: Columbia University Press, 1988.

Monson, Craig A., ed. *The Crannied Wall: Women, Religion, and the Arts in Early Modern Europe.* Ann Arbor: University of Michigan Press, 1992.

Müller, Armand. *La poésie religieuse catholique de Marot à Malherbe.* Paris: Imprimerie R. Foulon, 1950.

Nelson, John. *Renaissance Theory of Love.* New York: Columbia University Press, 1958.

Okin, Susan Moller. *Women in Western Political Thought.* Princeton: Princeton University Press, 1979.

Pagels, Elaine. *Adam, Eve, and the Serpent.* New York: Harper Collins, 1988.

Patterson, W. F. *Three Centuries of French Poetic Theory.* Ann Arbor: University of Michigan Press, 1935.

Pomeroy, Sarah. *Goddesses, Whores, Wives, and Slaves: Women in Classical Antiquity.* New York: Schocken Books, 1976.

Ranft, Patricia. *Women and the Religious Life in Premodern Europe.* New York: St. Martin's Press, 1996.

Raymond, Marcel. *L'influence de Ronsard sur la poésie française, 1550–1585.* Genève: Droz, 1965.

Read, Kirk. "Women of the French Renaissance in Search of Literary Community: A Prolegomenon to Early Modern Women's Participation in Letters." *Romance Languages Annual* 5 (1993): 95–102.

Régnier-Bohler, Danille. "Literary and Mystical Voices." Translated by Arthur Goldhammer. In *A History of Women in the West.* Volume 2, *Silences of the Middle Ages,* edited by Christiane Klapisch-Zuber. Cambridge, Mass.: Harvard University Press, 1992.

Reynolds-Cornell, Régine. "Reflets d'une époque: *Les Devises ou emblèmes chrestiennes* de Georgette de Montenay." *Bibliothèque d'Humanisme et Renaissance* 48, no. 2 (1986): 373–86.

———. *Witnessing an Era: Georgette de Montenay and the Emblèmes ou Devises Chrestiennes.* Birmingham: Summa Publications, 1989.

Richardson, Lula McDowell. *The Forerunners of Feminism in French Literature of the Renaissance from Christine of Pisa to Marie de Gournay.* New York: Johnson Reprint Corp., 1973.

Rigolot, François. "Ecrire au féminin à la Renaissance: Problèmes et perspectives." *Esprit Créateur* 30, no. 4 (winter 1990): 3–10.

———. "La préface à la Renaissance: un discours sexué?" *Cahiers de l'Association Internationale des Études Françaises* 42 (May 1990): 121–35.

Rose, Mary Beth, ed. *Women in the Middle Ages and the Renaissance: Literary and Historical Perspectives.* Syracuse: Syracuse University Press, 1986.

Rousselot, Paul. *Histoire de l'éducation des femmes en France.* 2 vols. Paris: Didier et Cie, 1883.

Russell, Rinaldina, ed. *Italian Women Writers: A Bio-Bibliographical Sourcebook.* Westport, Conn.: Greenwood Press, 1994.

Salies, Pierre. "Gabrielle de Coignard: Poétesse toulousaine du XVIe siècle." *Archistra* 79 (March–April 1987): 33–43.

Sankovitch, Tilde. *French Women Writers and the Book: Myths of Access and Desire.* Syracuse, N.Y.: Syracuse University Press, 1988.

Sartori, Eva, ed. *Feminist Encyclopedia of French Literature.* Westport, Conn.: Greenwood Press, 1999.

Seiler, Sister Mary Hilarine. *Anne de Marquets: Poétesse religieuse du XVIe siècle.* Washington, D.C.: Catholic University of America Press, 1931.

Skenazi, Cynthia. "Marie Dentière et la predication des femmes." *Renaissance and Reformation* 21, no. 1 (winter 1997): 5–18.

Sommers, Paula. *Celestial Ladders: Readings in Marguerite de Navarre's Poetry of Spiritual Ascent.* Geneva: Droz, 1989.

Sommers, Paula. "Female Subjectivity and the Distaff: Louise Labé, Catherine Des Roches, and Gabrielle de Coignard." *Explorations in Renaissance Culture* 25 (1999): 139–50.

———. "Gendered Distaffs: Gabrielle de Coignard's Revision of Classical Tradition." *Classical and Modern Literature* 18, no. 13 (spring 1998): 203–10.

Sommerville, Margaret. *Sex and Subjectivity: Attitudes to Women in Early Modern Society.* London: Arnold, 1995.

Stephens, Sonya. *A History of Women's Writing in France.* Cambridge: Cambridge University Press, 2000.

Tetel, Marcel. *Marguerite de Navarre's Heptameron: Themes, Language and Structure.* Durham, N.C.: Duke University Press, 1973.

Tuana, Nancy. *The Less Noble Sex: Scientific, Religious, and Philosophical Conceptions of Woman's Nature.* Bloomington, Ind.: Indiana University Press, 1993.

Tucoo-Chala, Pierre. *Catherine de Bourbon: Une calviniste exemplaire.* Biarritz: Atlantica, 1997.

Vüy, Jules. *Jeanne de Jussie et les Soeurs de Sainte Claire.* Geneva: Henri Trembleu, 1881.

Weber, Henri. *La création poétique au XVIe siècle en France.* Paris: Librairie A.-G. Nizet, 1994.

Wiesner, Merry E. *Women and Gender in Early Modern Europe.* Cambridge: Cambridge University Press, 1993.

Wiethaus, Ulrike, ed. *Maps of Flesh and Light: The Religious Experience of Medieval Women Mystics.* Syracuse, N.Y.: Syracuse University Press, 1993.

Winn, Colette H. "Early Modern Women and the Poetics of Lamentation: Mourning, Revenge, and Art." *Mediævalia* 22 (1999): 127–55.

———. "La femme écrivain au XVIe siècle: Ecriture et transgression." In *Poétique: Revue de théorie et d'analyse littéraires* 21, no. 4 (1990): 435–52.

———. *Imitation of the Victory of Judith.* In *Writings by Pre-Revolutionary French Women: From Marie de France to Elizabeth Vigée-Le Brun,* edited by Anne Larsen and Colette Winn, 171–211. New York: Garland, 2000.

———. "Une lecture au féminin: L'Imitation de la victoire de Judich par Gabrielle de Coignard (1594) in L'Exégèse biblique au seizième siècle. Edited by Colette Winn. *Oeuvres et Critiques* 20, no. 2 (1995): 123–42.

———. "Mirrors of the Subject: Women Poets of the Renaissance." In *Understanding*

French Poetry: Essays for the New Millenium, edited by Stamos Metzidakis, 121–38. New York: Garland, 1994.

Winn, Colette H., and Donna Kuizenga. *Women Writers in Pre-Revolutionary France: Strategies of Emancipation.* New York: Garland, 1997.

Zinguer, Ilana. *Misères et grandeur de la femme au XVIe siècle.* Geneva: Slatkine, 1982.

SONNETS SPIRITUELS
GABRIELLE DE COIGNARD

AUX DAMES DEVOTIEUSES

Car, à qui sont plus justement deus ces vers devotieux? Et mesme d'une Dame devotieuse, laquelle durant son vefvage ayant à commander des filles et à gouverner sa maison sceut si bien mesnager et les heures du jour et les graces d'entendement qu'elle avoit receu du ciel, qu'elle en fit ces vers chrestiens tesmoins des vertueuses pensées dont elle entretenoit son esprit et son loisir. Or ne nous est il pas à l'avanture bien seant de la louer, puis que nous sommes ses enfans. Aussi n'en est il nul besoin: ceux qui l'ont cogneue, ont assez veu ce qu'elle avoit de louable et ses escrits la feront assez cognoistre à ceux qui ne l'ont jamais veue; mais osons nous bien dire (puis que la verité nous en donne la hardiesse) qu'elle fit ce que vous lirez en cest oeuvre, avec un extreme ardeur de devotion et quant et quant avec une extreme facilité. Elle n'estoit ny n'avoit desiré d'estre une grande clergesse, non qu'elle n'honorat les sçavantes dames, mais elle disoit que c'estoit savoir tout que n'ignorer point les moyens de son salut. C'estoit là sa science, ses preceptes et maximes, les commandemens de Dieu; sa theorique, cognoistre et contempler la bonté, sagesse et puissance divine; sa pratique, les oeuvres de misericorde; ses propos et ses escrits, les louanges de Dieu. Si elle estoit en vie et vouloit publier ses vers, nous ne doutons point qu'elle n'eust fait mesme chois que nous pour les dedier et peut estre qu'assez loin d'icy elle eut choisi de l'oeil du penser ceste illustre et si devotieuse Princesse enfermée dans son Usson, laquelle vivant et marchant encore sur la terre, ne vit et ne hante qu'aux cieux, et que dans ceste ville mesme de sa naissance, elle n'eust eu garde d'oublier ceste venerable Dame mere de nos Prelatz et Gouverneurs, l'exemple et le vray miroir de toute devotion et vertu. On lict dans les Actes des Apostres que ces bonnes et devotes Dames, pour esmouvoir davantage et susciter le

SPIRITUAL SONNETS
GABRIELLE DE COIGNARD

TO DEVOUT LADIES

For to whom are these devout verses more rightly due? And especially these [since they were written] by a devout lady, who was forced during her widowhood to raise daughters and govern her house, and who knew so well how to manage both the hours of the day and the graces of understanding she had received from above that she made of these Christian verses witnesses of virtuous thoughts with which she occupied her mind and her free time. Now, is it not well suited to the occasion to praise her since we are her children? Indeed, it is not even necessary: those who knew her have seen in what ways she is praiseworthy, and her writings will make her well-known to those who have never met her. But dare we say (since the truth gives us the audacity) that she wrote this work with an extreme ardor of devotion and at the same time with tremendous facility? She was not nor did she desire to be a great scholar. Not that she did not honor learned ladies, but she said that to know the means of one's salvation was to know everything. In this belief she found her knowledge, her precepts, and maxims: the commandments of God. She found her theory: to know and contemplate divine bounty, wisdom, and power. She found her practice: works of mercy. She discovered her words and her writings: the praise of God. If she were alive now and wanted to publish her poems, we do not doubt that she would have made the same choice as we did in their dedication. Perhaps far from here she would have chosen with sound consideration this illustrious and devout Princess[1] enclosed in her Usson,[2] who, still living and walking on the earth, in truth inhabits and contemplates the heavens, and perhaps in this very city of her[3] birth, she would have also taken good care not to forget this venerable lady, mother of our prelates and governors,[4] the example and true mirror of all devotion and virtue. One reads in the Acts of the Apostles[5] that those good and devout ladies, in order to move and incite the greatest of the disciples[6] to plus grand des Disciples à ramener en vie par ses prieres et par la vertu de Dieu qui l'assistoit, la bonne et devote d'Orcas (de laquelle, celle qui a fait ces vers, fait mention en quelque lieu de ses escrits) luy monstroient les ouvrages qu'elle souloit faire. Nous en userons de mesme et vous viendrons icy desployer et estaler les plus beaux ouvrages d'une Dame devote à fin de vous inciter à luy moyenner encore sur la terre par vos sainctes faveurs, une seconde et plus belle vie de renommée. Recevez donc d'aussi bon coeur qu'ils vous sont offerts ces monumens devotieux de l'esprit de la mere (Dame devotieuses) avec la devotion des filles à vostre obeissance, qui demeureront tousjours, s'il vous plaist,

Vos humbles et affectionnées servantes,
Jane et Catherine de Mansencal

AU LECTEUR

Amy Lecteur, n'ignorant point que tu ne trouves beaucoup de petites fautes et quelquefois d'assez remarquables en ce livre, que tu pourras taxer et reprendre (ce qui est tousjours tres-aisé), nous t'avons voulu briefvement advertir par ce mot que ce n'est point la faute de celle qui a faict cest oeuvre, comme tu recognoistras facilement, ains de l'imprimeur. Mais tant y a que si tu aymes tant soit peu la lecture des bons livres et à repaistre sainctement ton ame, sans t'amuser à la mesdisance, tu en raporteras un contentement et consolation incroyable, lisant diligemment ceste oeuvre spirituelle, et trouveras que le tout est raporté par ceste honneste et vertueuse Dame, à l'honneur et gloire de Dieu, le seul but et la fin de son entreprinse. Une chose te puis je bien encore asseurer que parmi tant de rares et excellens poetes de nostre temps à peine y en a-il aucun qui se puisse vanter d'avoir mieux parlé de Dieu ny escrit plus sainctement ses hauts et sacrez mysteres. Tache donc lisant et relisant journellement ce petit livre d'en faire ton profit, à fin que ce que les vains et lascifs discours de tant d'autres autheurs ont corrompu en toy de bonnes moeurs, tu le puisses corriger par le remede salutaire de ceste poesie spirituelle. A Dieu.

SUR LES VERS DE FEU MADAME DE MIREMONT

Sonnet
Honneur de ma Patrie, esprit de tant de graces,
Et de tant de beautez sainctement revestu,

bring back to life, by his prayers and by the virtue of God who assisted him, the good and devout woman Dorcas (whom our mother mentions in some of her verses), showed to Saint Peter the works that the woman wanted to accomplish. We will use these works as well and come to you here to deploy and spread the most beautiful verses of a devout lady in order to incite you to procure again for her on earth by your holy favors a second and more beautiful life of renown. Receive then, devout ladies, with as good a heart, these pious monuments of the spirit of our mother, which are offered to you in deference to your authority with the devotion of her daughters, who will always remain, if it pleases you,

Your humble and affectionate servants,
Jane and Catherine de Mansencal

TO THE READER

Gentle reader, as we are aware that you will find many small mistakes and occasionally some fairly remarkable errors in this book that you will be likely to criticize and condemn (which is always very easy to do), we wanted to warn you briefly by this note that this is not the fault of the author, as you will easily recognize, as did the printer. But the situation is such that if you even remotely like the reading of good books and piously nourish your soul without amusing yourself with malicious gossip, you will find contentment and incredible consolation in diligently reading this spiritual book, and you will find that the entire thing has been delivered by this honest and virtuous lady for the honor and glory of God, the sole ambition and end of her enterprise. One thing of which I can reassure you is that among so many rare and excellent poets of our time there is hardly one who can boast to have spoken better of God or written more reverently about His high and sacred mysteries. Try, then, reading and rereading daily this little book to profit from it, in order that the good mores that the vain and lascivious discourses of so many other authors have corrupted in you may be corrected by the salutary remedy of this spiritual poetry.[7] Adieu.

ON THE VERSE OF THE LATE MADAME DE MIREMONT

Sonnet
Honor of my country, spirit of so many graces,
Devoutly vested in so much beauty,

Parangon de ton sexe, estoille de vertu,
Fleur de devotion dont je baise les traces,

Lors que tu t'envolas dans les celestes places,
Triomphant du peché soubs tes pieds abbatu,
Quel fut nostre heritage? Et que nous laissas-tu,
Que le dueil et les pleurs dont nous baignons nos faces?

Sçais-tu que nous faisons pour le seul reconfort
De nos coeurs affligez despuis ta triste mort?
Flattez de la douceur de ta vive memoire,

Nous lisons tes beaux vers que les Anges aux cieux
Chantent avecque toy d'un air melodieux,
Louans de Dieu sans fin les oeuvres et la gloire.

DIALOGUE: PHILANDRE ET TOLOSE

Philandre
Genereuse cité, pour m'enfler le courage,
Tu presentes encor ce beau monstre à mes yeux,
Ces escripts d'une femme, esprit prodigieux,
Outre tant de grands dons qui decorent nostre aage!

Mais dy moy, je te pry, (car un chacun t'outrage)
Puisque riche tu es d'enfans si pretieux,
Beaux thresors de la terre et beaux presens des cieux,
Que ne leur es tu douce et non pas si sauvage?

Tolose
Je te diray que c'est: c'est le ciel envieux,
Qui cognoit bien, voyant fleurir si glorieux
Le don que j'ay receu de luy mesme en partage,

De meint enfantement si celebre en touts lieux,
Que s'il m'avoit encor donné cest advantage,
Au lieu d'esprits divins j'enfanterois des Dieux.

Paragon of your sex, star of virtue,
Flower of devotion whose memory I kiss,

When you took flight to celestial places,
Triumphing over sin trampled beneath your feet,
What did we inherit? And what did you leave us
But the grief and the tears with which we bathe our faces?

Do you know what we do to comfort
Our afflicted hearts since your sad death?
Flattered by the sweetness of your vivid memory,

We read your beautiful verses that the angels in heaven
Sing with you on a melodious air,
Praising without end the works and the glory of God.

DIALOGUE: PHILANDRE AND TOULOUSE

Philandre[8]
Generous city, to swell courage in me,
You present again this beautiful spectacle to my eyes,
These writings of a woman, a prodigious spirit
Beyond so many grand gifts that adorn our age!

But tell me, I beg you (for everyone now insults you[9]),
Since you are rich with such precious children,[10]
Beautiful treasures of the earth and beautiful gifts from heaven,
Why are you not sweet to them instead of being so savage?

Toulouse
I will tell you what it is: heaven is envious,
And knows well, seeing blossom so gloriously
The gift that I received from him in sharing

So many children known the world over
That if this advantage were given to me again,
Instead of divine spirits, I would give birth to gods.

SONNETS SPIRITUELS DE FEU
MADAME LA PRESIDENTE DE MIRAMONT

1.
Je n'ay jamais gousté de l'eau de la fontaine,
Que le cheval aeslé fit sortir du rocher.
A ses payennes eaux je ne veux point toucher,
Je cerche autre liqueur pour soulager ma peine.

Du celeste ruisseau de grace souveraine,
Qui peut des alterez la grand soif estancher:
Je desire ardemment me pouvoir approcher,
Pour y laver mon coeur de sa tasche mondaine.

Je ne veux point porter le glorieux laurier,
La couronne de myrte ou celle d'olivier,
Honneurs que l'on reserve aux testes plus insines.

Ayant l'angoisse en l'ame, ayant la larme à l'oeil,
M'irois-je couronnant de ces marques d'orgueil,
Puis que mon Sauveur mesme est couronné d'espines?

2.
Guide mon coeur, donne moy la science,
O Seigneur Dieu, pour chanter sainctement
Ton haut honneur que j'adore humblement,
Recognoissant assez mon impuissance.

Je n'ay nul art, grace, ny eloquence,
Pour ton sainct nom entonner dignement,
Mais ton clair feu de mon entendement
Escartera les ombres d'ignorance.

SPIRITUAL SONNETS OF THE LATE
MADAME LA PRÉSIDENTE DE MIRAMONT

1.

I have never tasted the water of the fountain
That the winged horse[11] set free from the rock.[12]
I do not want to touch its pagan waters;
I seek a different liquor to relieve my pain.

So that I may wash my heart of its worldly stain,*
I long to draw near to
The heavenly stream of sovereign grace,
Which quenches the thirst of any who desire it.[13]

I do not want to wear the glorious laurel,
The crown of myrrh or that of the olive tree;[14]
Such honors are reserved for more distinguished heads.

With anguish in my soul, with a tear in my eye,
Dare I crown myself with these marks of pride,
When my Savior Himself was crowned with thorns?

2.

Guide my heart, grant me the knowledge,
O Lord God, to praise Your glory,*
Which I humbly adore;
For, in my weakness, I am unable.

I have no art, grace, or eloquence
To do justice to Your name in song.
But Your resplendent fire will force
The shadows of ignorance from my mind.

Je ne veux point la Muse des payens,
Qu'elle s'en voise aux esprits qui sont siens,
Je suis Chrestienne et bruslant de ta flamme.

Et reclamant ton nom à haute voix,
Je sacrifie à l'ombre de ta croix,
Mon tout, mon corps, mes escrits, et mon ame.

3.
O desirs, mes mignons, qui sur vos sainctes aisles,
Volez plus vistement que le vent plus leger,
C'est ores, mes mignons, qu'il vous faut desloger,
Sans plus que vous arrester aux choses temporelles.

Çà bas tout est laideur pour les ames plus belles,
Ne poursuivez donc rien du monde passager,
Les objects terriens ne vous font qu'affliger,
Il faut cercher au ciel les graces eternelles.

Mais quand vous y serez, ô desirs bienheureux,
Ne retournes jamais en ce val douloureux,
Mais attendez là haut que mon heure ait bornée:

La vie de ce corps, et tandis beauz desirs,
Faictes un grand amas des eternels plaisirs,
Pour festoyer là haut mon ame retournée.

4.
Le clair soleil par sa chaleur ardente
Fait destiller la neige d'un rocher,
Et je me fons en sentant approcher
Le doux rayon de ta flamme excellente.

Mon oeil devient une source coulante,
Et l'ame à lors commande sur la chair,
Deliberant de jamais ne cercher,
L'occasion à l'offence coulante.

Mais quant ce feu de moy s'en est allé,
Mon pauvre coeur demeure plus gelé
Qu'un jour d'hyver tout blanchissant de glace,

I do not desire the Muse of the pagans;
Let her go to the spirits that are hers.
I am a Christian woman, burning with Your flame.[15]

And as I call Your name out loud,
I lay down my all, my body, my writings, and my soul,*
In the shadow of Your cross.[16]

3.
O desires, my darlings, who on holy wings
Fly faster than the lightest wind,
It is now, my darlings, that you must depart,
Without stopping for temporal things.

Down here, everything is ugly for the most beautiful souls.
Therefore, pursue nothing of the ephemeral world;
Things of this world will only afflict you.
You must seek eternal graces in heaven.

But, when you arrive there, O blessed desires,
Never return to this sorrowful vale.[17]
Wait in heaven instead until my fate brings to an end

The life of this body, and so many beautiful desires.
Gather an abundance of these eternal pleasures,
So that you may celebrate on high the return of my soul.

4.
The bright sun by its ardent warmth
Distills the snow of a rock,
And I melt, sensing the approach
Of the sweet ray of Your brilliant flame.[18]

My eye becomes a flowing spring,
And the soul then commands the flesh,
Determining never to seek
An occasion to offend.[19]

But when this fire was extinguished in me,
My barren heart froze harder
Than a day of winter all white with ice.

Revien, Seigneur, ne m'abandonne pas,
Si je te pers, las je voy mon trespas,
Car je ne vy qu'aux douceurs de ta grace.

5.
Ha! mon Dieu, qu'est cecy? ay-je perdu courage?
Où sont les bons desirs que j'allois poursuivant?
Seray-je point subjecte à la pluye et au vent,
Suivant les passions maistresses de nostre age?

Ce n'est pas le chemin d'une jeunesse sage,
De reculer arriere au lieu d'aller avant.
Où est ce bon espoir qui m'animoit devant,
Et ce chaste project d'un resolu vefvage?

Helas! Je cognois bien quand ta douce bonté
Me soustient, qu'en mon coeur par ta grace indompté
La constance fleurit, et que rien ne l'empesche.

Mais quant tu viens de moy ta faveur retirer,
Mon ame qui se sent de son tronc separer,
Chet comme quelque branche ou quelque feuille seiche.

6.
Ni les desirs d'une jeunesse tendre,
Ny les appas des humaines grandeurs,
Ny l'hameçon des superbes honneurs,
Ny les plaisirs qu'au monde l'on peut prendre,

Ne me pourroient contente jamais rendre,
Ny m'arrester à ces songes trompeurs.
Je veux fuyr ces ameres douceurs,
Autre loyer mon ame veut attendre.

Aille bien loin le thresor precieux
Rassasier quelque avaricieux:
Que les honneurs soient à qui les desire.

O mon vray bien, je ne veux rien avoir,
Au lieu d'espoux, de richesse, et pouvoir,
Que ton amour où seulement j'aspire.

Come back, Lord, do not abandon me.[20]
If I lose You, alas, I see my demise,
For I live only by the sweetness of Your grace.

5.
Ah! My God, what is this? Have I lost courage?
What happened to the good desires that I was pursuing?
Will I not be subject to the wind and the rain
If I follow the governing passions of our age?

It is not the path of a wise youth
To withdraw instead of going forth.
What happened to the good hope that animated me before,
And the chaste plan of a resolute widowhood?

Alas! I know that when Your sweet goodness
Sustains me, by Your unyielding grace,*
Constancy flowers unhindered in my heart.

But when You come to take back Your favor from me,
My soul, feeling severed from its trunk,[21]
Falls like a branch or some withered leaf.

6.
Neither the desires of a tender youth,
Nor the seduction of human splendors,
Nor the snare of distinguished honors,
Nor the pleasures one can procure in the world,[22]

Could ever render me content,
Or delay me with deceitful thoughts.
I want to flee these bitter sweetnesses.[23]
My soul awaits a different recompense.

May the precious treasure go far away
To satisfy some miser;
Let the honor go to him who desires it.

O my True Goodness, instead of husband, riches, and power,*
I want Your love alone,
The only thing to which I aspire.

7.
Plustost le ciel perdra ses clairs flambeaux,
Et l'esté chaut sera roidy de glace,
L'hyver aura du printemps les rameaux,
Et les mortels n'auront plus de fallace.

Plustost la mer environnant la masse,
Et seiche et froide, ayant perdu ses eaux,
N'aura poissons, ne portera batteaux,
Que de chanter ta gloire je me lasse.

Je chanteray, ô Dieu de mon salut,
Je chanteray ton los dessus mon lut,
Jamais au coeur ne sera que je n'aye

Un trait fiché de ton doux souvenir,
Pour le combat hardiment soustenir,
Contre le mal qui mes forces essaye.

8.
Monarque des hauts cieux, à ton honneur et gloire,
Je chanteray tousjours, quoy qu'il puisse advenir:
Car j'ay le coeur si plain de ton doux souvenir,
Que tu seras tousjours escript en ma memoire.

Je voudrois manier ceste lire d'ivoire,
Que le grand Vandomois fait si haut retentir,
Je ferois de mes chants les rochers mi-partir,
Si j'avois le laurier, marque de sa victoire.

Mon Dieu! que j'ay le coeur plain d'admiration,
Lisant parmy ses vers la docte invention,
D'un Hercule Chrestien r'apportant ta semblance.

Ah! non divin Ronsard, je ne puis advouer
Telle comparaison: leur payenne insolence
Offence le Seigneur au lieu de le louer.

9.
Qu'on aye opinion que je suis hypocrite,
Ayant le coeur rempli de ruse et fiction,

7.

The sky will sooner lose its bright torches,[24]
The hot summer stiffen with ice;
Winter will sooner overtake the branches of spring,
And mortals abandon their fallacies;

The sea that surrounds the land,
Will sooner lose its water, fish, and boats,*
Turning dry and cold,
Than I will ever tire of singing Your glory.

I will sing, O God, of my salvation,[25]
I will sing Your glory on my lute.
Always in my heart will there be

A line carved of Your sweet memory
That valiantly upholds the combat
Against the evil that tries my forces.

8.

King of the high heavens, no matter what may come,*
I will always sing to Your honor and glory.
My heart is so full of Your sweet memory
That Your name will forever be written in my thoughts.

I would like to hold this lyre of ivory
That the grand Vandomois[26] plays so sweetly.
I would sunder rocks with my songs,[27]
If I had the laurel, the mark of his victory.

My God! My heart is full of admiration
As I read among his verses the learned invention
Of a Christian Hercules bearing Your semblance.[28]

Ah! Not divine Ronsard, I cannot admit
Such a comparison: his pagan insolence
Offends the Lord instead of praising Him.

9.[29]

Let them say that I am a hypocrite,
That my heart brims with deceit and guile.

Que tout ce que je fais est ostentation,
Que je suis envieuse, arrogante, et despite:

J'advoue tout cela, plus encor' je merite
Qu'on publie par tout mon imperfection.
Toutesfois le haut but de mon intention
Ne se changera point, quoy qu'on m'aye descrite.

Que l'on die de moy tout ce que l'on voudra,
Je m'asseure qu'en fin matiere leur faudra:
Car Dieu qui voit à clair la verité celée,

Permettra que ceux-là, qui blasment les vertus,
Seront de leur baston à la parfin battus,
Ayant d'un repentir leur ame bourrelée.

10.
Obscure nuit, laisse ton noir manteau,
Va reveiller la gracieuse aurore,
Chasse bien loin le soin qui me devore,
Et le discours qui trouble mon cerveau.

Voicy le jour gracieux, clair et beau,
Et le soleil qui la terre decore,
Et je n'ay point fermé les yeux encore,
Qui font nager ma couche toute en eau.

Ombreuse nuit, paisible et sommeillante,
Qui sçais les pleurs de l'ame travaillante,
J'ay ma douleur cachée dans ton sein,

Ne voulant point que le monde le sçache,
Mais toutefois je te pry' sans relasche,
De l'apporter aux pieds du Souverain.

11.
Si ce mien corps estoit de plus forte nature,
Et mes pauvres enfans n'eussent de moy besoing,
Hors des soucis mondains, je m'en irois bien loin
Choisir pour mon logis une forest obscure.

That everything I do is ostentatious,
That I am envious, arrogant, and insolent.

I admit all that and concede that I deserve
To have my imperfection proclaimed the world over.
Nonetheless, the high purpose of my intention
Will not change, no matter how they describe me.

They may say anything they want about me.
I assure myself that they will be speechless in the end:
For God, who clearly sees the hidden truth,

Will ensure that those who reproach virtues
Will be beaten to the end by their own staff,
Their souls racked with remorse.

10.
Dark night, take leave of your black cloak;
Go awaken the gracious dawn.
Chase far away the care that devours me
And the chatter that troubles my mind.

The gracious day, beautiful and bright, is here
With the sun that adorns the earth,
And I have yet to close my eyes,
Which flood my bed with water.[30]

Shadowy night, slumberous and quiet,[31]
You who know the tears of the laboring soul,
I have hidden my pain in your breast,[32]

Not wanting the world to know of it.
Nonetheless, I implore you without reprieve
To carry it to the feet of the Sovereign One.

11.
If my body were of a stronger nature
And my poor children did not need me,[33]
I would go far away from worldly worries
And choose a dark forest for my lodging.

Las! je ne verrois plus aucune creature,
Ayant abandonné de ce monde le soing,
Dans quelque creux rocher je choisirois un coing,
Et les sauvages fruicts seroient ma nourriture.

Et là j'admirerois en repos gracieux
Les oeuvres du haut Dieu, l'air, la terre et les cieux,
Les benefices siens sainctement admirables.

Et en pleurs et souspirs requerant son secours,
Je passerois ainsi le reste de mes jours,
Recevant de mon Dieu les graces secourables.

12.
Fauche Seigneur de ton glaive trenchant
Tous les chardons qui prennent accroissance
Aux plus beaux lieux de nostre conscience,
Et vont tousjours les vertus empeschant.

Ce sont les grains que l'ennemy meschant
Jette sur nous par sa fauce semence.
Vien donc, Seigneur, car la moisson s'avance,
Vient de ta main ces herbes arrachant:

Ne permets point que la ronce et l'espine
Gastent le fruict de la bonne racine:
Envoye nous de la pluye d'en haut,

Pour arroser ceste terre infertille,
Qui dans son champ ne porte rien d'utile,
S'il ne te plaist reparer son deffaut.

13.
Mon ame, dormez vous? mon corps, vous sommeilles,
Assoupi lourdement sur la plume otieuse:
La sombre obscurité de la nuict oublieuse,
D'un voile paresseux vous tient les yeux sillez.

Les animaux des champs, les poissons escaillez,
Voyent plustost que vous la clarté gracieuse,

Alas! I would not see a single creature.
Having abandoned the cares of this world,
I would choose a corner in some hollow rock
And take wild fruits for nourishment.

And there I would admire in pleasant repose,
The works of the God on high: the air, the earth, and the skies,
His holy and admirable blessings.

And in tears and sighs, invoking His succor,
I would thus spend the rest of my days,
Receiving the merciful grace from my God.

12.
Cut down, Lord, with Your sharp sword,
All of the thistles that grow
In the most beautiful places of our conscience,
Always hindering the growth of virtues.

These are the seeds that the wicked enemy
Throws on us by his perfidious dissemination.
Come then, Lord, for the harvest is advancing.
Come with Your hand to tear away these grasses.[34]

Do not permit the branch or the thorn
To spoil the fruit of the good root.
Send us rain from above

To water this infertile earth,
Which cannot produce anything useful in its field[35]
Unless You repair its imperfection.

13.
My soul, are you sleeping? My body, you doze,
Heavily lulled on the idle feather.
The somber obscurity of the forgetful night
Keeps your eyes closed with a lazy veil.

The animals of the fields and the scaled fish
Will see the gracious clarity sooner than you.

Le chariot pesant de la chair vicieuse
Garde que nous n'ayons nos esprits esveillez.

Mais sus, c'est trop dormy en ma paresse extreme,
Je me veux esveiller en ce temps de caresme,
Me levant de matin pour ouyr les sermons.

Mon ame conduira par la raison active
Ce corps appesanti de sa charge retive
A servir le Seigneur et gaigner les pardons.

14.
Mes vers, demeurez coys dedans mon cabinet,
Et ne sortez jamais, pour chose qu'on vous die,
Ne volez point trop haut, d'une aesle trop hardie,
Arrestez vous plus bas sur quelque buissonnet.

Il faut estre sçavant pour bien faire un sonet,
Qu'on lise nuit et jour, qu'Homere on estudie,
Et le riche pinceau des muses l'on mandie
Pour peindre leurs beautez sur un tableau bien net.

Demeurez donc mes vers enclos dedans mon coffre,
Je vous ay façonnez pource que je vous offre
Aux pieds de l'Eternel, qui m'a fait entonner

Tout ce que j'ay chanté sur ma lire enrouée:
Je me suis à luy seul entierement vouée,
Ne voulant mes labeurs à nul autre donner.

15.
Perce moy l'estomach d'une amoureuse fleche,
Brusle tous mes desirs d'un feu estincellant,
Esleve mon esprit d'un desir excellent,
Foudroye de ton bras l'obstacle qui l'empesche.

Si le divin brandon de ta flamme me seiche,
Fay sourdre de mes yeux un fleuve ruisselant,
Qu'au plus profond du coeur je porte recelant
Des traits de ton amour la gracieuse breche.

The heavy chariot of depraved flesh[36]
Makes certain that we do not awaken our minds.[37]

But, come now, it is too much to sleep in my extreme laziness.[38]
I want to awaken myself in this time of Lent,
And rise early each morning to hear the sermons.

By active reason, my soul will guide
This body weighed down by its unruly charge,
To serve the Lord and earn forgiveness.

14.
My verse, stay quiet in my room,[39]
And never leave, no matter what anyone says to you.
Do not fly too high on a wing too bold,[40]
But stop lower on some small bush.[41]

One must be learned to compose a sonnet well,
Read night and day and study Homer,[42]
And beg for the rich brush of the muses
To capture their beauty within a flawless painting.

Stay then, my verse, enclosed in my coffer;
I made you so that I might offer you
At the feet of the Eternal One, who incited me to sing

All that I sang on my rusty lyre.
I have devoted myself entirely to Him,
Not wanting to give my labors to any other.

15.
Pierce my stomach with an amorous arrow,[43]
Burn all my desires with a scintillant fire,
Lift my spirit with an excellent desire,
With Your arm, strike down the obstacle that entangles it.

If the divine brand of Your flame desiccates me,
Make a streaming river spring up from my eyes,
So that I carry concealed in the depths of my heart
The gracious opening forged by the traces of your love.

Puis que tu n'es qu'amour, ô douce charité,
Puis que pour trop aymer tu nous as merité
Tant de biens infinis et d'admirables graces,

Je te veux supplier par ce puissant effort
De l'amour infini qui t'a causé la mort,
Qu'en tes rets amoureux mon ame tu enlasses.

16.
Fleuve coulant par ce pays fertille,
Qui enrichis les champs et les citez,
Nous apportant mille commodités,
Battant les murs de ma fameuse ville.

O si j'avois un doux et grave stile,
Dessus le bort de tes concavités,
Je chanterois tes grandes raritez,
Et du rocher ta source qui distile.

Tu as nourris maints excellents esprits
Qui font tes eaux jaillir dans leurs escrits,
Ja l'Indien sçait le nom de Guaronne.

Puis que je suis née dessus tes bors,
Ayant apprins quelques simples accorts,
A ton honneur ma muse les entonne.

17.
Je beniray tousjours l'an, le jour et le moys,
Le temps et la saison, que la bonté divine
Lança ses doux attraits au fonds de ma poitrine,
Arrachant de mon sein le coeur que je portois.

Un soir il me sembla ainsi que je dormois
Dessous l'obscurité de ma sombre courtine,
Que je me submergeois dedans la mer mutine,
Hallettant à la mort peu à peu je mourois.

J'avois mille regrets de mes fautes commises,
Je promettois à Dieu des sainctes entreprises,
S'il me donnoit loisir de vivre encor un peu.

Since You are only love, O Sweet Charity,[44]
Since You secured for us*
Infinite goods and admirable graces by loving too much,

I beseech You, by this powerful exertion
Of the infinite love that caused Your death,
To ensnare my soul in Your amorous nets.

16.
River flowing through this fertile country,
You who enrich the fields and the cities,
Bring us a thousand commodities,
Beating the walls of my famous city.

Oh, if only I had a sweet and grave style,
I would sing of your great rarities;*
Above the banks of your hollows,
I would sing of the rock distilled by your source.

You have nourished many excellent minds[45]
Who make your waters gush forth in their writings.
The Indian already knows the name Garonne.[46]

Since I was born above your banks,[47]
Having learned some simple lessons,
My muse proclaims them in your honor.

17.
I will always bless the year, the day, and the month,[48]
As well as the time and the season, that divine bounty
Thrust its sweet charms into the depths of my chest,
Tearing from my breast the heart I carried.

While I was sleeping beneath the obscurity*
Of my somber curtain one evening,
It seemed that I was submerging into the seditious sea.
Inhaling death, little by little, I was dying.[49]

I had a thousand regrets for the faults I had committed.
I promised holy undertakings to God
In exchange for the opportunity to live a little longer.

Je m'esveille en sur-saut, et mon ame advertie
Par ce songe divin de corriger ma vie,
Demande ton secours pour accomplir son voeu.

18.

Perisse la grandeur qui trompe les plus sages,
Enfle les plus sçavans, charme les plus devots,
Elle attire chacun au bruit de son beau los,
Puis des liens d'orgueil enlasse nos courages.

Mais las! tous ces honneurs et ces grans heritages
Ne nous peuvent donner un moment de repos,
Agitant nos esprits tout ainsi que les flos,
Guindés jusques au ciel, par mille et mille orages.

Bien-heureux donc celuy qui n'est point engeollé
En sa douce prison et n'est point affollé
Des Circeans appas dont plusieurs elle trompe.

Fuyez, humbles d'esprit, ses vaines passions,
La croix soit le subjet de vos affections,
Car c'est un traict volant, que le monde et sa pompe.

19.

Amour est un enfant, ce disent les poetes,
Qui a les yeux sillés par un obscur bandeau:
C'est un cruel serpent, un devorant flambeau,
Qui brusle les humains par les flammes secrettes:

Dardant à tous propos des mortelles sagettes,
Il donne en nous flattant la mort et le tombeau,
Il vole dans nos coeurs tout ainsi qu'un oyseau,
C'est un foudre tonnant, racine de tempestes.

Chassons donc vistement cest aveugle estranger,
Avant que dans nos coeurs il se puisse loger,
Cherchons cest autre amour qui fait la vertu suivre,

Qui est chaste et parfaict, modeste, et gracieux,
Dardant ses trais dorez de la voute des cieux,
Non pour nous massacrer, mais pour nous faire vivre.

I awakened with a start, and my soul,*
Inspired by this divine dream to correct my life,
Asks for Your help in order to accomplish its wish.

18.
May the greatness that fools the wisest,*
Inflates the most learned, charms the most devout, perish.
It attracts each one to the din of its alluring glory.
Then, by the tethers of pride, it bridles our courage.

But alas! All these honors and these grand legacies
Cannot grant us one moment of repose,
Stirring our spirits like torrents
Raised to the sky by a thousand storms.

Blessed, therefore, is he who is not held captive
In its sweet prison and is not terror stricken
By the Circean charms that fool so many.[50]

You who are humble of spirit, flee its vain passions.
May the Cross be the subject of your affections,
For the world and its pomp are but a flying arrow.

19.
The poets say love is a child
Whose eyes are closed by a dark blindfold.[51]
It is a cruel serpent,[52] a devouring torch
That burns humans by secret flames.

Shooting mortal arrows at the slightest thing,
It sends us to our death and tomb by flattering us.
It flies into our hearts like a bird.
It is a thunderous bolt of lightning, a wellspring of storms.

Therefore, let us hasten to chase away this blind stranger
Before he lodges himself in our hearts.
Let us search for this other love that incites virtue,

Which is chaste and perfect, modest and gracious,
Shooting its golden arrows from the canopy of heaven,
Not to massacre us, but to make us live.

20.

Furieuse amitié qu'on nomme jalousie,
Venimeuse poison des sens plus arrestez,
Qui peints dans nos cerveaux mille meschancetez,
Dont l'apprehension est follement saisie.

Ce n'est point amitié, c'est une frenaisie,
Un transport enragé, forgeur de cruautez:
Ceux qui ont ce malheur demeurent hebetez,
Perdans toute raison et toute courtoisie.

O farouche amitié, fuyez de ma maison,
J'aymerois plus humer un verre de poison,
Qu'avoir ces passions qui bourrellent nos ames.

L'affligé soupçonneux qui porte ceste croix,
De son propre cousteau se tue mille fois,
Et blesse la vertu des innocentes ames.

21. Pour le jour de l'exaltation de la Croix

O saincte Croix, enseigne glorieuse,
Je te salue, à deux genoux flechis,
Offrant mon coeur, aux pieds du Crucifix,
Qui sur ton bois mit sa chair precieuse.

Tu as porté, ô Croix victorieuse,
Le restaurant pour guerir nos soucis,
Tu es la clef ouvrant le Paradis,
Nous delivrant de la mort furieuse.

O douce Croix, sous tes sacrez rameaux,
Je veux porter mes peines et travaux,
Sans m'eslongner de l'ombre de tes aesles.

Car le vaincqueur qui te fait triompher,
Nous a sauvez du gouffre de l'enfer,
Et nous conduict aux joyes eternelles.

22. Pour le jour de l'invention de la Croix

J'ay le coeur tout esmeu et l'ame travaillée,

20.
Furious friendship, otherwise known as jealousy,
Venomous poison of the most constant senses,
You paint a thousand ignobilities in our brains
That frantically seize our understanding.[53]

It is not friendship; it is a frenzy,
An enraged rapture, a maker of cruelty.
Those who have this misfortune remain dazed,
Losing all reason and all courtesy.

O fierce friendship, flee my house!
I would prefer to inhale a vial of poison
Than be afflicted by these passions that rack our souls.

The suspicious, afflicted one who bears your cross
Slays himself a thousand times with his own knife
And wounds the virtue of innocent souls.

21. For the Day of the Exaltation of the Cross[54]
O holy Cross, glorious ensign,[55]
I salute you on bended knee
And offer my heart at the feet of the Crucifix,
Where, on your wood, His precious flesh was hung.

You have borne, O victorious Cross,
The remedy that will assuage our cares.
You are the key that opens Paradise
And delivers us from furious death.

O sweet Cross,[56] I want to carry my pains and travails*
Beneath your sacred branches,
Without leaving the shadow of your wings.[57]

For the conqueror who makes you triumph
Saved us from the abyss of hell
And leads us to eternal joy.

22. For the Day of the Invention of the Cross[58]
My heart is wholly moved and my soul tormented.

Quel ombrage plaisant me pourra resjouyr?
Car je ne cerche pas le gracieux plaisir
D'une verte forest ou riante valée.

Ce n'est point le repos de ma longue journée,
J'ay bien plus hautement appuyé mon desir,
A l'ombre de la Croix je me veux r'afraichir,
Et gouster la douceur qu'elle nous a donnée.

Soubs cest arbre sacré je feray ma demeure,
Y mettant mon espoir, soit que je vive ou meure,
Car il est arrosé de la saincte liqueur.

Dessus ce grand autel nostre Seigneur et maistre
A respandu son sang pour nous faire renaistre,
Comme estant de la mort heureusement vainqueur.

23.
Douce virginité, nourrice d'innocence,
Mignonne du haut Dieu, tresoriere des cieux,
Qui portes le laurier pris du victorieux,
Et l'habillement blanc, marque de continence.

Ceux qui sont guerdonnez de ta grand recompence,
Compaignons de l'aigneau, le suivent en tous lieux,
O parfaicte vertu, ô tresor precieux,
Qui rapportes le cent de ton humble semence.

Bien-heureux sont ceux-là qui forçant leurs desirs,
Quittent joyeusement du monde les plaisirs,
Pour avoir les vertus de celuy qui les donne.

Leurs lampes brusleront d'un feu continuel,
Attendant le retour de l'espoux eternel,
Recevant pour loyer une riche couronne.

24.
Mon coeur estoit de douleur oppressé,
Je n'avois plus parole ny langage,
Mon estomach ressembloit à l'orage,
Qu'eleve en mer Aquilon courroucé.

In what pleasant shade may I delight?
For I seek not the gracious pleasure
Of a green forest or a cheerful valley.

This is not the repose of my long day.
I have pressed my desire much higher.
I want to refresh myself in the shadow of the Cross
And savor the sweetness it has given us.

I will make my dwelling beneath this sacred tree,
Putting my hope there, whether I live or die,
For it is sprinkled with the holy liquor.[59]

Our Lord and Master spilled His blood*
Above the grand altar so that we might be reborn,[60]
As He was the fortunate conqueror of death.

23.
Sweet virginity, nurturer of innocence,
Darling of the God on high, treasurer of the heavens,[61]
You bear the laurels, the prize of the victorious one,
And white clothing, the symbol of chastity.

Those who are awarded your great recompense
Are companions of the Lamb and follow Him everywhere.
O perfect virtue! O precious treasure!
You yield all of your humble fruit.

Blessed are they who, forcing their desires,
Joyfully leave the pleasures of the world
To win the virtues of Him who gives them.

Their lamps will burn with a continual fire.
And as they await the return of the eternal spouse,[62]
They will receive a rich crown for recompense.

24.
My heart was oppressed with pain;
I no longer had words or language;
My stomach resembled the storm
That rises up in the angry Aquilon sea.[63]

Mille sanglots vers le ciel j'ay poussé,
Vrais tourbillons eschelans ce nuage,
Et me sauvant d'un plus triste naufrage,
J'ay submergé mon courage lassé,

Non pas des eaux d'une claire fontaine,
Mais du torrent des larmes de ma peine,
Qui m'ont servi beaucoup pour ceste fois:

Car le bon Dieu voyant sa creature
Souffrir à tort quelque inhumaine injure,
Par sa paix saincte appaise ses esmois.

25.
O de tous mes labeurs, le repos desirable,
O de tous mes desirs, le desiré bon-heur,
O de tout mon espoir, et le comble et l'honneur,
O de tous mes plaisirs, la joye perdurable.

O de tout mon pouvoir, la force secourable,
O de tous mes biensfaits, le liberal donneur,
O de tous mes desseins, le sage gouverneur,
O de tous mes dangers, le Sauveur favorable.

O le tout de mon tout, ô ma fin et mon but,
O celuy qui conduis mon ame à son salut,
O pere liberal à qui je dois mon estre.

O humain Redempteur qui as souffert pour nous,
O tres-haut Fils de Dieu qui t'es fait nostre espous,
O seul bien souverain, à toy seul je veux estre.

26.
Arrestez vous, mon coeur, reposez vous, mon ame,
Il n'est plus ores temps de vaguer et courir,
Vous estes chasque fois en danger de perir,
Vivant dedans le las de la mondaine trame.

Embrassez ardemment ceste divine rame,
Qui sur ces flots mondains vous pourra secourir,

I have pushed a thousand sobs toward the sky,
True whirlwinds climbing the clouds.
Saving myself from a more devastating shipwreck,
I submerged my wearied courage,

Not in the waters of a clear fountain,
But in the torrent of the tears of my pain,
Which served me well this time.[64]

For the good God, seeing His creature
Suffer unjustly some inhuman injury,
Appeases her torments with His holy peace.

25.[65]
O the desirable repose from all my labors!
O the desired happiness of all my desires!
O both the height and the honor of all my hope!
O the never-ending joy of all my pleasures!

O the redeeming force of all my power!
O the bountiful giver of all my good deeds!
O the wise governor of all my designs!
O the favorable Savior from all my dangers!

O the all of my all, o my end and my purpose!
O the one who leads my soul to its salvation!
O liberal Father to whom I owe my being!

O human Redemptor who has suffered for us![66]
O very high Son of God who made You our spouse![67]
O singular, sovereign goodness! I want to belong to You alone.

26.
Stop, my heart; rest, my soul.
It is no longer time to wander and run.
You are in danger of perishing each time,
Living in the trap of the worldly web.

Embrace with ardor this divine oar,
Which will save you on these terrestrial waves

Où le Fils du treshaut voulut pour nous mourir,
Monstrant la charité de sa divine flame.

Attachez à ces clous l'espoir de vos desirs,
Atterez sous la Croix vos joyes et plaisirs,
Tenant les yeux fichez sur sa liqueur vermeille.

Voyez ce gouvernail qui vous conduit au port,
Apres estre sauvez des abismes de mort:
C'est l'arbre où se brancha la plus haute merveille.

27.
Je n'attens des mortels ceste paix desirée,
Car si le Tout Puissant n'y met sa saincte main,
Elle se changera du jour au lendemain,
Et son plaisir sera de bien courte durée.

Mais si le long travail de la guerre endurée,
Nous est ores changé en un repos certain,
Sans qu'on offence en rien l'honneur du Souverain,
Ceste divine paix sera toute asseurée.

Mais pour gouster le fruict de la tranquillité,
Je voudrois que mon coeur ne fut point agité,
Reposant ses desirs sous la haute puissance.

Je voudrois que mon corps fut subject à l'esprit,
Embrassant ardemment la Croix de Jesus Christ,
Pour enfermer la paix dedans ma conscience.

28. Sur la coqueluche
Les efforts inhumains de la guerre heretique,
Renversoient l'univers d'un estrange pouvoir,
Et sans baigner les yeux, l'on ne pouvoit plus voir
Les persecutions de la foy catholique.

Dieu regardant nostre courage inique,
Qui pour tous ces malheurs ne pouvoit s'esmouvoir,
Nous dit en son courroux: je vous feray sçavoir
Comme je sçay punir la lascheté publique.

Where the Son of the God on high was willing to die for us,
Showing the charity of His divine flame.

Attach the hope of your desires to these nails,
Anchor your joys and pleasures beneath the Cross
While fixing your eyes on His vermilion liquor.

Behold the rudder that guides you to the port
After having been saved from the depths of death:
It is the tree upon which the greatest marvel sacrificed Himself.[68]

27.
I do not expect this desired peace from mortals.
For if the Almighty does not put His holy hand therein,
This peace will change from one day to the next,
And its pleasure will be short-lived.

But if the long labor of the war endured[69]
Is then changed for us into certain repose,
Without offending in any way the honor of the Sovereign One,
This divine peace will be fully guaranteed.

But in order to taste the fruit of tranquility,
I would like for my heart to be free of turmoil
And rest its desires beneath the high power.

I would like for my body to be subject to the spirit,
Ardently embracing the Cross of Jesus Christ
In order that peace be enclosed within my conscience.

28. On the Whooping Cough[70]
The inhuman efforts of the heretic war
Upset the universe with a strange power,
And, without bathing our eyes, we could no longer see
The persecution of the Catholic faith.[71]

God, observing our iniquitous disposition
Untouched by all these misfortunes,
Tells us in His wrath: I will show you
How I punish public cowardice.

Vous craignez d'hazarder vostre vie pour moy,
Laissant si prez de vous perdre ma saincte loy,
Vous ne mourrez donc point en me faisant service,

Mais je vous frapperay dans vos fortes citez,
Car le nombre infini de vos iniquitez,
Offence ma pitié, provoque ma justice.

29.
Trois ans sont ja passez qu'en ceste mesme place,
Nous avions resolu de nous bien amander,
Ce puissant donnateur nous pourra demander
Le talent mesprisé de sa divine grace.

Le temps s'en va glissant, nostre vie se passe,
Voicy la pasle mort qu'on doit apprehender,
Il nous faut à ce coup nos desirs commander,
Proposant un dessein qui sainctement se fasse.

C'est le temps de pleurer, de prier et gemir,
De chastier le corps, sur la cendre dormir.
Mais si nous ne pouvons faire ces exercices,

Au moins que nous jeunions des inclinations
Qui mettent en nos coeurs ces fortes passions,
Et d'un hardi vouloir faisons la guerre aux vices.

30.
Tousjours au coeur le souvenir me ronge,
Du temps heureux que je vay regrettant,
Où je vivois ayant l'esprit content,
Sans les ennuis où mon ame se plonge.

Tout le passé ne me semble qu'un songe,
Et le present s'eschappe en un instant,
Le sovenir me demeure pourtant,
Du bien, du mal, du vray, et du mensonge.

Mets en oubly, ô pauvre coeur lassé,
Tous les destrois ausquels tu as passé,
Et les plaisirs de ceste vie humaine.

You fear risking your life for me,
Letting my holy law, so close to you, suffer loss.
Therefore, you will not die in doing service to me.

But I will strike you in your strong cities,
For the infinite number of your iniquities
Offends my pity and provokes my justice.

29.
Three years have already passed in this same place
Since we had resolved to amend ourselves.
This powerful donor will be able to ask us
For the talent scorned by His divine grace.

Time slips away, our life passes,[72]
Here is the pale death that we must apprehend.
Now we must command our desires
And propose to undertake a pious plan.

It is time to cry, to pray, to groan,
To chastise the body, to sleep on ashes.[73]
But if we cannot do these exercises,

We should at least refrain from the inclinations
That put these strong passions in our hearts,
And boldly make war on our vices.

30.
The memory always gnaws away at my heart,
Of the happy time that I regret,
When I lived with a contented spirit
Without the troubles that immerse my soul.

The past seems only a dream to me,
And the present escapes in an instant.
The memory of the good, the bad, the true, and the false*
Remains with me nonetheless.

Put into oblivion, O poor, weary heart,
All the torments you have endured
And the pleasures of this human life.

Marche tout droit, de rien ne t'esbahis,
Voyant de loin le celeste pays
Qui t'est promis pour loyer de ta peine.

31.
Cependant que l'ardeur d'une fievre bruslante,
De sa forte douleur tient mon coeur tout enclos,
Et qu'un rheume picquant me consomme les os,
Me tenant attachée en ma couche dolente,

Je dresse au Tout Puissant l'espoir de mon attente,
En reclamant ainsi sa grace à tous propos:
Vous estes ma santé, ma vie et mon repos,
Secoures, s'il vous plaist, vostre pauvre servante.

O mon doux Redempteur, que je suis importune,
Je ne puis endurer affliction aucune,
Et ne puis supporter une petite croix,

Et pour cinq ou six jours que ceste maladie
A privé de santé ma delicate vie,
Il me semble des-ja qu'elle a duré dix mois.

32.
Que j'aye dans le coeur une amere tristesse,
Et qu'on jette sur moy des mots injurieux,
Que j'endure des maux cruels et furieux,
Et que tous mes plaisirs se changent en destresse.

Que je n'aye jamais en ce monde liesse,
Que nuit et jour les pleurs descoulent de mes yeux,
Que le regret m'assaille et me suive en tous lieux,
Et que ce corps mortel soit affligé sans cesse.

Pourveu qu'au dernier jour quand la machine ronde,
Recevra jugement du Redempteur du monde,
Je sois du nombre esleu des bien-heureux esprits.

Ce n'est rien d'endurer en la vie mortelle,
Pour avoir le repos de la gloire eternelle,
Et combattant en terre, au ciel avoir le pris.

Walk straight ahead, and let nothing intimidate you
As you see from afar the celestial country
Promised to you as compensation for your pain.[74]

31.
While the ardor of a burning fever
Keeps my heart shut tight with its strong pain,
And while a biting cold consumes my bones,
Binding me to my doleful bed,

I raise the hope of my expectation to the Almighty,
Reclaiming His grace in every matter:
You are my health, my life, and my repose;
Save Your poor servant,[75] if it pleases you.

O my sweet Redeemer! I am so troublesome
That I cannot endure a single affliction;
I cannot even bear a little cross.[76]

The five or six days that this sickness
Has deprived my delicate life of health
Seem like ten months.

32.
May I have a bitter sadness in my heart;
May they cast injurious words upon me;
May I endure cruel and furious harms;
And may all my pleasures turn into distress.

May I never have jubilation in this world;
May tears run from my eyes night and day;
May regret assail and follow me in every place,
And may this mortal body be unceasingly afflicted,[77]

Provided that on the last day when the terrestrial globe
Will receive judgment from the Redeemer of the World,
I be among the elected number of the blessed spirits.

It is nothing to suffer through mortal life
In order to obtain the repose of eternal glory,[78]
To combat on earth to secure the prize in heaven.

33.
Celuy qui veut aymer d'une amour toute pure,
Sans recevoir travail, angoisse ni douleur,
Qu'il tienne roidement la bride de son coeur,
N'aimant point ce vil corps subject à pourriture.

Çà bas ne loge pas l'amour qui tousjours dure,
Ainçois volant plus haut pense au plus haut honneur,
Mettant tous ses desirs aux pieds de son Seigneur,
Aymant avecque luy la simple creature.

Donc si nous desirons aimer parfaictement,
Aymons ce Dieu benin, plain de contentement,
Il est la charité, l'amour, et l'esperance

De ceux qui l'ayment bien, et par tout l'univers,
Chantons de son amour cent mille et mille vers,
Et de nostre amitié nous aurons recompense.

34.
Ha! quel regret encore me tourmente,
Ay-je perdu le souvenir si doux
Que Jesus-Christ est mon loyal espoux,
Et que je suis sa tres-humble servante?

Ay-je perdu l'espoir de mon attente,
Et le loyer que Dieu promet à tous?
Heureux celuy qui flechit les genoux,
Pour requerir sa faveur si constante.

Non, Seigneur Dieu, Redempteur de mon ame,
Tu brusleras par ta divine flame,
Mes vains desirs et folles passions,

Et chasseras hors de ma fantasie,
Les vanitez qui la tiennent saisie,
Pour n'aimer rien que tes perfections.

35.
Celuy qui domptera, comme dit l'Escriture,
Et qui vaincra constant ses divers ennemis,

33.
He who wants to love with the purest of loves
Without receiving labor, anguish, or pain,
Should hold firmly the rein of his heart,
Loving not this vile body subject to decay.

The love that endures forever does not tarry here below,
But, soaring higher, thinks of the supreme honor,
Putting all its desires at the feet of the Lord and
Loving with Him the simple creature.

So if we desire to love perfectly,[79]
Let us love this kind God, who is full of contentment;
He is the charity, the love, and the hope of those who love well.*[80]

Throughout the entire universe,
Let us sing thousands of verses about His love,
And we will obtain recompense for our friendship.

34.
Ah! What regret torments me still?
Have I lost the sweet memory
That Jesus Christ is my loyal spouse,[81]
And that I am His humble servant?

Have I lost the hope of my expectation?
And the recompense that God promises to all?[82]
Blessed is he who bends his knees
To pray for His constant favor.

No, Lord God, Redeemer of my soul,
With Your divine flame You will burn
My vain desires and foolish passions,

And You will chase from my vision
The vanities that hold it captive,
So that I love nothing but Your perfections.

35.
As the Scriptures say, he who will subdue
And constantly vanquish His various enemies[83]

Recevra le loyer que Dieu luy a promis,
Non en ce monde icy subject à pourriture.

Ce monde est lasche, aveugle, errant à l'aventure,
Que tout coeur genereux doit avoir à mespris,
Pour avoir ce guerdon d'inestimable pris,
Que Dieu garde au vainqueur en la vie future.

Ha! qu'il nous payera pour un peu de constance,
Que nous luy garderons en la perseverance
De sa divine loy, nous conduisans au port,

Et havre de salut, de sa gloire infinie,
Apres avoir couppé le fil de nostre vie,
Revivans dans le ciel, affranchis de la mort.

36.
Le papillon, qui s'eslance en la flamme,
Sans se vouloir esloigner de ses feux,
Me doit servir d'un patron vertueux,
Pour rechauffer la glace de mon ame.

Cest element luy est plus doux que basme,
Bien qu'il luy soit nuisible et dangereux,
Il ne craint point le tourment chaleureux,
Mais de mourir dans l'amoureuse trame.

Helas! mon Dieu, subject de mes amours,
Helas! combien devrois-je ardre tousjours,
Me souvenant de la flamme divine,

Dont vous purgez ceux qu'il vous plaist toucher,
Brusles mon coeur, mes pechez, et ma chair,
Et de vos feux embrases ma poitrine.

37. Pour le jour de sainct Gabriel
Ange de qui le nom au baptesme j'ay pris,
Fidelle messager de l'heureuse nouvelle,
Qui triomphes au ciel en la gloire eternelle,
Parmy le sainct troupeau des biens-heureux esprits.

Will receive the recompense that God promised to him,
Though not in this world subject to decay.[84]

This world is cowardly and blind, wandering to the adventure
That every generous heart must disdain
In order to obtain the recompense of inestimable value
That God keeps in the future life for the victor.

Ah! He will pay us for the little constancy
That we keep for Him in the perseverance
Of His divine law, leading us to the port[85]

And haven of salvation, of His infinite glory,
After having cut the threads of our life,
Liberated from death, reborn in heaven.

36.
The butterfly that thrusts itself into the flame
Without seeking to flee from the fire
Must serve as a model of virtue for me
To melt the ice of my soul.

This element is sweeter to the butterfly than balm,
Even though it is harmful and dangerous.
It is not the torment of the heat he fears,
But rather dying in the amorous snare.

Alas! My God, subject of my loves.
Alas! How much more must I burn
Remembering the divine flame

With which You purge those whom it pleases You to touch.[86]
Burn my heart, my sins, and my flesh,
And set my chest on fire with Your flames.[87]

37. For Saint Gabriel's Day[88]
Angel, whose name I took at my baptism,
Faithful messenger of the good news[89]
Who triumphed in heaven in eternal glory
Among the holy flock of blessed spirits,

Garde bien que mon coeur çà bas ne soit surpris,
O benoist Gabriel, ayme ta Gabrielle,
Et la guide au despart de la vie mortelle,
Au seul bien, seul amour, dont son coeur est espris.

Impetre moy de luy, que tu sois ma deffence,
Et de mon ennemy surmonte la puissance,
Ne m'abandonne poinct par ce chemin tortu,

Et comme Raphael conduit le bon Tobie,
Vueilles prendre le soin de ma dolente vie,
Et addresse mon coeur à suivre la vertu.

38. Pour le jour de sainct Hierosme
Pour un peu de travail qui passe avec la vie,
Nous pouvons acquerir un repos eternel,
Bien qu'en ce monde icy il soit continuel,
Le guerdon est suivy d'une joye infinie.

Nous devons bien aimer tout ce qui nous convie,
A cercher ardemment le beau chemin du ciel,
Et tant que nous trainons ce chariot mortel,
D'offencer nostre Dieu n'ayons jamais envie.

Mettant devant nos yeux et nous representant
Le benoist sainct Hierosme au desert penitent,
Passant austerement sa vie tres-dolente,

Ah! que ce peu de temps, qu'il affligea son corps,
Luy fut recompencé de precieux thresors,
Jouyssant dans le ciel du fruict de son attente.

39.
Saincte mere de Dieu, entens à mes clameurs,
J'ay le coeur oppressé d'une amere tristesse,
Presente, s'il te plaist, ô ma seule maistresse,
A ton fils Jesus Christ, mes larmes et mes pleurs.

Une mer de regrets, un torrent de douleurs,
Submerge ma raison dans l'abisme d'angoisse.

Make sure that my heart is not surprised here below.
O blessed Gabriel, love your Gabrielle
And guide her to the departure from mortal life ,
To the sole good, the sole love, that impassions her heart.

Ask Him to let you be my defense.
Surmount the strength of my enemy;
Do not abandon me on this tortuous path.

As Raphael leads the good Tobit,[90]
Take care of my doleful life
And direct my heart to follow virtue.

38. For Saint Jerome's Day[91]
For the little labor that passes with life,
We can acquire an eternal repose.
Even though in this world the work is continual,
The recompense is followed by infinite joy.[92]

We must love all that urges us
To search ardently for the beautiful path of heaven.
And as long as we drag this mortal chariot,
Let us never seek to offend our God.

Let us put before our eyes and imagine
The blessed Saint Jerome in the desert of penitence,
Where he spent his miserable life in austerity.[93]

Ah! Know that he was repaid with precious treasures*
For the little time he afflicted his body;
For he delighted in the fruit of his endurance in heaven.[94]

39.
Holy Mother of God, hear my cries.
My heart is oppressed with a bitter sadness.
If it pleases you, my sole mistress, present
My tears and cries to your son Jesus Christ.[95]

A sea of regrets and a torrent of pains[96]
Submerge my reason in the abyss of anguish.

Helas! s'il ne te plaist me donner quelque adresse,
Je perdray le doux fruict des celestes douceurs.

Car je vois mes pechez et mortelles offences,
Qui bourrellent mon coeur de mille et mille trances,
Mettant devant mes yeux tous mes fortaits commis.

Tousjours cela me suit, et par mer, et par terre,
Me livrant à tous coups une mortelle guerre:
Chasse bien loin de moy ces cruels ennemis.

40.
Ni des vers prez les fleurettes riantes,
Ny d'un ruisseau le doux flot argentin,
Ny le long cours d'un fleuve serpentin,
Ny les rameaux des forests verdoyantes,

Ny de Ceres les pleines blondoyantes,
Ny ce beau ciel d'où vient nostre destin,
Ny la fraischeur du soir et du matin,
Ny du printemps les beautez differentes,

Las! ne m'ont point le regret allenty
De mes pechez: je l'ay plus ressenti,
Considerant cest ouvrage admirable

De ce grand Dieu, qui par ses beaux objects,
Fait que mon coeur recognoist ses forfaicts:
Forfaits, l'horreur de mon ame coulpable.

41.
Ha! que je suis extreme en ma condition,
Je ne garde jamais le milieu de la voye:
Car en mes actions quelque part que je soye,
Je n'ay jamais le sel de la discretion.

Je suis ores trop douce, or' sans compassion,
Ores j'ay trop de pleurs, ores j'ay trop de joye,
Je ne me puis facher pour chose que je voye,
Et puis je suis esmeue à toute occasion.

Alas! If it does not please you to give me some guidance,
I will lose the fruit of celestial sweetnesses.

For I see my sins and mortal offenses
That slash my heart with a thousand gashes,
Putting before my eyes all the betrayals I have committed.

They always follow me, by sea and by land,
Delivering me incessantly to a mortal war:
Chase these cruel enemies away from me.[97]

40.
Not the cheerful flowerets of green meadows,
Not the gentle, silvery wave of a stream,
Not the long course of a serpentine river,
Not the branches of verdant forests,

Not the whitening plains of Ceres,[98]
Not this beautiful sky from whence our destiny comes,
Not the freshness of the evening and morning,
Nor the myriad beauties of springtime.

Alas! Nothing has eased my regret
For my sins; I have felt it more intensely,
Considering the admirable work

Of this great God, who makes my heart recognize its crimes*
Through His beautiful creation:
Crimes, the horror of my guilty soul.

41.
Ah! I am extreme in my condition;
I never keep to the middle of the road.
In my actions, no matter where I am,
I never have the salt of discretion.[99]

First I am too sweet, then I am without compassion;
In one instant I have too many tears, the next I have too much joy.
I avoid getting angry over the things I might see,
And then I am moved by the slightest little thing.

Helas! qui domtera ces passions estranges?
Ce sera toy, bon Dieu, qui façonnes et changes,
Les coeurs plus inconstans en un ferme rocher.

Delivre moy, Seigneur, de l'orage et tempeste,
Qui pour me submerger s'eslance sur ma teste:
Car tu es mon espoir, ma nef, et mon nocher.

42.
Fuyés de moy esperances mondaines,
Je ne veux plus surgir à vostre port,
Vous ne pourriez mettre ma nef à bort,
Tous vos desseins sont choses incertaines:

C'est un amas de tromperies vaines,
Qui doucement nous meinent à la mort.
Il faut cercher quelque meilleur support,
Pour soulager le travail de nos peines.

Je veux ancrer le navire inconstant
De ce mien coeur qui va tousjours flottant
Dessoubs l'abry d'un gracieux rivage,

Où le bon Dieu, nostre seul conducteur,
De nos dangers s'est rendu protecteur,
Et nous deffend de tempeste et d'orage.

43.
Faut il tant marchander, ô mon ame couarde,
Pour ton advancement, à te faire enrooller
Sous la Croix, d'où tu veux ce semble reculer?
Non, il faut s'asseurer soubs la divine garde.

Le soldat n'a point peur, car la guerre luy tarde,
Si son grand Coronnel le prie d'y aller:
Ainsi nos ennemis ne nous peuvent troubler,
Si le Dieu tout puissant est nostre sauve-garde.

Il ne me fache pas, ô mon doux Redempteur,
De combattre hardiment sous ta saincte faveur;
Mais quand pour mes pechez tu me quittes et laisses,

Alas! Who will temper these strange passions?
It will be You, beneficent God, who fashion and change
The most inconstant hearts into solid rock.

Deliver me, Lord, from the storm and the tempest
That thrust themselves onto my head to submerge me:
For You are my hope, my ship, and my captain.

42.
Worldly hopes, flee from me;[100]
I no longer wish to appear at your port.
You could not put my vessel on shore;
All of your plans are mere incertitudes:

They are a mass of vain deceptions
That gently lead us to death.
We must seek some better support
To relieve the pains of our labor.

I want to anchor the unsteady ship
Of my heart that floats aimlessly
Beneath the shelter of a gracious shore,

Where the beneficent God, our sole leader,
Made Himself our protector against danger
And shields us from tempest and storm.

43.
Is it necessary to haggle so much, O my cowardly soul,
For your advancement, to make yourself curl up
Under the Cross from where it seems you seek to withdraw?
No, you must protect yourself under the divine guard.

The soldier is not afraid; he is eager for war,
If his great Colonel summons him there.[101]
Thus our enemies cannot trouble us,
If the Almighty God is our protection.[102]

It does not bother me, O my Sweet Redeemer,
To fight boldly under Your holy protection.
But when You leave and abandon me because of my sins,

J'endure la rigueur de mes fiers ennemis,
A juste occasion pour mes forfaicts commis:
Donne doncques secours à toutes mes foiblesses.

44.
A chaque mot, que mon ame attentive
Va recueillant des predications,
Je sens en moy mille mutations,
Las! qui me font triste, morne et pensive.

Ores j'espere, ores je suis craintive,
Quand je ne puis vaincre mes passions:
Car les liens de mes affections
Serrent mon coeur et me tiennent captive.

Mon Dieu! que j'ay de liesse et plaisir,
Lors que je suis pleine d'un bon desir,
D'aller au ciel et mespriser la terre,

Mais ce dessein ne dure pas tousjours,
Vien donc, mon Dieu, j'implore ton secours,
Estant sans toy plus fragile qu'un verre.

45.
M'esveillant à minuit, dessillant la paupiere,
Je voy tout assoupi au centre du repos,
L'on n'entend plus de bruit, le travail est enclos
Dans l'ombre de la terre, attendant la lumiere.

Le silence est par tout, la lune est belle et claire,
Le ciel calme et serain, la mer retient ses flots,
Et tout ce qui se voit dedans ce large clos
Est plein de majesté et grace singuliere.

La nuit qui va roulant ses tours continuels,
Represente à nos yeux les siecles eternels,
Le silence profond du Royaume celeste.

En fin le jour, la nuit, la lumiere et l'obscur,
A louer le haut Dieu incitent nostre coeur,
Voyant reluire en tout sa grandeur manifeste.

I endure the rigor of my proud enemies,
And justly so, for I have committed crimes.
Assist me, then, in all my weaknesses.

44.
For each word that my attentive soul
Gathers from sermons,
I feel in me a thousand transformations
That make me sad, alas, mournful and brooding.

First I am hopeful, then I grow fearful[103]
When I cannot conquer my passions,
For the ties of my affections
Grip my heart and hold me captive.

My God! I have such delight and pleasure
When I am filled with a wholesome desire
To go to heaven and to despise the earth,

But this aspiration does not always last.
Come then, my God, I implore Your help.
Without You, I am more fragile than glass.

45.
Waking myself at midnight, forcing my eyes open
In the midst of slumberous repose, I see.
There is not the slightest sound; toil is engulfed
In the shadow of the earth, waiting for the light.

Silence is everywhere, the moon beautiful and bright,
The sky calm and serene, the sea motionless and quiet.
Everything in this vast expanse
Is full of majesty and singular grace.

The endlessly revolving night
Represents eternity to our eyes,
The profound silence of the celestial kingdom.

At last, the day, the night, the light, and the dark,
Incite our heart to praise the God on high,
Seeing his magnificence illuminate the world.

46. A sainct Pierre
J'ay veu le temps que sainctement esmeue,
Mon ame alloit bruslant de saincts desirs,
J'ay veu le temps que tous les vains plaisirs,
Je desirois esloigner de ma veue.

De tout cela je suis or' despourveue,
Je n'ay rien plus que larmes et souspirs,
Je veux prier quelqu'un des saincts Martyrs,
Qui sont au ciel parmy la troupe esleue.

Ce sera toy, Apostre glorieux,
De qui le nom me fut si gracieux,
A qui je veux presenter ma requeste,

Pour obtenir à ma necessité,
Du Tout Puissant la liberalité,
Pour soulager ma trop longue disette.

47.
Qui eust bien contemplé la Marthe soucieuse
A servir Jesus Christ logé dans sa maison,
Eust dit qu'elle faisoit mieux sans comparaison
Que Marie, sa soeur, demeurant otieuse.

Mais celuy qui cognoist la vie plus heureuse,
Jugea bien autrement avec bonne raison,
Car Marie à ses pieds escoutoit sa leçon,
Sans distraire son coeur à chose curieuse.

Aussi la deffend il contre Marthe sa soeur,
Disant qu'elle a choisi le party le plus seur,
Laissant tous les soucis de ceste vie active.

Bien-heureux donc celuy qui du monde bien loin,
A servir son Seigneur met son unique soing,
Pour jouyr du repos de la contemplative.

48.
Mon coeur plain de soucis cerche quelque retraite,
Prens pour t'y façonner ce miroir reluisant

46. To Saint Peter[104]
I remember the time when, moved like a saint,
My soul was ablaze with holy desires.
I remember the time when I yearned to push*
All vain pleasures from my view.

I am now deprived of all that;
I have nothing more than tears and sighs.
I want to pray to some of the holy martyrs
Who are in heaven among the elected flock.

It is you, glorious apostle,
Whose name has been so gracious to me,[105]
To whom I want to present my request

To obtain from the Almighty*
The generosity that is necessary
To relieve my interminable deprivation.

47.
He who has fully contemplated Martha,*
Careful to serve Jesus Christ, a guest in her house,
Has said that her service was beyond that of
Mary, her sister, who remained idle.[106]

But he who knows the more fortunate life,
Rightfully judged otherwise with good reason.
For Mary listened to His lesson at His feet,
Without distracting her heart with curious things.

Moreover, He defends her against her sister Martha,
Arguing that she chose the more certain role,
Abandoning all the worries of this active life.

Blessed then is he who places his unique concern[107]*
Far from the world in order to serve his Lord,
To delight in the repose of the contemplative life.

48.
My heart, full of worries, seek some retreat.
Take this shiny mirror to fashion yourself

De Marthe qui poursuit son travail diligent,
Et Marie, sa soeur, qui n'est en rien distraite.

Elle a l'esprit ravy d'une grace secrette,
Oyant le sainct parler du Sauveur tout puissant,
Son coeur est abaissé, contrit et penitent,
Suivant le doux repos de la vie parfaicte.

Je voudrois que mon corps fut au chemin actif,
Et mon ame eslevée au bien contemplatif,
Mais helas! de tous deux je suis fort esloignée:

Car Marie et sa soeur ne logeant point chez moy,
Je ne les cerche pas tout ainsi que je doy:
Voila pourquoy je suis tres-mal accompagnée.

49. Pour le jour de la Magdaleine
Saincte amye de Dieu, heureuse Magdaleine,
Qui as si bien servi ton doux maistre et Seigneur,
Et tousjours assisté à l'amere douleur,
Qu'il souffrit à la Croix pour nous oster de peine.

Tu as faict de tes pleurs une large fontaine,
Arrosant les saincts piedz de nostre Redempteur,
Sur luy as espandu la tresriche liqueur,
Que l'avaritieux estimoit chose vaine.

Tu as vescu trente ans parmy les Roches hautes,
Nourrie du Seigneur qui pardonna tes fautes,
Parce que tu l'aymois de parfaicte amitié:

Tu montres le chemin de vraie penitence,
Prie le, s'il te plaist, qu'il nous doint repentence,
Et que de nos pechez il veuille avoir pitié.

50. Sur le verset: Averte faciem tuam a peccatis meis
Destournez, s'il vous plaist, vostre divine face
De ceste enormité de mon forfaict commis,
Ne veuillez pas conter mes pechez infinis,
Mais effacez les tous par vostre saincte grace.

After Martha, who pursues her diligent work,
And after Mary, her sister, who lets nothing distract her,[108]

And whose spirit is delighted with a secret grace,
Hearing the holy words of the Almighty Savior.
Her heart is humbled, contrite, and penitent,
Following the sweet repose of the perfect life.

I would like for my body to be an active path
And for my soul to be raised to the contemplative good.[109]
But alas! I am rather distant from both.

For since Mary and her sister do not dwell in my home,
I do not seek them in the way that I should:
That is why I am so terribly forlorn.

49. For Mary Magdalene's Day[110]
Holy friend of God, blessed Magdalene,[111]
You who have served your sweet Master and Lord so well[112]
And have always attended to the bitter pain
That He suffered on the Cross to relieve our pain,[113]

You have made a large fountain of your tears
In which to bathe the holy feet of our Redeemer.
You have spilled on Him the very rich liquor
That the miserly esteemed vain.[114]

You have lived thirty years among the high rocks,[115]
Nourished by the Lord, who forgave your mistakes
Because you loved Him with perfect friendship.

You show the way of true penitence.[116]
Entreat Him, if it pleases you, to give us repentance
And to take pity on us for our sins.

50. On the verse, "Averte faciem tuam a peccatis meis"[117]
Please turn Your divine face away
From this enormous crime I have committed.
Please do not count my infinite sins,
But erase them all with Your holy grace.

Mon corps est tout fondu comme un monceau de glace,
Je sers de passetemps à tous mes ennemis,
Nuict et jour je me plains, je lamente et gemis,
Envoyez le pardon qui mes pechez efface.

Voudriez vous bien monstrer la force de vos bras,
Sur un corps affligé qui attend son trespas?
Foudroiez l'orgueilleux, le mutin et rebelle.

Regardez que mes os se tiennent à ma peau,
Mon ame est toute preste à descendre au tombeau,
He! destournes voz yeux de ma faute mortelle.

51. Sur le verset: Audi tui meo dabis gaudium
Le peché rend tousjours celuy-là qui le porte,
Triste, morne et pensif, chagrin et malcontent,
Comme nous dit tresbien ce bon Roy penitent,
Ayant bien esprouvé sa violence forte,

Et s'est aneanty d'une piteuse sorte,
Esperant neantmoins au Seigneur tout clement,
Ses os humiliez requierent ardamment
Quelque douce faveur qui son ame conforte.

Il n'esperoit rien plus pour son plaisir parfaict
Que la remission de son grave forfaict
Pour resjouir ses os courbez de penitence.

Les pecheurs penitents n'ont jamais tel plaisir,
Qu'alors qu'ils sont espris de quelque bon desir,
Qui monstre ses effects dedans leur conscience.

52.
S'esbahit-on de me voir souspirer
A chasque mot sans penser à moy-mesme?
S'esbahit-on de me voir pasle et blesme,
Et tous les jours je ne fais qu'empirer?

S'esbahit-on de me voir desirer,
D'un coeur ardent d'affection extreme,

My body is melted like a piece of ice;[118]
I serve as an amusement for all my enemies;
Night and day I complain, I lament and moan.[119]
Deliver the pardon that blots out my sins.

Would You like to show the force of Your arm
On an afflicted body that awaits its death?
Strike down the proud, the mutinous, and the rebellious.

Behold how my bones cling to my skin.
My soul is ready to descend to the tomb.
Oh! Turn Your eyes away from my mortal imperfection.

51. On the verse, "Audi tui meo dabis gaudium"[120]
Sin always renders the one who bears it
Sad, mournful, and pensive; chagrined and malcontent,
As this good, penitent king[121] tells us most eloquently,
Having admirably endured its mighty violence.

Having abased himself in a piteous way,
Believing nonetheless in the all-merciful Lord,
His humbled bones ardently sought
Some gentle favor to comfort his soul.

He did not hope for anything more for his perfect pleasure
Than the absolution of his grave misdeed,
To delight his bones, contorted with remorse.

The penitent sinners never have such pleasure,
Unless they are enthralled by some good desire
That manifests its effects in their conscience.

52.
Are they surprised to see me sigh
At each word without thinking of myself?
Are they surprised to see me pallid and wan?
And every day I only get worse.

Are they surprised to see me desire
With an ardent heart and extreme affection

Le doux repos de la vie supreme,
Où le Chrestien doibt tousjours aspirer?

Parmy le cours de mon pelerinage,
Durant l'Avril verdoyant de mon aage,
J'ay tout perdu ce que j'avois ça bas.

Tant qu'ay vescu en ce val de misere,
Je n'eus jamais une année prospere,
Je veux chercher mon bien par le trespas.

53.
Grand passion est une maladie,
Qui fait sentir au corps mille douleurs,
Poignantz ennuys sont les humains labeurs,
Qui vont genant nostre dolente vie.

Mais bien encor ce qui plus nous ennuye,
C'est le travail de l'ame en ses langueurs,
C'est le tourment qui plus ronge nos coeurs,
Tenant le corps et son ame asservie.

Mais, ô bon Dieu, sur ces calamitez
Regne la mort en ses extremitez,
Sur tous les maux emportant la victoire,

Donnant au corps cruelle affliction,
Regret au coeur, en l'ame passion,
Obscurcissant au tombeau nostre gloire.

54.
Amere et douce mort, bien que tu sois cruelle,
Et que fuye le coup de ton dard rigoureux,
Si est-ce toutesfois que les saincts bien heureux
Ont desiré le choc de ta lance mortelle.

Entre les actions, c'est la plus saincte et belle
Pour guider tout d'un vol nostre ame dans les cieux,
Et la faire jouyr du repos gracieux,
Ravissant le loyer de la vie eternelle.

The sweet repose of the supreme life
To which the Christian must always aspire?

During the course of my pilgrimage,[122]
During the verdant April of my age,
I lost everything I had down here.[123]

As long as I have lived in this valley of misery,
I have never had one prosperous year.
I want to seek my fortune through death.

53.
Great passion is a sickness
That makes the body suffer a thousand torments.
Trenchant adversities are the human labors
That plague our wretched lives.

But what troubles us even more
Is the work of the soul in its languors;
The torment that eats away at our hearts,
Restraining the body and enslaving its soul.

But, O beneficent God, death reigns in its farthest reaches*
Over all these calamities
Carrying victory over all the evils,

Thrusting cruel affliction on the body,
Regret on the heart, passion on the soul,
And darkening our glory in the tomb.

54.
Bittersweet death, even though you are cruel,
And I flee the blow of your rigorous dart,
The blessed saints have nonetheless
Desired the shock of your mortal lance.

It is the most godly and beautiful of actions
To guide our soul all at once into the heavens
And to make it delight in gracious repose,
Ravishing the recompense of eternal life.

Nous sommes bien-heureux si nous pouvons souffrir,
Puis que Dieu nous monstra le chemin de mourir
Et, tout bruslant d'amour, avalla ce brevage.

Laissant ce sainct hanap à ceux qui l'aymeront,
Et qui pour le servir leur vie employeront,
Du sainct et vray Nectar enyvrans leur courage.

55.
Ha! mon Dieu, je me meurs! Ha! mon Dieu, je trespasse,
Mettant devant mes yeux ce dernier jugement,
Et la grand majesté de ton advenement,
Quand le feu sortira des clairtez de ta face.

A ce jour de douleur où trouveray-je place,
Affin de me sauver de l'eternel tourment?
Je te presenteray pour tout mon payement,
Ta mort et passion qui mes pechez efface.

Quelle estrange clameur, quelle horrible tempeste,
Quand l'Ange sonnera la bruyante trompette,
Assemblant les vivans et morts resuscitez!

L'univers bruslera par un ardant deluge,
Nous serons presentez devant le juste Juge,
Effroyez et tremblans pour nos iniquités.

56.
La crainte de la mort incessamment me trouble,
En enfer il n'y a nulle redemption,
Je n'ay de mes pechez une contrition,
Tant plus je vais avant, plus ma peine redouble.

Tu me consommeras comme une seiche estouble,
A ce terrible jour de tribulation,
Laisse moy repentir de ma transgression,
Car l'amere douleur à mon ame s'accouple.

Tu as basti mon corps de chair, d'os et tendons,
De peau, veines et sang, ratte, foye et poulmons,
Souvienne toy, Seigneur, que je suis pouldre et cendre,

We are blessed if we can suffer,
Since God showed us the path to death.
Burning with love, He swallowed that drink,[124]

Leaving this holy chalice to those who will cherish it,
To those who will use their lives to serve it,[125]
Intoxicating their hearts with the true and holy nectar.[126]

55.
Ah! My God, I am dying! Ah! My God, I am expiring,
Putting before my eyes this last judgment[127]
And the grand majesty of Your coming,
When the fire will emanate from the brilliance of Your face.[128]

Where will I find a place on this painful day
To save myself from eternal torment?
I will present to You for my entire payment
Your death and passion, which will erase my sins.

What a strange clamor there will be, what a horrible storm
When the angel sounds the noisy trumpet,[129]
Assembling the living and the resurrected dead.

The universe will burn in an ardent deluge.
We will be presented before the Judge,
Afraid and trembling for our iniquities.[130]

56.
The fear of death troubles me incessantly;
In hell there is no redemption.
I do not have the slightest contrition for my sins;
The more I advance, the more my pain sharpens.

You will consume me as dry straw[131]
On this terrible day of tribulation.
Let me repent for my transgression,
For the bitter pain cleaves to my soul.

You built my body of flesh, bones, and tendons;
Of skin, veins, and blood; spleen, liver, and lungs.
Remember, Lord, that I am dust and ash.[132]

Comme un festu poussé par la rigueur du vent,
Tu me peux basloyer et reduire à neant,
He! ne me laisse pas aux abismes descendre.

57. Pour le jour de Noel
Je m'estonne de voir ceste machine ronde,
Ornée richement de ses dons precieux.
Je m'estonne de voir ce bon Dieu soucieux
D'estre si liberal à ce terrestre monde.

Je m'estonne de voir le ciel, la terre, l'onde,
La lune et le soleil, et la voute des cieux,
Les diverses saisons d'un printemps gracieux,
Tout regi par compas et sagesse profonde.

Mais j'ay le coeur ravy en admiration,
Voyant le sainct exces de la redemption,
Et Dieu se revestir de nostre chair mortelle.

Luy qui est adoré de tous esprits vivans,
Porté des Cherubins et des aesles des vents,
Se repose au giron d'une saincte pucelle.

58.
Je voy le fils de Dieu dans la loge champestre,
Plié dans ses drappeaux, dans le sein virginal,
Sucçant le laict sacré de ce divin canal,
Se voulant comme enfant de ses liqueurs repaistre.

Luy qui de tous vivans est le Seigneur et maistre,
Endure la froideur du retour hyvernal,
C'est luy qui jugera par son arrest final
Tous les hommes creés qui eurent jamais estre.

Mais or' nous le voyons humble, petit et doux,
Abbaissant sa grandeur, habitant parmy nous,
Prenant l'habit de serf pour nous vestir de gloire.

Il adopte pour siens les pauvres fugitifs,
Et brise les liens des prisonniers captifs
Aux abysmes profonds de la province noire.

Like a wisp of straw pushed by the rigor of the wind,[133]
You can whisk me away and reduce me to nothing,
Oh! Do not let me descend into the abyss.

57. For Christmas Day[134]
I am surprised to see this terrestrial sphere
Richly adorned with His precious gifts.
I am surprised to see this good God careful
To be so generous to this earthly world.

I am surprised to see the sky, the earth, the waves,
The moon and the sun, and the canopy of heaven;
The diverse seasons of a gracious spring,
All ruled by profound wisdom and measure.[135]

My heart is delighted in admiration,
Seeing the holy excess of redemption,
Seeing God don our mortal flesh.

He who is adored by all living spirits,
Carried by the cherubim and by the wings of the winds,[136]
Rests in the lap of a holy virgin.

58.
I see the Son of God in the country lodge[137]
Folded in his swaddling clothes at the virginal breast,
Sucking the sacred milk from this divine canal,
Wanting to nourish himself with its liquors like a child.

He, who is Lord and Master of all living things,
Endures the cold of the hibernal return.
It is He, at His final stop, who will judge
All the created men who have ever existed.

But now we see Him humble, little and sweet,
Shedding His grandeur to live among us,
Taking the clothes of the serf to dress us in glory.

He takes the poor fugitives as His people
And breaks the bonds of the prisoners held captive[138]
In the profound abyss of the black province.[139]

59. Pour le jour de Noel
Beniste soit l'excellente venue
De ceste nuict plus claire que le jour!
C'est le rayon de l'eternelle amour,
Que nous avons si long temps attendue.

Du Tout Puissant la grandeur est cognue,
Que les mortels le louent à leur tour,
Il nous reluit dedans l'obscur sejour,
Nous delivrant de la mort pretendue.

O saincte nuict si claire à nos desirs,
Portant le fruict qui porte tous plaisirs!
Les Pastoreaux, et les Roys et les Anges

Chantent le los de ton heur nompareil,
Terres et mers, le ciel et le soleil
Bruyent partout cantiques de louanges.

60. Pour le jour de sainct Estienne
Prothomartir plain de force admirable,
Remply de dons de ce divin esprit,
Qui le premier patiemment souffrit,
D'un coeur ardent, la mort intollerable:

Les durs rochers du torrent effroyable,
Te furent doux, ainsi qu'il est escript,
En contemplant ton Sauveur Jesus-Christ,
Tu t'endormis au repos desirable.

Nous celebrons au retour annuel,
Au nom de Dieu ton martyre cruel,
Et que chascun tes merites cognoisse:

Tu as prié pour les ennemis tiens,
Presente à Dieu l'oraison des Chrestiens,
Et sois Patron de ma grande parroisse.

61. Pour le jour de sainct Jean l'Evangeliste
C'est le disciple aymé qui au sacré repas,

59. For Christmas Day[140]
Blessed be the excellent arrival
Of this night brighter than the day!
It is the ray of the eternal love
That we have awaited so long.

The grandeur of the Almighty is known.
May the mortals praise Him in turn.
He shines on us throughout the obscure journey,
Delivering us from presumed death.

O holy night, so clear to our desires,
Carrying the fruit that bears every pleasure!
Shepherds and kings and angels all,

Sing the praise of your singular good fortune.
Land and sea, sky and sun,
Resound songs of praise the whole world over.

60. For Saint Stephen's Day[141]
Protomartyr, full of admirable force,
Filled with gifts of the Divine Spirit,
You were the first to suffer intolerable death*
Patiently, with an ardent heart.[142]

The hard rocks of the terrifying torrent
Were soft to you, so it is written.
In contemplating your Savior Jesus Christ,
You fell asleep in desirable repose.

We annually celebrate
Your cruel martyrdom in the name of God.
May everyone know your merits:

You prayed for your enemies.
Present the prayer of the Christians to God
And be the patron of my great parish.[143]

61. For Saint John the Evangelist's Day[144]
He is the beloved disciple who, at the sacred meal,

Reposa doucement sur la saincte poitrine,
Ayant de son Seigneur tant de faveur divine
Qu'il estoit le plus pres accompagnant ses pas.

La crainte de la mort ne le recula pas
De ce divin Soleil qui le monde illumine,
Recevant les rayons de sa saincte doctrine,
Il demeura tousjours present à son trespas.

Aussi fut-il pourveu d'une charge honorable,
D'estre le conducteur de la Vierge admirable,
Estant sur tous esleu pour ses perfections:

C'est le benoist sainct Jean et dans l'isle deserte,
Dieu luy a hautement sa grace descouverte
Par ses divins secrets et revelations.

62.
Tu es ma portion, mon loier, ma fiance,
Mon appuy, mon repos, mon amour, mon desir,
Ma consolation, ma joye, mon plaisir,
Mon pere, mon espoux, ma foy, mon esperance,

Mon liberal Sauveur, ma force, ma constance,
D'où je ne veux jamais mon ame dessaisir.
Puis que tu es mon tout, escoute le souspir,
Qui sans oser parler te faict tres-humble instance.

Je ne merite pas d'avoir ce doux accueil,
Comme tes familiers regardes de bon oeil,
Ny les sainctes douceurs des ames favorittes,

Ny les contentemens des divins mets du ciel,
Trop indigne je suis de gouster de ce miel,
Je veux tant seulement des miettes petittes.

63.
Combien d'occasions nous donne l'Eternel
De marcher hardiment au chemin difficile,
Sans estre effarouchez d'une crainte servile,
Puis qu'en tous nos combats il s'est fait Coronel?

Rested gently on the holy breast.
Having received such divine favor from his Lord,[145]
He was the one who followed His steps most closely.

He did not retreat in fear of death
From this divine sun that illuminates the world.
Receiving the rays from His holy doctrine,
He remained fully present at this passing.

He was, moreover, endowed with an honorable charge
To be the guide of the admirable virgin,[146]
Being elected above all for his perfections.

He is the blessed Saint John to whom[147]*
God openly unveiled His grace on the deserted island
By His divine secrets and revelations.[148]

62.
You are my portion, my recompense, my confidence;[149]
My support, my repose, my love, my desire;
My consolation, my joy, my pleasure;
My father, my spouse,[150] my faith, my hope,

My generous Savior, my strength, my constancy,
From where I never want to relinquish my soul.
Since You are my all, listen to the sigh,
Which, without daring to speak, very humbly entreats You.

I do not deserve to have this sweet welcome,
Nor Your loving and gentle regard,
Nor the holy sweetnesses granted to the favorite souls,

Nor the contentments of the divine repast from heaven.
Too unworthy am I to taste of this honey;
I desire only the smallest of crumbs.[151]

63.
How many occasions does the Eternal One give us
To walk boldly on the difficult path
Without taking fright in slavish fear,
Since He has made himself Colonel in all our combats?

Lors que les vanitez de ce monde charnel
Nous viennent desrober ce qui nous est utile,
Il se tient pres de nous car il garde sa ville,
Et recognoit les siens de son oeil paternel.

C'est le divin Pasteur qui garde ses ouailles,
Et les va repaissant de graces nompareilles,
Les chastiant aussi s'il les voit esgarer:

Ne nous esloignons point de la trouppe cherie,
Demeurons en ce parc de la grand bergerie,
Et ne veuillons jamais ce chemin ignorer.

64.
Ton nom est espandu comme l'huyle amiable,
O nom plein de douceur et consolation,
Seigneur, tu as souffert la circoncision,
Prenons l'excellent nom de Jesus pitoyable.

Tout ce qui est en toy est sainct et desirable,
Et tu es au conseil plein d'admiration,
Ton nom est tout l'espoir de ma redemption,
Et ton sang precieux mon pleige inviolable.

Je veux avoir ce nom gravé dedans mon coeur,
Et ma bouche louera le nom de mon Sauveur,
Jesus sera tousjours escrit en ma memoire:

Ce sera mon appuy, ma joye, mon support,
Jesus me sauvera du gouffre de la mort,
Jesus me conduira au Royaume de gloire.

65. L'adoration des Roys
L'unique fils de Dieu, venant pour nous sauver,
Fut trouvé de ceux-là qui cerchoient sa presence,
L'estoille fit cognoistre aux Rois sa demeurance,
Qui pleins de vive foy le desiroyent trouver.

Du pays d'Orient, ils firent aporter
Forces riches presens, ayant ceste esperance

When the vanities of this carnal world
Come to steal from us what is useful,
He keeps Himself close to us to guard His city
And recognizes His people with a paternal eye.

He is the Divine Shepherd who keeps His sheep[152]
And nourishes them with incomparable graces.
He chastises them, too, if He sees them stray.

Let us not distance ourselves from the cherished troop;
Let us stay in this meadow of the great sheepfold,
And let us never seek to ignore this path.

64.
Your name is poured forth like pleasant oil,[153]
O name, full of sweetness and consolation.
Lord, You have suffered circumcision;[154]
Let us take the excellent name of merciful Jesus.

All that is in You is holy and desirable,
And, in deliberation, You are full of admiration.
Your name is all the hope of my redemption
And Your precious blood my inviolable guarantor.

I want to have this name engraved in my heart,[155]
And my mouth will praise the name of my Savior.
Jesus will always be written in my memory:

This will be my sustenance, my joy, my support.[156]
Jesus will save me from the chasm of death.
Jesus will lead me to the Kingdom of Glory.

65. The Adoration of the Kings[157]
The only Son of God, coming to save us,
Was found by those who were seeking His presence.
The star informed the kings of His stay,
Where, full of lively faith, they desired to find Him.

They had brought many rich presents*
From the country of the Orient, bearing this hope

D'adorer le grand Roy au lieu de sa naissance,
Et luy offrir leurs corps et leurs dons presenter.

Escoute moy, Seigneur, entens à ma demande,
Je n'ay rien ce beau jour pour te faire une offrande,
Je ne t'apporte point or, myrrhe, ny encens.

Que t'offriray-je donc à ta saincte venue?
Un corps plein de pechez, une ame despourveue,
Affin de recevoir quelqu'un de tes presens.

66. De la Presentation
Je veux accompagner ceste excellente Dame,
Et son divin enfant entre ses bras porté,
A son Pere eternel au temple presenté,
Pour rompre le lien de la mortelle trame.

Le vieillart Simeon seul esjouyt son ame,
Voyant de ses deux yeux d'Israel la clarté,
Et plein du Sainct Esprit, doucement a chanté
Ce cantique si sainct que l'Eglise reclame,

Puis en prophetisant dit à la Vierge Saincte:
Vous serez de douleur cruellement attaincte,
Et ce glaive poinctu vous percera le coeur:

Cest enfant bien-heureux sera pour la ruine
De ceux qui blasmeront sa parfaicte doctrine,
Mais des humbles Chrestiens il sera protecteur.

67. Sur le verset: Tibi soli peccavi
C'est moy qui ay peché, c'est mon ame coulpable,
Laquelle a transgressé tes saincts commandemens,
C'est moy qui ay peché par tous mes sentimens,
Engouffrant mes desirs au monde variable.

Pitoyable Seigneur, ma playe est incurable,
Qui par mille regrets redouble mes tourmentz,
Si tu ne la gueris de tes doux oignementz,
Delivrant de la mort ma vie miserable.

Of adoring the great King at the place of His birth,
And to offer their bodies and to present their gifts to Him.[158]

Listen to me, Lord; hear my request.
I have nothing to offer You this fine day.
I do not bring You gold, myrrh, or frankincense.[159]

What will I offer You at Your holy arrival?
A body full of sin and a broken soul,[160]
In the hope of receiving one of Your gifts.

66. On the Presentation[161]
I want to accompany this excellent Lady
And her divine child, whom she carried in her arms,
And presented to her eternal Father at the temple[162]
To break the tie of the mortal web.

The old man Simeon alone delighted in his soul,
Seeing with his two eyes the brightness of Israel,
And, full of the Holy Spirit, he softly sang
This holy song called for by the church.[163]

Then in prophesying, he said to the Holy Virgin:
You will be cruelly stricken with pain,
And this sharp sword will pierce your heart.[164]

This blessed child will be the ruin
Of those who blame His perfect doctrine,
But He will be the protector of humble Christians.[165]

67. On the verse, "Tibi soli peccavi"[166]
It is I who have sinned; my guilty soul is
The one that has transgressed His holy commandments.
It is I who have sinned in all my sentiments,
Devouring my every desire in this inconstant world.

Merciful Lord, my wound is incurable
And will intensify my torments with a thousand regrets,
If You do not heal it with Your gentle ointments
And deliver my miserable life from death.

Las! c'est devant tes yeux, las! c'est devant toy seul,
Contre qui j'ay meffaict par mon superbe orgueil,
Pourtant tu puniras justement ma pauvre ame,

Et seras recogneu veritable et entier,
Si equitablement tu me veux chastier,
Des plus aspres douleurs de l'infernale flame.

68.
Tout ce grand univers incessamment travaille,
Mais l'homme est paresseux et ne veut faire rien,
Tout ce qui est enclos en ce val terrien,
Cent mille enseignemens et doctrines nous baille.

La mer va produisant ses nourrissons d'escaille,
Le ciel tournant tousjours suit son cours ancien,
Et la terre produit pour l'humain entretien
Les plantes, animaux et toute la volaille.

Et nous qui cognoissons cest ouvrage excellent,
Avons l'esprit remis, ingrat et nonchalant,
Vivant oysivement en cest ouvrier du monde,

Et où tant d'instrumentz travaillent sans cesser,
Et où nous nous devrions à l'esgal exercer,
Nostre ame de paresse et voluptez abonde.

69.
Je ne sçaurois escrire d'autre chose
Que de la croix, où j'ay le coeur fiché,
En cest object mon amour est niché,
Autre chanson ma muse ne compose.

Soit que j'escrive ou en vers ou en prose,
J'ay mon discours à la croix attaché,
C'est mon escu, defenseur de peché,
Soubz ses rameaux mon ame se repose.

C'est bien raison qu'en ce siecle pervers,
Où nous voions tant d'ennemis divers
Contre la croix hausser leur arrogance.

Alas! It is before Your eyes, alas! It is before You alone
That I have done wrong by my superb pride.[167]
Nevertheless, You will justly punish my poor soul.

You seek to punish me so fairly*
With the bitterest pains of the infernal flame
That You will be considered veritable and whole.

68.
This entire great universe works incessantly,
But man is lazy and wants to do nothing.
All that is enclosed in this earthly valley
Imparts a hundred thousand teachings and doctrines.

The sea produces nourishment of shells;
The revolving sky always follows its ancient course;
And, for the sustenance of men, the earth produces
Plants, animals, and all the fowl.

And we who know this excellent work
Have negligent, ungrateful, and apathetic spirits,
Living lazily in this workshop of the world.

And where so many instruments work without ceasing,
And where we should apply ourselves just as much,
Our soul abounds with laziness and delight.

69.
I would not know how to write about anything else
But the Cross, where I have fixed my heart.
Within this object, my love is deeply nestled.
My muse does not compose any other song.

Whether I am writing in verse or in prose,
My speech is attached to the Cross.
It is my shield, my defender against sin;
My soul rests beneath its branches.

It is quite right that in this perverted century,
Where we see so many diverse enemies
Raise their arrogance against the Cross,[168]

Les bons Chrestiens d'une commune voix
Chantent l'honneur de la divine croix,
Qui contre tous sera nostre deffence.

70.
Vous estes mort pour moy, ô Sauveur de ma vie,
Vous estes mort pour moy, ô desir de mon coeur,
Vous estes mort pour moy, de la mort le vainqueur,
Vous estes mort pour moy d'une amour infinie.

Vous avez surmonté toute force ennemie,
Vous avez triomphé, ô parfaicte valeur,
Vous nous avez sauvez du gouffre de douleur,
Vous avez accablé l'inique tyrannie.

Voudrions nous bien aymer jamais autre que vous,
Vous estes si benin, si gratieux et doux,
Vous ne cessez jamais de nous faire largesse:

Vous estes tout clement, piteux et liberal,
Vous nous donnez du bien et nous gardez de mal.
Heureux qui hait le vice et vous ayme sans cesse.

71.
Estant haut eslevé sur la montaigne saincte,
Tu as tout attiré en tes doux oignements,
Le ciel s'est obscurci regardant tes tourments,
Et la terre s'esmeut de grande frayeur attainte.

Tout ce pole arrondi gemissoit sa complaincte,
Qui s'entendoit muette en tous les elemens.
Seuls estoient les Hebrieux ces choses regardans,
Sans loger dans leurs coeurs compassion ny crainte.

Mais nous, tes serviteurs, gemissans nos pechez,
Avons nos tristes yeux sur tes playes fichez,
Playes, de nos langueurs les vrayes medecines:

Playes qui ont produit les pommes et les fleurs,
Du celeste jardin de tes douces faveurs,
Pour ceux de qui ton feu embrase les poictrines.

The good Christians, with a common voice,
Sing the honor of the divine Cross,
Which will be our defense against all.

70.
You have died for me, O Savior of my life!
You have died for me, O Desire of my heart!
You have died for me, Conqueror of death;
You have died for me with infinite love.

You have surmounted every enemy force;
You have triumphed, O Perfect Valor!
You have saved us from the abyss of pain;
You have overwhelmed the iniquitous tyranny.

May we never want to love any other than You.
You are so kind, so gracious and sweet;
You never stop giving us generous gifts.

You are all merciful, compassionate, and tolerant;[169]
You bestow goodness upon us and keep us from harm.[170]
Blessed is he who hates vice and loves You without end.

71.
Being raised high on the holy mountain,
You have attracted all by Your sweet ointments.
The sky has darkened looking upon Your torments;
The earth, too, has been touched, stricken with great fear.

This whole round world moaned its complaint,
Which remained mute in all elements.[171]
The Hebrews alone looked upon these things,
Without harboring compassion or fear in their hearts.

But we, Your servants, bemoaning our sins,
Have our sad eyes fixed on Your wounds,
Wounds that are the true remedy for our languor,[172]

Wounds that have produced the apples and the flowers
From the celestial garden of Your sweet favors
For those in whose chests Your fire burns.

72. Pater ignosce illis, quia nesciunt quid faciunt

L'on t'avoit couronné de poignantes espines,
Sanglant et deschiré de tourmens inhumains,
Estant dessus la Croix encloué pieds et mains,
D'un vouloir furieux par ces ames malignes.

Tu voyois les pechez de leurs noires poictrines,
Et les intentions de leurs mauvais desseins,
Et nonobstant cela, ô Sauveur des humains,
Tu leur voulois donner de tes graces divines.

Criant à haute voix par un desir profond:
Pere pardonne leur, ils ne sçavent qu'ils font.
Ceste saincte oraison les Anges admirerent,

Les Demons reprouvés l'ouyrent des enfers,
Demeurants effroyez, mais les hommes pervers,
En leurs vices obstinez, ce pardon refuserent.

73.

Je ne puis plus chanter, je ne puis plus escrire,
J'ay le coeur oppressé, j'ay l'estomach pantoix,
Je ne puis r'appeller la parole et la voix,
Je ne puis remonster les cordes de ma lire.

J'ay les yeux esblouys, je lamente et souspire,
Je veux ores mourir sous la divine croix,
Je ne veux plus bouger de l'ombre de ce bois,
Je veux estre à jamais subjecte à son empire.

Je voy le Sainct des Saincts sur la terre eslever,
Je voy son sang bouillant, où je me veux laver,
Je voy son corps divin, chargé de cicatrices.

Je voys ses bras cloués qu'il tend aux esgarez,
Je voy son coeur ouvert aux pauvres alterez,
Je le voy trespasser pour l'amour de nos vices.

74. Sur le verset: O vos omnes qui

O vous humains, qui passez par la voye,

72. Pater ignosce illis, quia nesciunt quid faciunt[173]
They had crowned You with painful thorns.[174]
Bleeding and torn with inhuman torments,[175]
Your feet and hands were nailed to the Cross
With a furious will by these malicious souls.

You saw the sins of their blackened chests
And the intentions of their evil plans.
Despite that, O Savior of humans,
You wanted to give them Your divine graces.

You cried out loud with a profound desire:
Father, forgive them, they know not what they do.
The angels admired this holy prayer;

Reproved demons heard it in hell
And remained full of fear; but perverted men,
Obstinate in their vices, refused this forgiveness.

73.
I can no longer sing; I can no longer write;
My heart is oppressed; my stomach is all aflutter;
I cannot recall any words or rouse my voice;
I cannot raise the strings of my lyre.

My eyes are blurry; I lament and sigh;
I want now to die beneath the divine Cross;
I no longer want to move from the shadow of this wood;
I want to be subject to its empire forever.

I see the Saint of Saints rise up on the earth;
I see His boiling blood, in which I want to wash myself;
I see His divine body, covered with scars;

I see His arms pierced with nails that He stretches toward the lost ones;
I see His heart open to the thirsty poor,
I see Him die because of our love for our vices.

74. On the verse, "O vos omnes qui"[176]
O you humans, who pass by the way

Et qui courez sans regarder vos pas:
Arrestez vous et voyez mon trespas,
Et ma douleur qui ciel et terre effroye.

Ores vos pleurs sont convertis en joye,
Et vos labeurs en repos et soulas:
A ce grand jour je porte sur mes bras
Le payement d'excellente monnoye.

J'ay presenté à mon Pere eternel
Vostre rançon sur ce sanglant autel,
Vous delivrant des lacs de servitude:

Arrestez vous et voyez le tourment,
Que j'ay souffert pour vostre sauvement,
Et ne soyez taschez d'ingratitude.

75.
He! que j'ay trop dormy en ceste nuict amere,
Où nostre Redempteur a souffert passion,
Si j'eusse prins ces maux pour contemplation,
Le somme paresseux ne m'en eust peu distraire.

Mais si j'eusse porté le cilice ou la haire,
Ayant de mes pechez vive contrition,
Ou bien que j'eusse prins quelque autre affliction,
Je n'aurois tant dormy ceste nuict salutaire.

Qui ne s'esveillera quant les cieux s'obscurcirent,
Que la terre s'esmeut et les pierres fendirent,
Quant les tombeaux cachez rendirent leur butin?

Las! le seul fils de Dieu sur la croix glorieuse,
Rachepte les humains par sa mort douloureuse,
Tandis que lachement je dors jusque au matin.

76.
Il est fort grief de jeusner de viandes,
Porter le sac, coucher tout revestu,
Aller piedz nudz apres s'estre battu,
Et faire encore d'austeritez plus grandes.

And run without looking at your steps,
Stop and behold my death
And my pain that frightens the land and sky.

Now your tears are turned to joy,
And your labors to rest and relief.
On this great day, I carry in my arms
The excellent payment.

I presented your ransom[177] to my eternal Father*
On this blood-soaked altar,
Delivering you from the lakes of servitude.

Stop and behold the torment
That I suffered for your salvation,
And be not stained with ingratitude.

75.
Oh! I have slept too much on this bitter night[178]
That our Redeemer suffered passion.
If I had taken these pains for contemplation,
Lazy sleep could not have overcome me.[179]

But if I had borne the hair shirt,[180]
Having great remorse for my sins,
Or if I had withstood some other affliction,
I would not have slept so much during this salutary night.

Who will not wake up when the skies darken,
When the earth trembles and the rocks split open,
When the hidden tombs render their plunder?[181]

Alas! The only Son of God redeems mankind*
Through His painful death on the glorious Cross,
While I sleep like a coward until morning.

76.
It is exceedingly unpleasant to abstain from meats,
To carry the sack, to lie down fully clothed,
To go barefooted after having beaten oneself,
And to inflict on oneself even greater austerities.[182]

Il est fort grief aux penitantes bandes
D'estre de faim et de froid combattu,
Mais le loyer qu'apporte la vertu,
Faict adoucir l'aigreur de ces offrandes.

Heureux troupeau qui d'un commun accort,
Vous affligez d'un merveilleux effort
Pour surmonter ceste escorce charnelle:

Perseverez en voz devotions,
Pour le guerdon de voz afflictions,
Vous recevrez la couronne eternelle.

77.
Toute felicité que l'homme peut cognoistre,
Et desire jouir au monde passager,
Consiste à sainctement sa volonté ranger,
Unissant son vouloir à celuy de son maistre.

L'air, la terre et le ciel, et tout ce qui a estre,
Suit comme son troupeau ce haut et grand berger,
Tout ce qui doit ça bas nostre exil soulager,
C'est ce bien de le suivre et de le recognoistre.

Bien-heureux sont ceux-là qui voyent clairement
Ce que nostre bon Dieu nous monstre incessamment,
Nous dirons à jamais: heureuses les oreilles

Qui escoutent parler l'esprit de verité,
Bien-heureux sont les coeurs en toute eternité,
Adorans, plains d'amour, ses bontez nompareilles.

78.
Gouverne donc, Seigneur, tout ce que je doy faire,
Adresse mon esprit, manie mon dessain,
A fin qu'estant conduit par ta divine main,
J'acheve à ton honneur cest importun affaire.

S'il ne faut point parler, apprens moy de me taire,
Et s'il faut discourir, que ce ne soit en vain,

It is exceedingly unpleasant to the penitent groups[183]
To be assaulted with hunger and cold.
But the recompense that virtue brings
Sweetens the bitterness of these offerings.

Blessed troop, you who afflict yourselves*
With common accord and marvelous effort
In order to surmount this carnal skin,

Persevere in your devotions,
For you will receive the eternal crown*[184]
As recompense for your afflictions.

77.
All the felicity that man can know
And desire to enjoy in the ephemeral world
Consists of piously ordering his volition,
Uniting his will with that of his Master.[185]

The air, the earth, and the sky, and all that is to be,
Follow this high and grand shepherd[186] like His flock.
All that is supposed to relieve our exile here below
Is found in the good of following Him and recognizing who He is.

Blessed are they[187] who see clearly
What our good God shows us incessantly.
We will say forever: blessed are the ears

That listen to words of the spirit of truth.
Blessed are the hearts in all eternity
Who adore, full of love, His incomparable bounty.

78.
Govern then, Lord, all that I must do,
Guide my spirit, direct my plan,[188]
So that being led by Your divine hand,
I achieve in Your honor this pressing affair.

If one must not speak, teach me to be silent,
And if one must converse, let it not be in vain.

Mais sur tout je te pry, cache dedans mon sain,
Ta saincte volonté sans que j'aille au contraire.

Mon corps est affligé, mon ame est aux abois,
Je traine sans support ceste pesante croix,
Pressant dedans mon coeur un torrent d'amertume.

Rien que le seul travail ne me sert de repos,
Mes regrets sont des dartz qui me percent les os,
Mes maux sont des marteaux et mon coeur un enclume.

79.
Cheminant lentement, j'erre par un boccage,
Cerchant pour reposer quelque ombrageux halier
D'aubespin fleurissant, de chesne ou de peuplier,
Où le gay rossignol fredonne son ramage.

Las je veux arroser de larmes mon visage,
Pour allenter le mal que je veux oublier.
Aux villes je ne veux ma douleur publier,
Je la veux enterrer en ce desert sauvage.

Mais qui sera tesmoin de l'ennuy que je sens?
Ce sera toy, Seigneur, espoir des innocens,
Support des orphelins, et consolant la vefve.

Tu daigneras secher les larmes de mes yeux,
Appaisant de mon coeur les regrets soucieux,
Donnant à mes combats ou la paix ou la treve.

80.
Je trouve le lict dur, la nuict m'est une année,
Il semble que mes draps soient de chardons poignans,
Que mon corps soit pressé dans des ceps estraignans,
Tant je suis de souci cruellement genée.

Apres m'estre en tous lieux cent et cent fois tournée,
Et faisant enfanter à mes pensers preignans
Tant d'ennuys et regrets, mon repos esloignans,
Je passe ainsi la nuict au sommeil ordonnée.

But above all, I beg, conceal your holy will*
In my breast, and let me not resist it.

My body is afflicted; my soul is hard-pressed;[189]
I drag this heavy cross without support,
Pressing a torrent of bitterness into my heart.

Nothing but this toil allows me any repose.
My regrets are darts that pierce my bones;
My pains are hammers, my heart, an anvil.

79.
Making my way slowly, I wander through a grove
Seeking to rest in some shady thicket
Of blooming hawthorn, oak, or poplar,
Where the gay nightingale hums his tune.[190]

Weary, I want to wet my face with tears
To alleviate the pain that I long to forget.
I do not want to disclose my pain in the cities;
I want to bury it in this wild desert.

But who will be witness to the grief I feel?
It will be you, Lord, Hope of the innocent,
Support of the orphans, and Consoler of widows.[191]

You will deign to dry the tears from my eyes,[192]
Appeasing the worrisome regrets of my heart,
Giving either peace or truce to my struggles.

80.[193]
My bed is hard; the night seems like a year to me;
It seems that my sheets are sharp thistles,
That my body is constrained in shackles
So that I am cruelly troubled with worry.

After having tossed and turned hundreds of times,
Delivering so many troubles and regrets*
To my pregnant thoughts,
Restlessly, I spend the hours of darkness that are designed for sleep.

Heureux sont les bergers qui dorment sans soucy,
Sur le vert matelas du printemps adoucy,
Ayant pour pavillon le feuillage d'un chesne,

Sans craindre que la nuict et l'humide serain
Offence tant soit peu leur corps allegre et sain,
Et nous trop delicats, vivons tousjours en peine.

81.
Chacun me dit: vous estes en mes-aise,
Vos pas sont lentz, vostre haleine se pert,
Despuis six mois, despuis le printemps vert,
Que vous avez la couleur fort mauvaise.

La fiere mort jalouse de nostre aise,
Desja pour vous a le sepulchre ouvert.
C'est quelque ennuy que vous tenez couvert,
Qui faict aussi que chose ne vous plaise.

Je leur responds: vous vous abusez fort,
Me menaçant de ce pas de la mort,
C'est le repos de l'ame qui desire

Se delivrer de son fardeau charnel,
Pour s'en aller au pais eternel
Jouyr du bien où tousjours elle aspire.

82.
C'est fort peu advancé en ceste saincte escole,
Ou j'esperois un jour grandement profiter,
C'est fort peu advancé, faudra-il tout quitter?
Porteray-je tousjours le regret qui m'affole?

Helas! sans y penser, ma jeunesse s'en volle,
Et l'âge qui survient ne se peut eviter,
Mon paresseux esprit je ne puis exciter,
Par les divins attraitz de ta douce parolle.

Mon Dieu, le temps passé, si tost que j'entendois
Parler de ton sainct nom ou de la saincte Croix,
Mon ame se brusloit d'une flame amoureuse,

Blessed are the shepherds who sleep without worry[194]
On the green mattress of softened springtime,
Having the foliage of an oak for a pavilion,

Without fearing that the night and dank eventide
Will even slightly harm their lively and healthy bodies.[195]
And we, too delicate, always live in pain.

81.
Everyone says to me: you are in pain;
Your steps are slow; you are out of breath.
For six months, since the green springtime,
You have had very bad color.

Proud death, jealous of our ease,
Has already opened the sepulcher for you.
It is some trouble that you are concealing
That also makes it so that nothing pleases you.

I answer them: You delude yourselves greatly,
Threatening me with this approach of death.
Tranquil is the soul that desires

To deliver itself from its carnal burden
In order to flee to the eternal kingdom
To delight in the goodness to which it always aspires.

82.
I have gained nothing in this holy group
Where I was hoping to profit greatly one day.
I have gained nothing; must I leave everything?
Will I always carry this regret that distresses me?

Alas! Without my realizing it, my youth is stealing away,
And I cannot avoid the age that succeeds it.
I cannot excite my lazy spirit
With the divine appeal of Your sweet word.[196]

My God, in the past, as soon as I heard
Mention of Your holy name or the holy Cross,
My soul would ignite with a passionate flame;

Mon coeur s'esjouissoit de dans mon estomac,
Mes yeux humiliez versoient un tiede lac,
Recevant du haut Ciel la Manne savoureuse.

83.
Non je ne veux aucunement me plaindre,
Non je ne veux mes ennuis racompter,
Non je ne veux mon esprit contenter,
Pour en parlant faire ma douleur moindre.

Je veux plustost dissimuler et feindre,
En me taisant ma langue surmonter,
Il faut ce corps severement dompter
Par la raison qui se doit faire craindre.

Que me sert il de me plaindre aux humains?
C'est l'Eternel qui change leurs dessains,
Il les deffaict ainsi qu'un pot d'Argile.

Devant ses yeux toute chose se voit,
Sans luy parler noz desirs il cognoit,
Prenant pitié de nostre chair fragile.

84. Pour le jour des Trespassez
Ames qui vous purgez dans la flame bruslante,
Et paiez aigrement vos debtes emportez,
Recevez aujourd'huy les bonnes volontez
Que va faisant pour vous l'Eglise militante.

Elle presente à Dieu son oraison fervente,
Mandiant humblement les hautes sainctetez
Des Apostres, Martyrs, Anges, principautez,
Et tout l'ordre sacré et bande triomphante.

Helas! il m'est advis que je voy sainct Michel
Par le comandement du grand Dieu eternel
Eslever dans le ciel mainte ame repurgée.

O vous heureux esprits qui ce celebre jour,
Estes faicts habitans du celeste sejour,
Priez pour le repos de l'Eglise affligée.

Elatedly, my heart would flutter in my stomach;
My eyes, humbled, would pour forth a warm lake,
Receiving the savory manna from heaven.

83.
No, I do not want to complain at all;
No, I do not want to recount my troubles;
No, I do not want to content my spirit
In order to lessen my pain in speaking.

I would rather dissemble and feign,
And surmount my tongue by silencing myself.[197]
I must severely break this body
With the reason that must be feared.

What good is it to me to complain to humans?
It is the Eternal One who changes their designs;
He undoes them like a pot of clay.[198]

Before His eyes, all things are seen;
Without our speaking to Him, He knows our desires[199]
And takes pity on our fragile flesh.[200]

84. For the Day of the Dead[201]
Souls who purge yourselves in the burning flame[202]
And pay dearly for your debts incurred,
Receive today the good wishes
That the militant church makes on your behalf,

Presenting to God its fervent prayer,
Humbly beseeching the high godly ones,
The apostles, the martyrs, the angels, and the sovereign ones,
And all the holy order and triumphant troop.

Alas! It seems to me that I see Saint Michael,[203]
Who raises many purified souls into heaven*
By the commandment of the great eternal God.

O you blessed spirits, who are made inhabitants*
Of the celestial kingdom this famous day,
Pray for the peace of the afflicted church.

85.
Vous le voulez, et je le veux aussi,
Vous le voulez, ô ma douce lumiere,
Vous le voulez, que je sois coustumiere
A receler maint ennuyeux souci.

Mon coeur se deult, mon corps est tout transi,
Estant privé de sa santé premiere.
Apprenez moy, quelque douce maniere,
Pour supporter tous ces travaux icy.

Je veux la Croix et puis elle me fache,
Je veux souffrir et puis apres je tache
Par tous moyens à recouvrer santé:

Je sens en moy une guerre intestine,
Contre le corps mon ame se mutine,
Et chacun d'eux n'est jamais contenté.

86.
Je veux quicter les vers, je veux laisser la muse,
J'abandonne le lut, je ne veux plus chanter,
Je hay ce que souloit mon esprit contenter,
Et qui entretenoit ma vie langoureuse:

Puis que pour m'affliger l'envie dangereuse,
Dessus mes actions ose bien attenter,
Ores je quicte tout, je me veux absenter,
Pour trouver le repos, solitaire et recluse.

Nous sommes quelque fois de tous favorisez,
Et puis en mesme temps de chacun mesprisez,
Il nous faut recevoir le blasme et les louanges.

Dieu le permet aussi pour nous humilier,
Et nous faire sçavoir qu'il ne faut oublier
Que nous sommes pecheurs et ne sommes point Anges.

87.
Le ciel tout obscurcy d'un nuage liquide,
Embrunit l'air serain de ces coulantes eaux,

85.
You want it, and I want it, too.[204]
You want it, O my gentle Light!
You want me to become accustomed
To concealing many troublesome worries.

My heart grieves; my body is frozen to the marrow,
Deprived of its initial health.
Teach me some gentle manner
In which to endure these many labors here.

I want the Cross, and then it angers me.
I want to suffer, and then I try
To recover health by every means.

I feel in me an intestine war.
My soul revolts against my body,
And neither one of them is ever contented.

86.[205]
I want to quit these verses; I want to leave the muse;[206]
I am abandoning the lute; I shall not sing any longer.
I hate that which sought to content my spirit
And which maintained my languorous life.

Since dangerous envy*
Dares to violate my actions in order to afflict me,
I am taking leave of everything, I am absenting myself,
To find repose, solitary and reclusive.

We are sometimes favored by all,
And then, at the same time, by each despised.
We must receive the blame and the praise.

God permits this in order to humble us[207]
And to remind us of what we must not forget:
We are not angels; we are sinners.

87.
The sky, all blackened with a liquid cloud,
Darkens the evening air with these running waters;

Les tourbillons venteux frappent les arbrisseaux,
Rien n'est plus verdissant en la saison humide.

L'on ne voit plus les rais du grand flambeau lucide,
Ni le chant gracieux des voletantz oyseaux,
Tout demeure enfermé aux villes et chasteaux,
Pour l'amour d'Aquilon qui sur les ventz preside.

Plus que l'hyver glacé, mon coeur est refroidy,
D'un paresseux sommeil mon corps est refroidy,
Je ne sentz plus l'ardeur de la flame celeste.

Tous les ventz outrageux me frappent rudement,
Les brouillats ont saisi mon foible entendement,
Delivre moy, Seigneur, de ce qui me moleste.

88.
Helas! tout aussi tost qu'une guerre sanglante,
A cessé la rigueur de ses cruelz effaitz,
Et lors que nous pensons nous veoir un peu deffaitz
De la calamité et douleur precedente,

Nous sommes menassez de ceste main puissante,
Qui veut tresjustement chastier nos mesfaictz,
Nous voyans tous les jours estre plus imparfaictz,
Il monstre son courroux par une estoille ardente.

Las! nous pensions desja vivre tresseurement,
Sans avoir de noz maux aucun amendement,
N'en ayant desplaisir, regret ny repentance,

Mais nostre vain espoir nous pourra bien tromper,
Car ce juste Seigneur est prest à nous frapper,
Si nous ne l'appaisons par nostre penitence.

89.
Le coeur humilié, la conscience attaincte
D'un mordant repentir de nos graves pechez,
O Pere tout clement, nous sommes attachez
Comme des criminels devant ta face sainte.

The blustery whirlwinds strike the shrubbery;
Nothing is flourishing in this wet season.

One no longer sees the rays of the great, lucid torch,
Nor hears the graceful melody of the fluttering birds.
Everything remains enclosed within the cities and castles,
For the love of Aquilon, who presides over the winds.[208]

My heart is colder than the frosty winter.
My body is numbed with languorous slumber;
I no longer feel the ardor of the celestial flame.[209]

The brutal winds strike me harshly.
The fogs have seized my weak understanding.
Deliver me, Lord, from all my troubles.

88.
Alas! As soon as a bloody war
Has ceased the rigor of its cruel effects,
And we think we see ourselves a little ravaged
By the calamity and preceding pain,

We are threatened by this powerful hand
That wants quite justly to chastise our misdeeds.
Seeing us become more imperfect every day,
He shows His wrath by an ardent star.[210]

Alas! We were thinking that we were already living in security
Without receiving a single correction for our misdeeds,
Spared displeasure, regret, and repentance for our wrongs,

But our vain hope will be able to deceive us well,
For this just Lord is ready to strike us
If we do not appease Him through our contrition.[211]

89.
Our hearts humiliated, our consciences stricken
With biting remorse for our grave sins,
O merciful Father! We are bound
Like criminals before Your holy face.

Voy nos corps langoureuz, tous palissants de crainte,
Dans un lict ennuyeux dolentement couchez,
Tu es le medecin de nos maux plus cachez,
Vivifie dans nous nostre ame presque estainte.

Nous souffrons de ta main ce fleau commun à tous,
Confessant humblement qu'il est encor trop doux,
A nos transgressions la peyne n'est esgale.

Mais en nous chastiant tu nous corrigeras,
Et comme protecteur nostre ame garderas
De descendre au manoir de l'horreur infernale.

90.
Seigneur, si quelque fois mon amour diminue,
Et de ton feu divin mon coeur se refroidit,
L'on ne peut pas tousjours aussi comme l'on dit,
Estre en un mesme estat et force continue.

Il n'est rien d'asseuré qui soit dessoubz la nue,
Mesme l'astre nuictal descroit et s'arrondit,
Ainsi quand peu à peu mon desir s'attiedit,
Je sens un vray regret de ma faute cognue.

Or tant que la grand mer nourrira des poissons,
Et l'esté chaleureux meurira les moissons,
Et les bois porteront leurs espesses ramées,

Je te louray, Seigneur, et la posterité
Lira des vers de moy, qui chauds de charité,
Rendront de ton amour nos ames enflammées.

91.
Mes yeux sont esblouys de veoir la difference
Des champs, preds, bois et fleurs, herbes et arbrisseaux,
Rivieres et rochers, fontaines et ruisseaux,
Edifices pierreux, des hommes l'asseurance.

Et le jour se rouant par si grand temperance,
Mene l'obscure nuict ornée de flambeaux;

Behold our languorous bodies, all pallid with fear,
In a troubling bed dolefully laid,
You are the doctor of our most hidden pains.[212]
Vivify in us our nearly extinguished souls.

We suffer from Your hand this curse common to all,
Humbly confessing that it is still too sweet.
The pain is not equal to our transgressions.

But in punishing us, You will rectify us,
And as a protector, You will keep our souls
From descending to the manor of infernal horror.[213]

90.
Lord, if ever my love diminishes
Or my heart chills to Your divine fire,
One cannot always remain, as they say,
In the same state or maintain constant strength.[214]

Nothing is certain beneath the clouds.
Even the nocturnal star swells and wanes.
Thus when my desire cools little by little,
Recognizing my fault, I feel true remorse.

But, as long as the great sea nourishes the fish,
And the warm summer ripens the harvest,
And the woods bear their thick leafy boughs,

I will praise you, Lord, and posterity
Will read my verse, which, warm with charity,
Will render our souls enflamed with Your love.[215]

91.
My eyes are dazzled to see the variety
Of fields, prairies, woods and flowers, grasses and shrubs,
Rivers and rocks, fountains and streams,
Strong edifices, the assurance of men.[216]

And the day passing with such great temperance
Fades into the obscure night ornate with torches.

Tout ce qu'on voit creé sont de rares tableaux,
Qui nous peuvent donner une douce esperance.

Voyant ce grand ouvrier si soigneux des mortels,
Donnant si largement ses presens temporels,
Mesmes aux transgresseurs de ses loix equitables.

Tout ce grand univers pour nous il a basty,
A nos necessitez l'ayant assubjecty,
Nous gardant puis apres des places immuables.

92.
Je hay plus que la mort le bruit et les rumeurs
Des superbes citez abondamment peuplées,
Qui ressemblent aux flots des grands ondes salées,
Battant horriblement les roches et les murs.

Que de gens assemblez de diverses humeurs,
Qui me vont essourdant de clameurs redoublées,
Il n'y a jamais paix en ces grands assemblées,
Chacun est different de façons et de meurs.

Querelles et debats sont les plaisirs des villes,
Fureurs, seditions, paroles inutiles,
Estre conterollé mesmes jusqu'aux pensers.

J'aymerois plus aux champs manger du pain d'avoyne,
Et boire dans la main de l'eau d'une fontaine,
Qu'estre roine en la ville avec tant de dangers.

93.
Benissez le Seigneur, toutes choses creées,
Exaltez son sainct nom, ouvrage de ses mains,
Adorez sa grandeur, ô vous esprits humains,
Et vous divin troupeau des ames bien heurées.

Clair soleil revestu de tes flammes dorées,
Large et vaste univers qui rondement nous ceints,
Louez le Tout Puissant, et vous, astres hautains,
Servants de cloux luisants aux voultes azurées.

All that one sees created are rare scenes
That can give us a sweet hope,

Seeing this great workman so careful of mortals,
Giving His temporal presents so generously,
Even to the transgressors of His equitable laws.

He built this whole universe for us,
Having destined it to our necessities,
Saving unchanging places for us until after.

92.
More than death I hate the noise and rumors
Of the superb and abundantly peopled cities
That resemble the rush of the great salty waves,
Horribly beating the rocks and the walls.

People of diverse moods gather together
And deafen me with their bombastic clamors.
There is never peace in these great assemblies.
Each person is different in manners and mores.

Quarrels and debates are the pleasures of the cities:[217]
Furors, seditions, and useless words—
To be controlled right down to one's thoughts.

I would rather eat oat bread in the fields
And drink water from a fountain with my hand,
Than be queen in a city rife with danger.

93.
All things created, praise the Lord.[218]
Exalt His holy name and the work of His hands.
Adore His grandeur, O you human spirits!
And you, divine flock of blessed souls!

Bright sun vested in your golden flames,
Large and vast universe that surrounds us,
Praise the Almighty, and you, lofty stars,
Serving as glistening nails in the sapphire vault of heaven.

Benissez le Seigneur, terre, preds, bois et fleurs,
Rosées, eaux et vents, froidures et chaleurs,
Et bref tout ce qui est en toute la machine:

Admirez l'Eternel et son divin pouvoir,
Qui sa grand majesté par ses oeuvres faict veoir
Envers les clairs mirouers de sa bonté divine.

94.
A l'instant que je vy ceste belle lumiere,
Que tu monstres à ceux qu'il te plaist appeller,
Mon esprit tout esmeu pensoit desja voller
Au lieu delicieux de sa source premiere.

Mes yeux qui sommeilloyent ouvrirent la paupiere,
Et mes sens estonnez ne se pouvoyent saouler
D'admirer la bonté, qui m'a faicte enrouler
Au nombre des heureux qui suyvent ta baniere.

Lors que je m'esloignois de tes perfections,
Suyvant le vain object de mes affections,
Tu arrestas mon cours d'une plaisante haye,

Et de ta saincte main les infinis bien-faicts
Firent dedans mon coeur et mille et mille traicts,
Dont les coups sont si doux que j'en nourry ma playe.

95. Contre la chair
Enfleure d'un tombeau, cloaque de vermine,
Pasture des serpentz, taniere de la mort,
Oses tu desploier ton cauteleux effort
Pour vouloir offencer celle qui te domine?

As tu mis en oubly que nostre ame est divine,
Qu'elle remonste au ciel quand du corps elle sort?
Feignant l'amadouer, tu luy veux faire tort,
Et pour un vain plaisir tu cherches sa ruyne.

Servante de l'esprit, obeis promptement,
Tu n'es point icy bas que pour estre instrument
Du triomphe qu'obtient l'ame victorieuse:

Praise the Lord, earth, prairies, woods, and flowers,
Dew, waters and winds, cold and heat,
And in a word, all that the earth encompasses.

Admire the Eternal One and His divine power
That makes His great majesty visible through His works,
Through the resplendent examples of His divine bounty.

94.
In the instant I saw this beautiful light
That You show to those whom it pleases You to call,[219]
My spirit was so moved that it thought it was already in flight
To the delicious place of its birth.

My drowsy eyes raised their lids,
And my stunned senses could not satisfy themselves
In admiring the bounty that made me join
The blessed ones who follow Your banner.

When I distanced myself from Your perfections,
Following the vain object of my affections,
You impeded my course with a pleasant obstacle,

And, with the infinite good deeds of Your holy hand,
Made hundreds and thousands of piercings in my heart,
The blows so gentle that, with them, I nourish my wound.[220]

95.[221] Against the Flesh
Swelling of a tomb, cesspool of vermin,
Food of serpents, den of death,
Do you[222] dare deploy your cunning effort
To offend the one who dominates you?[223]

Have you forgotten that our soul is divine,
That she returns to the sky when she leaves the body?
Feigning the flatterer, you wish to do her wrong,
And for a vain pleasure you seek her ruin.

Servant of the spirit, obey promptly.
You are not down here to be an instrument
Of the triumph that the victorious soul obtains.

A supporter la croix tu luy sers d'un appuy,
Dieu l'a mise dans toy comme dans un estuy,
Si tu la veux servir tu seras glorieuse.

96.
Lors que je suis aux champs loing des tourbes mondaines,
Quand le fleury printemps deploie des thresors,
Estant le chaut passé, de ma maison je sors,
M'en allant promener sur les moittes arenes.

J'escoute le doux bruit des coulantes fontaines,
Et des doux oyseletz les differents accords,
Voyant tant de beautez je considere lors
De ce Dieu eternel les graces souveraines.

O espritz engourdis qui vous assoupissez
A l'esbat paresseux des logis tapissez,
Ayant de molz plaisirs l'ame toute enyvrée,

Laissez tout vostre orgueil, il n'est rien si plaisant
Que mener en repos la vie d'un paysant,
Ayant l'affection du monde delivrée.

97.
Donne, Seigneur, la douce patience
A tous ceux-là qu'il te plaist affliger,
Vien doucement nos peines soulager,
Garde nos coeurs en humble obeissance.

En nos travaux ta divine puissance
Sauve tousjours nostre ame du danger,
Nous ne cherchons le repos estranger,
Tu es le but de nostre confiance.

En ta maison celuy est bien traicté,
Qui pour ton nom a esté rejecté,
En s'honorant de la peine endurée:

Autre guidon tu ne monstres aux tiens,
Pour se monstrer obeissants Chrestiens,
Sinon la Croix, nostre enseigne honorée.

You serve her as a support to bear the cross.
God put her in you as a receptacle.
If you seek to serve her, you will be glorious.

96.
When I am in the fields far from the worldly crowds,
When the flowered springtime unveils its treasures,
The heat having passed, I go out of my house
To walk on the wet sand.

I listen to the soft noise of the running fountains
And to the various harmonies of the little birds.
Seeing so much beauty, I contemplate
The sovereign graces of this eternal God.

O benumbed spirits, who doze off
In lazy distractions at home,
Your souls drunk with many pleasures,

Leave all your pride, as there is nothing more pleasant
Than to lead the peaceful life of a peasant,
Having delivered yourself from the affection of the world.[224]

97.
Lord, give sweet patience
To all those whom You deign to afflict.
Come gently to relieve our pains.
Keep our hearts in humble obeisance.[225]

In our toil, Your divine power
Always saves our soul from danger.[226]
We do not seek some unknown tranquility:
You are the aim of our confidence.[227]

In Your house, he who has been rejected in Your name*
Is well treated,
And honors himself with the pain endured.[228]

Except for the Cross, our honored ensign,*
You do not show any other guide to Your people
To prove themselves obedient Christians.

98.

Ceste beauté à nulle autre pareille,
Qui embellit et la terre et les cieux,
Me mignarda d'un regard gracieux,
J'ouy sa voix sonner à mon oreille.

A ce doux bruit mon ame se reveille,
Se secouant du somme oblivieux,
Dressant au ciel ma pensée et mes yeux,
Je tressailli de si douce merveille.

Jamais mon coeur ne puisse retenir
Autre penser que le doux souvenir
De la beauté dont le feu me devore:

Heureux desirs dressez si hautement,
Heureux vouloir d'aymer parfaictement,
Ceste beauté qu'en silence j'adore.

99. Le jour de la Toussaincts

O Saints qui possedez le celeste heritage,
Ayant contre Sathan hardiment bataillé,
L'un a esté bruslé et l'autre tenaillé,
Souffrant mille tourments d'un genereux courage.

Vous regardez du port nostre mondain orage,
Et ce pauvre bateau des vagues travaillé,
Secourez le bien tost puis qu'il vous est baillé
L'aviron en la main pour surgir au rivage.

Chacun soit le patron de son pais aymé,
Ou vous avez si bien l'Evangile semé,
Ouvrez cest encensoir embasmé de prieres,

Impetrez du Seigneur qu'en sa saincte maison,
Nous puissions en tout temps faire nostre oraison,
Gardant sa saincte foy parmy tant de miseres.

100.

Si j'esleve les yeux de mon entendement,
Ou quand les yeux du corps exercent leur office,

98.
This beauty unlike any other
That embellishes both the earth and the skies
Caressed me with a gracious look.
I hear its voice resound in my ear.

At this sweet sonance, my soul awakens,
Stirring itself from oblivious sleep.
Raising my thought and my eyes to heaven,
I quiver in such sweet marvel.

May my heart never retain
Any other thought than the sweet memory
Of the beauty whose flames devour me:

Blessed desires with such high aspirations,
Blessed wish to love perfectly
This beauty that I adore in silence.

99. All Saints' Day
O saints, who possess the celestial heritage,
Having boldly battled against Satan;
One has been burned and the other tortured,
Suffering a thousand torments with tremendous courage.

You look from the port at our worldly storm
And at this poor boat, overworked by the waves.
Rescue it soon since the oar has been delivered*
To your hands to anchor it on shore.

May each one of you be the patron of the beloved country
Where you so successfully spread the Gospel.
Open this censer perfumed with prayer.

Ask and receive from the Lord that in His holy house
We might make our prayer at any time,
Keeping His holy faith amid so many miseries.

100.
If I raise the eyes of my understanding,[229]
Or when the eyes of my body exercise their duty,

Las! mon Dieu, je voudrois que jamais je ne visse
Figure ny object fors que toy seulement.

Que tu sois en tous lieux mon soigneux pensement,
Ma delectation, ma joye, mon delice,
Et que pour ton amour sans cesse je languisse,
Cerchant en toy mon bien et seul contentement.

Que tant que je vivray je n'aye en ma memoire,
Ny en ma bouche rien que ton honneur et gloire,
Meditant nuict et jour tes graces et bontez,

Et de ma volonté ceste libre puissance
Ne tende qu'à la seule et saincte obeissance
De tous autres desirs chassant les vanitez.

101.
Ce jour de sainct Thomas il y a dix années,
Que Dieu par sa bonté me choisit un espoux,
Plain de toutes vertus, sage, courtois et doux,
Fidelle observateur de ses loix ordonnées.

Mais comme le soleil rend les herbes fanées,
Apres que le faucheur leur a donné ses coups,
Ainsi la fiere mort du dard meurtrier de tous,
Rendit de ma moitié les graces moyssonnées.

Ce corps que j'aymois tant fut mis dans le tombeau,
L'ame se desliant de son pesant fardeau,
S'en volla dans le ciel par la divine grace,

Et portant mes amours, mon coeur et mes plaisirs,
Aux pieds du souverain attacha mes desirs,
Voila pourquoy despuis j'aspire à ceste place.

102.
La nuict qui couvre tout de ses aesles obscures,
Cacha les membres nuds de Jesus Christ mourant,
Nul des cruels Juifs ne le fut secourant,
Mais en le tourmentant luy disoyent mille injures.

Alas! My God, I would never want to see
Any figure or object, except You.

May You be the focus of my reflection wherever I go,
My delectation, my joy, my delight,
And may I languish incessantly for Your love,
Seeking in You my well-being and sole satisfaction.

As long as I live, may I have neither in my memory,
Nor in my mouth anything but Your honor and glory,
Meditating night and day on Your graces and bounties.

May I aspire solely to devout obeisance*
With the full power of my will
Chasing away the vanities of all other desires.

101.
Ten years ago, on this day of Saint Thomas,[230]
God, through His bounty, chose a spouse for me,[231]
Full of every virtue, wise, courteous, and sweet,
Faithful observer of the laws He commanded.

As the sun withers the grass,
After the reaper has administered his blows,
Thus proud death, murderer of all by its sting,
Harvested the graces of my other half.

This body that I loved so much was placed in the tomb.
The soul unbinding itself from its heavy burden,
Flew away, by divine grace, to the heavens

And, carrying my love, my heart, and my pleasures,
Attached my desires to the feet of the Sovereign One.
That is why from then on I have aspired to that place.

102.
The night, which covers everything with its obscure wings,
Hid the naked body of Jesus Christ as He was dying.
None of the cruel Jews brought Him any succor,
But tormented Him, uttering a thousand insults.[232]

La mere qui sentoit ces mortelles poinctures,
Ne luy pouvoit ayder sinon qu'en souspirant,
Mais ceste triste nuict son Seigneur honorant,
Desploya son manteau, repos des creatures.

O nuict, heureuse nuict qui as servy ton Dieu,
Faisant tous les meurtriers retirer de ce lieu,
A fin d'estre approché de ceux qui le desirent.

Venez tous travaillez et chargez de peché,
Voyez le Fils de Dieu sur la Croix attaché,
Qui oyt benignement les pecheurs qui souspirent.

103.
J'ay cent fois esprouvé mille herbes salutaires,
Et les drogues aussi qu'apporte le Levant,
Pour veoir si je pourrois ainsi qu'auparavant
Recouvrer ma santé et guerir mes miseres.

L'on m'a tiré le sang et seiché les arteres,
Me faisant avaller d'un breuvage puant,
Mais avec tout cela je suis pis que devant,
Endurant tous les jours des douleurs tres-ameres.

Je veux ores quitter tous ces medicaments,
Portant patiemment mes peines et torments,
Sans plus me soucier de mourir ou de vivre,

Mais de ta saincte main, ô Dieu plein de bonté,
J'embrasseray mon mal ou ma douce santé,
Car ton divin vouloir est ce que je veux suivre.

104. De l'Ascension de nostre Seigneur
C'est luy qui est passé sur les aesles venteuses,
Montant par sus les cieux par son divin pouvoir,
C'est ce triomphateur qui nous a fait r'avoir
L'heritage perdu par nos fautes honteuses.

A ce jour excellent les bandes glorieuses
Ont descendu du ciel pour mieux le recevoir,

His mother, who felt these mortal blows,
Could do nothing to help Him but sigh.
But the sad night, honoring her Lord,[233]
Unfurled her cloak, the repose of all creatures.[234]

O night! Blessed night who served Your God!
You forced all the murderers to withdraw from this place
In order to be approached by those who desired it.[235]

Come, all who are oppressed and burdened with sin.[236]
Behold the Son of God attached to the Cross:
He graciously heeds the sighs of sinners.

103.
I have tried a thousand salutary herbs a hundred times,
As well as the drugs that are brought from the East,[237]
To see if I could, as before,
Recover my health and heal my miseries.

My blood was drawn, and my arteries were dried;[238]
They made me swallow a stinking potion.
Despite all that, I am worse than before,
Enduring very bitter pains every day.

Now I want to stop all these medicines
And bear my pains and torments with patience,
Without worrying anymore about living or dying.

Instead, I will embrace my pain or my sweet health*
With Your holy hand, O God full of bounty!
For Your divine will is what I want to follow.

104. Of the Ascension of Our Lord[239]
It is He who passed on wind-swept wings,
Ascending to the heavens by His divine power.
He is the victor who helped us regain
The heritage lost by our shameful faults.

On this excellent day, the glorious groups
Descended from the sky in order better to receive him.

Les Apostres ravis ne le pouvans plus voir,
Tenoient les yeux fichez aux nues lumineuses.

Quand deux saincts messagers de ce Dieu nompareil,
Vestus d'habits tous blancs plus clairs que le soleil,
Sont venus consoler la troupe qui souspire

Disans: Galileens, nostre Dieu, nostre Christ,
Qui là haut est monté et qui pour nous souffrit,
Viendra juger un jour tout ce terrestre empire.

105.
Ne me parlez jamais de me remarier,
O vous, mes chers parens, si vous aymes ma vie,
Ne m'en parlez jamais, car je n'ay plus envie
A un second espoux oncques m'apparier.

Je veux garder ma foy sans jamais varier,
Ny rompre l'amitié que le ciel m'a ravie,
Encor qu'à maints travaux je puisse estre asservie,
Tousjours à la vertu on voit contrarier.

Je ne veux point cercher le repos de mes peines,
Non aux commoditez, ny aux grandeurs humaines,
Ny aux plaisirs trompeurs engeolant mes esprits.

Au seul Dieu tout benin j'ay mon certain refuge,
Il est mon advocat et pitoyable juge,
Qui bataillant pour moy m'adjuge le vray pris.

106.
Je veux chanter l'honneur de saincte Radegonde,
Qui a vescu ça bas en toute saincteté,
Ayant le coeur si plain de toute chasteté,
Qu'elle mit soubs les pieds tous les plaisirs du monde.

Elle est ores au ciel où toute gloire abonde,
Contemplant son Seigneur des yeux de pureté,
Qui l'a mise la haut au port de seureté,
La sauvant des dangers de ceste mer profonde.

The Apostles, entranced and no longer able to see Him,
Held their eyes fixed on the luminous cloud.

When two holy messengers from this incomparable God,
Dressed in white clothes brighter than the sun,
Came to console the sighing flock,

They declared to the Galileans, "Our God, our Christ,
Who has ascended above and suffered for us,
Will come one day to judge this entire terrestrial empire."[240]

105.
Never speak to me about remarrying.
And you, my dear relatives, if you love my life,
Never speak to me about it, for I will never desire
To pair myself with a second husband.[241]

I want to keep my faith without ever varying
Or breaking the friendship that the heavens took from me,
Even though I might be subject to many labors,
For virtue is never without its torments.[242]

I do not want to seek rest from my pains
In conveniences, in human grandeurs,
Or in the deceitful pleasures that imprison my mind.[243]

I have my assured refuge in the only all-merciful God.
He is my advocate and merciful judge
Who, battling on my behalf, discerns for me the true recompense.

106.
I want to sing the honor of Saint Radegonde,[244]
Who lived here below in all sanctity,
Having a heart so full of every chastity
That she put all the pleasures of the world under her feet.

She is now in heaven where all glory abounds,
Contemplating her Lord with eyes of purity,
Who put her up there at the port of certainty,
Saving her from the dangers of this deep sea.

Poyctiers, tu t'esjouys au los de ses vertus,
Et nous estans icy du peché combattus,
Mettons comme un tableau sa vie pour exemple:

Elle oyt nos oraisons et supplie pour nous
Le grand Dieu eternel qu'il nous conduise tous,
Au sejour glorieux de son celeste temple.

107.
Vous portez à bon droit la couleur azurée,
Monstrant que dans le ciel reposent vos desirs,
Separant vostre coeur de tous mondains plaisirs
Pour avoir du haut Dieu une joye asseurée.

Tout ce qui est de beau et de longue durée,
Est diapré de bleu comme les beaux saphirs,
La mer en est aussi quand les mouvans zephirs
Luy donnent la couleur de la voute aetherée.

Saincte societé qui par mille labeurs,
Jeusnes, austeritez, regrets, sanglots et pleurs,
Mandiez nuict et jour l'amour de vostre maistre:

Aux douleurs de sa croix vous vous glorifiez,
En luy sacrifiant vos corps mortifiez,
Pour les faire avec luy en la gloire renaistre.

108.
Ainsi que le berger qui veoit une tempeste
S'espessir dedans l'air d'une noire couleur,
Menassant les vers prez et la superbe fleur
De la rose et du lis qui esleve la teste.

Il serre les brebis dans sa basse logette,
Et triste veoit tomber l'orage et le malheur,
Puis revoyant Phoebus il chasse sa douleur,
Et fait sortir aux champs la bande camusette.

O Dieu! lors que j'entends comme un bruyant esclat
Menasser mes pechez par ton docte prelat,
Je m'en vay retirer à ta grand bergerie,

Poitiers,[245] you delight in the renown of her virtues,
And, with us being here defeated by sin,
Consider her life as an example like a painting.

She hears our prayers and supplicates the great eternal God*
On our behalf, praying that He might lead us all
To the glorious dwelling of His celestial temple.

107.
You rightly bear the azure color,
Showing that you place your desires in the sky,
Separating your heart from all worldly pleasures
In order to have an assured joy from God.

All that is of beautiful and long duration
Is mottled with blue like beautiful sapphires.
The sea bears it too when the moving zephyrs
Give it the color of the ethereal canopy.

Holy society, you who by a thousand labors,[246]
Fasts, austerities, regrets, sobs, and tears,
Beg for the love of your Master night and day,

Glorify yourselves in the pains of His Cross
And sacrifice to Him your mortified bodies
So that they might be reborn with Him in glory.

108.
Like the shepherd who sees a tempest
Thicken in the black air,
Threatening the green prairies and the superb flowers
Of the rose and the lily that raise their heads,

He clutches the sheep in his lowly little lodge,
Sadly watching the storm and misfortune descend.
Then, seeing Phoebus[247] again, he chases away his pain
And makes the contrite flock go out into the fields.

O God! When I hear such a noisy clamor
Threaten my sins through Your learned prelate,[248]
I withdraw into Your grand sheepfold,

Remachant l'aspreté de mes vices pervers,
Et puis à mon pasteur les ayant descouvers,
Tu monstres tes clairtez et mon ame est guerie.

109.
O Seigneur, ô grand Roy, n'avois tu point des louvres,
Las! tu n'euz onc logis, maison ny bastiment,
Toy qui as fabriqué ce large firmament,
Riche des grands tresors que benin tu nous ouvres.

Par quels divers effects ton amour tu descouvres,
O que nostre rachapt te cousta cherement,
Jusques à n'avoir point un pauvre habillement,
A fin que sur la croix tes membres nuds tu couvres.

Mourant tout alteré l'on te refuse l'eau,
Et pour t'ensevelir tu n'as point de tombeau,
Comme useray-je donc des choses superflues,

Te voyant souffreteux de ce qui est à toy?
Depouille, s'il te plaist, tout ce qui est à moy,
Retirant mes desirs des richesses pollues.

110. Pour l'Assumption de nostre Dame
Quel soleil radieux, quelle grande splendeur,
S'esleve doucement à ceste terre basse?
Mais qui est celle là qui hautement surpasse
De tous les bien-heureux la gloire et la grandeur?

C'est la mere de Dieu, luysante en sa candeur,
Parfaicte en sa beauté, toute pleine de grace,
Elle sort du desert et va prendre sa place
Au ciel voyant soubs soy du monde la rondeur.

Vous estes donc au ciel, ô Royne magnifique,
Vostre siege est posé sur le choeur Angelique,
L'Eglise s'esjouyt de vos felicitez.

Priez vostre cher fils, monstrez vous estre mere,
Nous vous benissons tous, la terre vous revere,
Et le ciel orgueilleux jouyt de voz beautez.

Chewing again the pungency of my perverted vices.
Then, after revealing them to my pastor,
You show Your brightness, and my soul is healed.[249]

109.
O Lord! O great King! Did You not have a royal palace?
Alas! You never had a dwelling, a house, or any sort of shelter,[250]
You, who have fabricated this large firmament,
Rich with grand treasures that You kindly open for us.

By what diverse effects You uncover Your love!
Oh, how our redemption cost You dearly:
You did not even have a ragged piece of clothing
To cover Your naked body on the Cross.[251]

Dying and thirsty, You were refused water,[252]
And You did not have a tomb for Your burial.[253]
How, then, will I use superfluous things,

Seeing You in need of what is Yours?
Strip me, please, of all that is mine,
And wipe out my desires for polluted riches.

110. For the Assumption of Our Lady[254]
What radiant sun, what grand splendor
Rises softly above this lowly land?
But who is it that supremely surpasses
The glory and the grandeur of all the blessed ones?

It is the Mother of God, stunning in her candor,
Perfect in her beauty, and full of grace.
She leaves the desert and goes to take her place
In the sky, seeing beneath her the roundness of the world.

You are in heaven, then, O magnificent queen!
Your seat is perched on the angelic choir.
The church delights in your felicities.

Pray to your dear son, and show yourself to be a mother.
We all bless you; the earth reveres you;
The proud sky delights in your beauty.

111.

J'avois un grand plaisir au plus chaut de l'esté
De prendre les zephirs le long d'une riviere,
Et soubs un orme espais à baisser la paupiere
En escoutant le bruit du doux flot argenté.

Puis dessillant les yeux, j'avois de tout costé
Mille parfaicts crayons de ceste main ouvriere,
Lors mon esprit va prendre une haute carriere,
Voulant de l'intellect fendre le ciel vouté.

Mais ainsi qu'il poursuit tout à coup le nuage,
Fit lors en se crevant tomber un tel ravage
Que mon esprit mouillé fut constrainct s'abaisser.

Ha! vaine, dis-je alors, voicy le vol d'Icare,
Il ne t'appartient pas de veoir chose si rare,
Ne monte point plus haut qu'on ne te veut hausser.

112. Sur la parole que Jesus-Christ dit en Croix: Pater dimitte illis

Le sang du juste Abel me demande vengeance,
Dit le Dieu tout puissant à Cain effrayé,
Comme s'il luy disoit: en bref sera payé
Le meurtre perpetré sur la simple innocence.

O juste Createur, tu passes soubs silence
La mort de Jesus-Christ cruellement playé,
Tu veux venger un sang par le temps essuyé,
Ou celuy de ton Fils ruisselle en ta presence.

Qui t'a faict oublier ceste grand trahison?
Ce fut de ce sauveur la parfaicte oraison,
Lors qu'il estoit mourant au bois du Sacrifice,

Disant: Pere eternel, pardonne leur ce tort,
Ne les chastie point pour leur donner la mort,
Ils ne sçavent qu'ils font, excuse leur malice.

113. Amen dico tibi

Le troupeau qui s'egare avoit laissé son maistre,

111.

I had the immense pleasure during the hottest days of summer
Of following the zephyrs along the river,
Of closing my eyes beneath a thick elm,
And of listening to the gentle, silvered wave.

Upon opening my eyes, I found a thousand perfect designs*
Fashioned by this Worker's hand all around me.
Then, my spirit aspired to a higher path,
Hoping to split the vaulted sky with its intellect.

But just as it was suddenly pursuing the cloud,
It collapsed, bringing down such destruction
That my dampened spirit was forced to humble itself.

"Ha! Vain one," I said then, "This is the flight of Icarus.[255]
It does not belong to you to see such a rare thing.
Do not go higher than you are raised."[256]

112. On the words that Jesus Christ said on the Cross: "Pater dimitte illis"[257]
"The blood of righteous Abel requires my vengeance,"
Says the God Almighty to frightened Cain,
As if He were saying to him, "In a word, the murder perpetrated*
On simple innocence will be paid."[258]

O just Creator! You pass under silence
The death of Jesus Christ cruelly wounded.
You want to avenge a blood wiped away by time,
Or that of Your son will stream in Your presence.

Who made You forget this great betrayal?
It was the perfect prayer of this Savior
When He was dying on the wood of sacrifice,

Saying, "Eternal Father, forgive them this wrong,
Do not chastise them with death,
They know not what they do; pardon their malice."[259]

113. Amen dico tibi[260]
The flock that wandered off had left its Master

Sans consolation en ses fortes douleurs,
Estant accompaigné de meurtriers et voleurs,
Qu'on avoit attachez à sa dextre et senestre.

Le voyant si meurtry qui eust peu recognoistre
Ceste douce beauté, lumiere des pecheurs?
Ses playes ont guari nos travaux et langueurs,
La vertu de sa mort commença d'apparoistre.

Lors il dit au larron: et vrayement je te dis
Qu'avec moy tu seras ce jour en paradis,
Que dictes vous, Seigneur, quelle grande promesse

Faites-vous à celuy qui meritoit l'enfer,
Voulant avecque vous le faire triompher?
C'est que les hauts bienfaicts sont deus à ta hautesse.

114. Mulier ecce filus tuus
Haussez vos tristes yeux, ô Vierge nompareille,
Dressez vostre regard sur la sanglante Croix,
Oyez de vostre fils la douloureuse voix,
Qui d'un son gemissant resonne à nostre oreille.

Celuy qui par sa mort tous les mourants esveille,
Effaçant le contract des rigoureuses loix,
Comme un cygne mourant chante sur le sainct boix
Ce cantique nouveau plain de grande merveille:

Femme, voilà ton fils, de Jean il dit cecy,
Et s'adressant à luy il parle encor ainsi:
C'est ta mere, et deslors il vous servit pour telle.

O sa mere, ô sa fille, il ne vous laisse pas,
Il se souvient de vous aux douleurs du trespas,
Vous gardant puis apres la couronne immortelle.

115. Deus meus Deus meus ut quid me dereliquisti
Eternel fils de Dieu, gloire de tous les Anges,
Lumiere du pecheur, force de l'oppressé,
Toy qui es le plus grand t'es le plus abaissé,
Tournant seul le pressoir des cruelles vendenges.

Without consolation in His severe pains,
Accompanied by murderers and thieves
Who were attached to His left and to His right.[261]

Seeing Him so wounded, who could have recognized
This gentle beauty, light of the sinners?[262]
His wounds have healed our languors and labors.[263]
The virtue of His death begins to appear.

Then He says to the thief, "And truly I say to you
That you will be with me in paradise this day."[264]
What do You say, Lord, what great promise

Do You make to one who deserved hell,
Wanting to make him triumph with You?
These noble deeds are owing to Your highness.

114. Mulier ecce filius tuus[265]
Raise your sad eyes, O singular Virgin!
Raise your gaze to the bloody Cross.
Hear the dolorous voice of your son
That resounds in our ears with a piteous moan.

He, who by His death awakens all the dying,
Effacing the contract of the rigorous laws,
Sings this new song full of great marvel*
On the holy wood like a dying swan:

"Woman, here is your son" speaking of John,
And addressing Himself to him He speaks still thus:
"This is your mother," and from then on He served you in this way.[266]

O His mother! O His daughter! He does not leave you.
He remembers you in the pains of death,
Keeping the immortal crown for you thereafter.

115. Deus meus Deus meus ut quid me dereliquisti[267]
Eternal Son of God, Glory of all the angels,
Light of the sinner, Strength of the oppressed,[268]
You, who are the greatest, lowered Yourself the most,[269]
Turning alone the winepress of the cruel grape harvest.[270]

En cryant hautement ta foible voix tu changes,
Disant: mon Dieu, mon Dieu, pourquoy m'as tu laissé?
Tous les flots du torrent sur ton chef ont passé,
Le pere t'a frappé pour nos pechez estranges.

Tu ne te plaignois pas de ce que tu souffrois,
Le supplice mortel aux branches de la Croix,
C'est pour moy que tu fis une plaincte si haute.

Pour me mettre en credit tu t'es faict oublier,
Pour rompre mes liens tu t'es voulu lier,
Bref tu verses ton sang pour en laver ma faute.

116. Sitio

Toy qui fais ondoyer la mer espouvantable,
Et donnes les liqueurs dont le monde se sert,
Toy qui fis ruisseler le rocher du desert,
Et comme un mur d'aerain as rendu l'eau estable.

Toy qui nous rafraichis de ta sacrée table,
Des-alterant nos coeurs dedans ton coeur ouvert,
Un pauvre verre d'eau ne te fut point offert,
Quand tu crias, j'ay soif, d'une voix lamentable.

Extreme fut l'ardeur qui sechoit ton gosier,
Mais tu avois au coeur un plus ardant brasier,
Un desir enflammé du salut de ma vie.

Ainsi tout alteré tu as rendu l'esprit,
Donne moy de ta soif, ô mon doux Jesus Christ,
Ou donne moy de l'eau de ta grace infinie.

117. Consummatum est

Dieu a tout faict par temps, par nombre et par mesure,
Luy mesme est le niveau, la regle et le compas,
Il dispose tout bien, mesmes à son trespas,
Il voulut accomplir de tout point l'Escripture.

La mort qui talonnoit son humaine nature,
Rendit son corps divin si mortellement las,

Yelling loudly, You alter Your feeble voice,
Crying, "My God, my God, why have You forsaken me?"
All the waves of the torrent have passed on Your head.
The Father has struck You for our sins.

You did not complain of what You suffered:
The mortal torture on the branches of the Cross.
It is for me that You made such a high complaint.

In order to give me credit, You made Yourself forgotten.
To break my ties, You sought to bind Yourself.
In a word, You spill Your blood to cleanse me of my sin.

116. Sitio[271]
You who make the waves of the terrifying sea[272]
And provide the liquids that the world consumes,
You who make water stream from the desert rock,[273]
And rendered the water stable like an aerial wall,[274]

You who refreshed us at Your sacred table,[275]
And quenched our hearts with Your open heart,
You were not even offered a glass of water
When You cried, in a pitiful voice, "I am thirsty."

The ardor that dried Your throat was extreme,
But You had a more ardent blaze in Your heart,
A desire inflamed with the salvation of my life.

Thus, completely parched, You rendered Your spirit.
Give Your thirst to me, O my sweet Jesus Christ!
Or give me some of the water of Your infinite grace.

117. Consummatum est[276]
God has made everything by time, by number, and by measure.
He is the level, the ruler, and the compass.
He prepared everything well, even at His death.
He wanted to carry out the Scriptures completely.

Death, who afflicted His human nature,
Rendered His divine body so mortally weary

Que ce verbe eternel, soustenant les combats,
Dict: tout est consommé, Pere, voicy mon heure.

J'ay ouvert les sept seaux du livre cacheté,
Satan est ruiné, mon peuple est racheté,
J'ay choisi dans mon coeur une espouse nouvelle.

Les portes de l'enfer soubs elles trembleront,
Et tant qu'à l'advenir les siecles dureront,
Elle doit estre en moy comme je suis en elle.

118. Pater in manus tuas commendo spiritum meum
Le celeste heritier, plain d'amour infinie,
Rengea son testament en sept mots excellens,
Il despartit son coeur en mille amours ardens,
A sa mere donna sainct Jean pour compagnie,

Son sang plain de valeur à qui en eust envie,
Au larron Paradis, ses robes aux sergens;
Ses merites sacrés il donne à toutes gens,
Se monstrant liberal des tresors de sa vie,

Disant: Pere eternel, reçoy entre tes mains
Mon esprit qui s'en va pour sauver les humains,
Et lors il expira en inclintant la teste.

Holocauste tressainct, plain de douce senteur,
Qui nous pacifiant te rends mediateur,
Sauve tous les captifs par ta rare conqueste.

119.
Le coeur plain de regret, les yeux chargés de pleurs,
Je passe ainsi les nuicts longues et solitaires,
Ayant comme un marteau mes importuns affaires,
Qui vont frappant le clou de mes fortes douleurs.

Mon mal estant causé de diverses humeurs,
Consomme peu à peu mes forces necessaires,
Mais j'attends du seul Dieu les graces salutaires,
A sa douce bonté j'adresse mes clameurs.

That this Eternal Word, enduring the struggles,
Said, "It is finished, Father, my time has come.

I broke open the book with the seven seals.[277]
Satan is ruined, and my people are redeemed.
I have chosen a new spouse in my heart.[278]

There will be trembling beneath the gates of hell,
And as long as the centuries will continue in the future,
She must be in me as I am in her."[279]

118.[280] Pater in manus tuas commendo spiritum meum[281]
The celestial heir, full of infinite love,
Arranged His testament in seven excellent words.
He divided His heart into a thousand ardent loves.
He gave Saint John to His mother for company,

His blood full of valor to those who desired it,
His sacred merits to all people,*
Paradise to the thief,[282] His robes to the sergeants,[283]
And proved Himself generous with the treasures of His life,

Saying, "Eternal Father, receive into Your hands
My spirit that departs this world to save mankind."[284]
And then, inclining His head, He expired.

Very holy Holocaust, full of sweet perfume,
Who render Yourself mediator in pacifying us,
Save all of the captives[285] by Your singular conquest.

119.
I spend the long, solitary nights*
With my heart full of regret and my eyes brimming with tears.
My importunate affairs are like a hammer
That strikes the nail of my trenchant pains.

My pain, caused by diverse moods,[286]
Consumes my necessary forces little by little,
But I await the salutary graces from the only God.
I address my clamors to His gentle goodness.

Mes amis estonnez ont crainte de ma vie,
Voyant mon pasle teint et ma face ternie,
Non, la peur de la mort ne m'espouvante pas:

Le souvenir de veoir mes filles en enfance,
Orphelines de pere et sans nulle defence,
M'est un plus grand tourment que le mesme trespas.

120.
Nous sommes viateurs, vous estes en repos,
Nous bataillons icy, vous avez la victoire,
Nous sommes en travail, vous estes en la gloire,
Vous estes dans le port, nous ramons sur les flots.

Nous sommes revestus de sang, de chair et d'os,
Vous avez despouillé ce qui est transitoire,
O vous, saints bien-heureux dont l'antique memoire
Consacre à l'Eternel l'honneur de vostre los,

Vous, Apostres, avez les chaires ordonnées
Pour juger à la fin les douze grands lignées,
Vous, Vierges et Martirs, Prophetes, Confesseurs,

Portez la palme en main, la robe blanchissante,
Dans le sang de l'aigneau faicte resplendissante,
Triomphans avec Dieu, de ses biens possesseurs.

121.
Le poisson vit en l'eau, la froide Salemandre
Demeure dans le feu sans jamais se brusler,
Le faux cameleon vit seulement de l'air,
La taupe se nourrit de la terre plus tendre.

Nous vivons dans les eaux lors que nous pouvons fendre
Le rocher de nos coeurs pour faire ruisseller
Une source de pleurs à fin de consoler
Nostre exil prolongé que Dieu nous faict attendre.

Nous vivons dans le feu sans alteration,
Si nous sommes constans en la tentation,
L'air nous sert de repas, de plaisirs et delices,

My astonished friends have fear for my life,
Seeing my pale color and my tarnished face.
No, the fear of death does not frighten me.

The memory of seeing my daughters in infancy,
Orphaned of father and without any defense,[287]
To me, is a greater torment than death.

120.
We are voyagers; you are at peace.
We battle here; victory is yours.
We are in labor; you are in glory.
You are in the port; we are rowing on the waves.

We are dressed in blood, flesh, and bone;
You have divested yourself of what is transitory.
O you blessed saints of whom the ancient memory
Devotes the honor of your glory to the Eternal One!

You, Apostles, have the ordained pulpits
To judge the twelve great tribes.[288]
You, virgins, martyrs, prophets, and confessors,

Carry the palm leaf in hand, and wear the white robe
Made resplendent in the blood of the lamb,
And triumph with God, sharing the goods He possesses.[289]

121.
The fish lives in the water;*
The cold salamander sits in fire without ever burning;[290]
The deceptive[291] chameleon lives on air alone;
The mole nourishes himself with the most tender earth.

We live in water when we can split
The rock of our hearts to make a spring of tears[292]*
Flow forth in order to ease
The prolonged exile imposed upon us by God.[293]

We live without thirst in the fire
If we are constant in the face of temptation;
The air nourishes us with pleasures and delights

Quand nous guindons là haut nos esprits dans le ciel,
Mais nous nous repaissons de ce terrestre fiel,
Quand nous nous arrestons au bourbier de nos vices.

122.
Instrument de Pallas, quenouille menagere,
Chargée de fin lin gentiment replyé,
Ton fardeau d'un lacet verdoyant est lyé,
Decorant le beau sein de la gaye bergere.

Par ton subtil moyen la soigneuse lingere,
Agence proprement son filet delié,
L'heur de ces grands effects ne doit estre oublié,
Despartant tes tresors à la rive estrangere.

Quenouille, s'il te plait m'aprendre la façon
De tordre le fuseau agravé du peson,
Mouiller les bouts des doigts, allonger ta despouille,

Et en pirouetant rendre les brins esgaux,
Faisant par ton mestier adoucir mes travaux,
Je t'aymeray tousjours, ô ma chere quenouille.

123.
Pallas se courrouça à l'ouvriere gentille,
Pour ce qu'elle avoit faict son ouvrage plus beau,
Deschirant le tissu et brisant le fuseau,
Et foulant à ses pieds la besongne subtille,

Frappa cruellement l'ingenieuse fille
Dont le sang ruissella du plus haut du cerveau,
Jupiter qui voyoit ce debat tout nouveau,
Aragnes transmua en l'aragne qui file.

Ainsi voit on souvent les plus grands se facher,
S'ils voyent les petits desireux d'approcher
La roche de vertu à grimper malaisée.

Mais Dieu qui prend plaisir à ses humbles ouvriers,
Leur donne bien souvent les triomphans lauriers,
Pource que des mondains leur toille est mesprisée.

When we raise our spirits to the sky.
But we feast on this terrestrial bile
When we stop at the quagmire of our vices.

122.
Instrument of Pallas,[294] domestic distaff[295]
Laden with fine, gently folded flax,
Your burden is tied with a verdant lace,
Adorning the beautiful breast of the lighthearted shepherdess.

By your subtle means, the careful linen maker,
Properly arranges her untied thread.
The success of these grand works must not be forgotten,
Leaving your treasures on the foreign shore.

Distaff, please teach me the way
To twist the spindle laden with weight,
To moisten my finger tips, to stretch out your threads,

And to spin in order to render equal strands,
Easing my task by your skill.
I will always love you, O my dear distaff![296]

123.
Pallas got angry at the kind workwoman,[297]
Because she had made her most beautiful work.
Tearing the fabric and breaking the spindle,
And treading on the fine work at her feet,

She cruelly struck the ingenious girl,
Whose blood streamed from the highest part of her brain.
Jupiter, who saw this completely new quarrel,
Changed Arachne into a spinning spider.[298]

Thus one often sees even the greatest ones get angry
If they see the little ones desirous of approaching
The rock of virtue so difficult to climb.

But God, who takes pleasure in His humble workers,[299]
Gives them quite often the triumphant laurels,
Because the worldly ones despise their cloth.

124.

Je ne veux rien sçavoir, pour sçavante paroistre,
Tres-heureux est celuy qui ne cognoist que soy,
Nous voulons tout sçavoir jusqu'aux secrets du Roy,
Les moeurs de nos voisins, le reglement du cloistre.

Ces curiositez font en nos ames croistre
Des mescontentements plains d'ennuyeux esmoy,
Rien que mon Redempteur Crucifié pour moy,
Je ne veux escouter, rien je ne veux cognoistre.

Venez doncques, Seigneur, posseder tous mes sens,
Attirez mes esprits, ha! desja je me sens
Plaine d'un chaut desir de vous louer sans cesse.

Je n'ay rien de ma part que ce foible vouloir,
Armez moy s'il vous plaist d'un asseuré pouvoir,
Et pour sauver mon ame animez ma foiblesse.

125. Pour la feste sainct Martin

Tout ainsi qu'un vert pré delicieux à veoir,
Aux jours du plus beau mois estale ses fleurettes,
Et comme le haut ciel esclaire ses planettes,
Quand sur nostre orizon on voit venir le soir.

Ainsi le Roy des Roys en son divin manoir
Desploye les rayons de ses graces parfaictes
Surtout les bienheureux Martirs, Vierges, Prophetes,
Et à chacun à part donne quelque pouvoir.

Le benoist sainct Martin dont la grand renommée
En l'Eglise de Dieu est aujourd'huy semée,
Prie pour le repos des pauvres souffreteus:

Lors qu'il vivoit icy sa robbe il a partie
Pour revestir les nuds, ores en l'autre vie,
Il est vestu d'honneur, de gloire et de vertus.

126.

Les jours me sont si doux en ce beau lieu champestre,
Voyant d'un fer tranchant fendre le long gueret,

124.
I do not want to know anything or appear as a learned woman.
Very blessed is he who knows only himself.
We want to know everything, right down to the secrets of the king,
The mores of our neighbors, and the regulations of the cloister.

The curiosities incite in our souls the growth of
Discontentments full of troublesome emotions.
I do not want to know anything or listen to anyone*
But my Redeemer, who was crucified for me.

Come then, Lord, possess all my senses.
Draw my spirits in. Ah! I already feel myself
Full of a hot desire to praise you without end.

I have nothing for my part except this feeble will.[300]
Arm me, please, with an assured power.[301]
And, in order to save my soul, animate my weakness.

125. For the Festival of Saint Martin[302]
Just as a green prairie, delicious to see,
Spreads its little flowers in the days of the most beautiful month,
And just as the high sky illuminates its planets
When the evening appears on our horizon,

So the King of Kings[303] in His divine manor
Deploys the rays of His perfect graces
Above all the blessed martyrs, virgins, and prophets,
And gives some power to each one separately.

The blessed Saint Martin, whose great renown
Is spread today in the church of God,
Prays for the peace of the suffering poor:[304]

When he lived here, he sacrificed his robe
To dress the naked. Now in the other life,
He is dressed in honor, glory, and virtue.

126.
The days are so sweet to me in this beautiful pastoral place,
Seeing the long tillage split with a trenchant iron

Et enterrer le bled jaunissant pur et net,
Puis le veoir tost apres tout verdoyant renaistre.

Mon Dieu, le grand plaisir de veoir sur l'herbe paistre
La frisée brebis portant son aignelet,
Et le cornu belier qui marche tout seulet
Au devant du troupeau comme patron et maistre.

L'air est delicieux, sans pluyes ne chaleurs,
Un petit vent mollet faict ondoyer les fleurs,
Les bois portent encor leur superbe coronne.

L'on n'oyt point la rumeur d'un vulgaire babil,
Sinon des oyselets le ramage gentil,
Loué soit l'Eternel qui tous ces biens nous donne.

127.
Combien ay je perdu de travail et de temps
A te suyvre par tout, ô monde miserable,
Tu faisois beau semblant de m'estre favorable,
Et puis tu m'as trompée en mes plus jeunes ans.

Je ne mandie plus tes dons ny tes presens,
Je quitte volontiers ta faveur variable,
Ores je veux chercher ce qui est perdurable,
Revien mon pauvre coeur et commande mes sens.

Qui m'a ouvert les yeux pour ces ruses cognoistre?
Ce n'est autre que toy, mon Createur et maistre,
Sans l'avoir merité tu as eu soing de moy.

Asseure donc mon coeur au sentier de ta grace,
Ne cache, s'il te plaist, la douceur de ta face,
Non, je ne suivray plus autre Seigneur que toy.

128.
Oyez les doux propos et mielleuse complainte
Que Dieu faict au pecheur à fin de l'attirer,
Mon peuple bien aymé, te veux tu retirer
De l'estroite union de mon amitié saincte.

And the yellowing fallow buried pure and simple,
Only to see it reborn all verdurous again soon after.

My God, it is a great pleasure to see the shaggy sheep*
Feeding on the grass, bearing her baby lamb,
And the horned ram that walks all alone
In front of the flock like a chief and master.

The air is delicious without rains or heat;
The flowers ripple in the soft, delicate wind;
The woods bear their superb crown again.

One does not hear the noise of vulgar chatter,
Only the gentle warble of little birds.
Praised be the Eternal One who gives us all of these good things.

127.
How much work and time have I lost
Following you everywhere, O miserable world!
You pretended quite successfully to be favorable to me,
And then you deceived me in my youngest years. [305]

I no longer plead for your gifts nor for your presents;
I voluntarily leave your variable favor.
Now I want to see what is eternal.
Come back, my poor heart, and command my senses.

Who opened my eyes in order to recognize these ruses?
It is no other than You, my Creator and Master.
Without my deserving it, You took care of me.

Steady my heart on the path of Your grace, then.
Please do not hide the sweetness of Your face. [306]
No, I will no longer follow any other Lord than You.

128.
Hear the sweet words and the mellifluous complaint
That God makes to the sinner so as to draw him near: [307]
"My beloved people, you want to withdraw
From the close union of my holy friendship.

Je ne veux rien de toy par force ny constrainte,
Tu as un franc vouloir dont tu dois m'honorer,
Obey moy tousjours sans jamais alterer
De mes commandemens la pieté non feinte.

Dy moy que t'ay je faict, je vois que tu t'enfuis,
Tu te vas engouffrer dedans l'infernal puis,
Revien dedans mon sein, ô ma pauvre facture.

Je suis ton pere doux qui te jure et promets
Que si d'un repentir tu laisses tes mesfaits,
Je lairay ma vengeance, oubliant ton injure.

129. Sur la mort de Ronsard
Muses, sçavez vous point la piteuse avanture,
Qui a d'un coup mortel affligé l'univers?
Ouy, vous la sçavez, d'un nuage couvers,
Vos beaux yeux vont pleurans ceste mesadvanture.

Vostre Apollon est mort, couvres sa sepulture
De vos cheveux dorez, faictes cent mille vers
A celuy qui premier planta vos lauriers vers,
Et vous faict honorer d'un los qui tousjours dure.

Dieu l'a voulu tirer du cloistre de ce corps,
Sa belle ame a trouvé les celestes accords,
Ayant vollé plus haut que le mont de Parnasse.

Ronsard est immortel en la terre et aux cieux,
Nous heritons icy ses labeurs precieux,
Il possede le ciel voyant Dieu face à face.

I do not want anything from you by force or by constraint.
You have a free will with which you must honor me.
Obey me always without ever altering
The unfeigned piety of my commandments.

I see that you flee; tell me what I have done to you.
You are going to engulf yourselves in the infernal well.
Come back into my breast, O my poor creation.

I am your sweet Father who swears to you and promises
That if you abandon your misdeeds through contrition,
I will abandon my vengeance, and your insult will be forgotten."

129. On the Death of Ronsard[308]
Muses, do you not know about the dreadful event
That has afflicted the universe with a mortal blow?
Yes, you know it. Covered with a cloud,
Your beautiful eyes shed tears over this misfortune.

Your Apollo[309] is dead; cover his sepulcher
With your golden hair; make a hundred thousand verses
For the one who first planted your green laurels
And honors you with a glory that will last forever.

God wanted to draw him from the cloister of this body;
His beautiful soul found heavenly harmonies,
Having flown higher than the mount of Parnassus.[310]

Ronsard is immortal on earth and in heaven.
We inherit here his precious labors.
Seeing God face to face, he possesses the sky.[311]

NOTES

The notes that I have incorporated from Winn and Fizet are often direct translations, sometimes bearing slight modifications and on other occasions exhibiting a more loosely paraphrased version of the original. When I have taken information in a note from Winn or Fizet, I indicate this within the text of the note itself or at the end with author's name in parentheses. To avoid encumbering the notes with frequent page references, I let the reader know here that any of the borrowed information in my notes can be located in the notes corresponding to the numbered sonnets in Winn's edition or in Fizet's thesis.

1. Marguerite de Valois.

2. Henri III banished Marguerite de Valois to the remote château d'Usson in 1586. See Jean H. Mariéjol, *La vie de Marguerite de Valois, reine de Navarre et de France, 1553–1615* (Paris: Hachette, 1928), 139.

3. "Her" refers here to their mother, Coignard.

4. Possibly Clémence Isaure.

5. See Acts 9:36–41.

6. The apostle Peter.

7. After having praised Coignard's honor and virtue, the author of the preface emphasizes her pious intentions and insists on the spiritual gains the public can expect from reading her work. Colette Winn points out that these comments are common to the prefatory pages of published works by women authors during the sixteenth century and serve as a strategic defense against censure. See François Rigolot, "La préface à la Renaissance: Un discours sexué?" *Cahiers de l'Association Internationale des Études Françaises* 42 (May 1990): 121–35; and Anne Larsen, "'Un honneste passetems': Strategies of Legitimation in French Renaissance Women's Prefaces," *L'Esprit Créateur* 30 (1990): 11–22.

8. According to Winn, Philandre was the twin brother of Phylacide and the son of Acacallis and Apollo.

9. Toulouse was a Catholic bastion in France during a time when the surrounding countryside was dominated by Huguenots (Winn). The city was the victim of con-

stant religious strife. See Philippe Wolff, *Histoire de Toulouse* (Toulouse: Privat, 1967), 271–92. The meaning of the phrase in parentheses in the first line of the second quatrain is unclear, as is the full meaning of the stanza as a whole. The verb "outrager" could be interpreted in a number of ways. Possible translations for the verb include "to outrage," "to violate," "to assault," "to offend," "to devastate," or "to attack." However, in light of the imprecise subject of this verb, "un chacun" (which refers most likely to "everyone" in the surrounding area who assails and offends the city in various ways), the verb "insult," with its numerous implications, allows for a broader interpretation of the verb "outrager," more appropriate to the context of the religious conflict of the period and its many manifestations. The final line of the stanza is also problematic: it is not clear in what way the city of Toulouse is mistreating its "precious children."

10.   Winn lists some of the "precious children" of Toulouse who were contemporaries of Gabrielle de Coignard: Gratien du Pont, sieur de Drusac, Guy Du Faur de Pibrac, and Pierre Paschal to whom Ronsard and Du Bellay dedicated numerous poems. Jean Bodin, Jean de Boyssoné, Etienne Dolet, Guillaume Salluste du Bartas, and Michel de Montaigne studied law at the University of Toulouse. The arrival of the printing press in 1476 in Toulouse brought about a rapid spread of humanism. The Parlement and the Collège de rhétorique et de poésie françaises, along with the *Jeux Floraux*, contributed significantly to the development of an intellectual milieu.

11.   The "winged horse" refers to Pegasus.

12.   Coignard is alluding to Hippocrene, the fountain of the Muses in Boeotia, which according to Greek mythology was exposed by Pegasus's kick (Fizet). See Hesiod *Theogony* 280–325, ed. Apostolos Athanassakis (Baltimore: Johns Hopkins University Press, 1983), 20–21; Pindar *Olympian Odes* 13.63–92, ed. William Race (Cambridge, Mass.: Harvard University Press, 1997), 195–99.

13.   Cf. Ex 17:6 Ps 78:15, 104:10–11, 105:41; Is 41:17–18; Mt 5:6; and Jn 4:13–14. Although the Exodus and Psalms references refer to physical provision and Coignard's poem is about spiritual nourishment, the imagery from these Biblical passages is echoed in this sonnet.

14.   Refusing to name the mythological gods, Coignard is content to designate them by their attributes (Winn). The laurel, the mark of poetic glory, was the emblem of Apollo, god of music and poetry. Myrrh was devoted to Venus, the goddess of love and beauty. The olive tree was the tree of Minerva, goddess of wisdom.

15.   For Biblical passages in which fire symbolizes divine presence and power, see, for example, Heb 12:29, Ez 22:20, Zec 13:9, Mal 3:2, and 1 Pt 1:7.

16.   Coignard frequently presents the Cross as a place of refuge. See also sonnets 21, 22, and 73.

17.   Cf. Ps 23:4 and 84:6.

18.   Cf. Heb 12:29. See also above, sonnet 2, note 15.

19.   The expression "offence coulante" is unclear in French. It is an unusual combination of terms. In Middle French, the adjective *coulant*, aside from its link to the verb *couler* (to flow), as it is used in the first line of this stanza, was related to the notion of

"inconstancy." Such a connotation does not make sense within the context of the preceding lines in combination with the noun "offence." It is clear that by "offence" the poet is referring to a behavior that should be avoided and therefore one that should not be undertaken intentionally (an issue Coignard also addresses in sonnet 38). In my efforts to grasp Coignard's meaning here, I stretched the adjective *coulant* (flowing) to mean "with ease or facility" and then to "with purpose" because of the verb "to seek" that introduces the line (for if one offends with ease, if one seeks an occasion to offend, one does so with intent). But instead of making interpretive leaps in order to translate this term, I decided that the meaning of the line was clearer without it. Therefore, I did not include the adjective in the translation, as I did not want to impose some imprecise equivalent for *coulante* that would further obscure the line.

20. Cf. Ps 71:9.

21. Cf. Rom 11:16–24.

22. This first stanza illustrates Coignard's affinity for the anaphora, a technique favored by Petrarch. See also sonnet 40. For a Biblical example of this rhetorical device that may have inspired Coignard in this sonnet, cf. Rom 8:38–39.

23. The oxymoron is another poetic device that Coignard draws from Petrarchan tradition.

24. The invocation of impossible natural occurrences is a poetic device found in Petrarchan verse.

25. For lines 9–10, cf. Ps 105:1–2.

26. Pierre de Ronsard.

27. An allusion to the enchanting power of Orpheus and an uncharacteristic pairing, in light of sonnet 1, of Christian and pagan imagery.

28. Ronsard's *Hercule chrestien*, published in *Hymnes* (1555–56).

29. This sonnet can be grouped with the other penitential compositions within this collection. Cf. sonnets 4, 5, 41, 46, 67, 82, 85, 87, and 90. Both Ignatius de Loyola and Louis of Granada encourage this type of self-examination. See the first week of Loyola's *Spiritual Exercises* and the Monday evening meditations of Granada's *Le Vray Chemin* (Winn). See also my introduction to this volume.

30. Recalls Ps 6:6–7 and is also, as Winn rightly maintains, reminiscent of the Petrarchan imagery of the lover in despair.

31. See Evelyne Berriot-Salvadore for commentary on night and shadow imagery in Coignard's sonnets (*Les Femmes dans la société française de la Renaissance* (Geneva: Droz, 1990), 439–40.

32. According to Marianne Fizet, the first tercet of this sonnet is one of the best examples of what might be called a "feminine sensibility" in the work of Coignard. The harmony of the liquid sounds and the intimacy conveyed in the vocabulary that is full of maternal connotations, such as the protective night, peace, sleep, tears, soul, pain, and breast, express a sensibility entirely her own, which contrasts with sonnet 80, for example, where the night assumes its common penitential image as a place of torment.

33.   Fizet points out that the two instances when Coignard mentions her daughters—in this sonnet and in sonnet 99—she links them to the discussion of her health and to her weariness of life.

34.   Paraphrase of the parable of the sower, Mt 13:3–23, Mk 4:3–20, and Lk 8:4–15.

35.   Cf. Gn 3:17–18, Mi 6:15.

36.   For Coignard, the body is merely an inconvenient obstacle between terrestrial and eternal life (Fizet). Consider the "mortal chariot" in line 7 of sonnet 38 and "the carnal skin" in line 12 of sonnet 76 for other examples of Coignard's conception of the body. See also, sonnet 129.

37.   Cf. Mt 26:36–46, Mk 14:32–42, Lk 22:40–46.

38.   Cf. Prv 6:9.

39.   *Cabinet* is a term that in middle French refers specifically to a private chamber (often attached to a larger room) to which one could retreat for work, reading, or reflection. A *cabinet* also served as a place to keep one's treasures or, as in Coignard's case, one's private papers or compositions.

40.   "[O]n a wing too bold" (*une aesle trop hardie*): a play on words with the term "pen," also referred to as "aile" in the Renaissance, a symbol of freedom and creative imagination.

41.   Cf. Ps 131:1, Rom 12:16, Phlm 2:3.

42.   These lines echo the recommendations of Joachim du Bellay, who states in *La deffence et illustration de la langue francoyse,* ed. Henri Chamard (Paris: Marcel Didier, 1970), that without the perfect mastery of the Greek and Latin languages, the imitation of the ancients is impossible (105–7). Fizet underlines that contemporary conceptions of women's education, formulated by such humanists as Vivès and Erasmus, did not encourage women to pursue this type of knowledge.

43.   Cf. Ps 38:2–3. These verses evoke the image of Saint Teresa at the moment when she is struck in the heart by the flaming arrow of the angel. Mystics throughout the centuries have noted that the spiritual wound gives both pain and pleasure (Winn).

44.   The Christian notion of *agape* ("God is charity") was developed by Saint John, as well as other New Testament figures, such as Peter and Paul. Cf. 1 Jn 4:8, 13:34–35, 14:15, 15:9–11, 12–13 (Winn).

45.   See note 10 for a list of a few of Coignard's contemporaries (the "excellent minds") nourished by the Garonne River.

46.   The Garonne is a river in southwest France.

47.   This is one of the rare biographical details Coignard includes in her poems.

48.   A reminiscence of Petrarch: "I bless the place and the time and the hour that my eyes looked so high . . . " *Rime sparse* 13.

49.   This stanza recalls Ps 69:1–3.

50.   An allusion to the magical powers that possessed Circe, the mystical Greek

goddess who charmed Ulysses and his companions with her sons in order to turn them into swine.

51.   She is referring to Eros, the Greek god of love. In this sonnet, love is linked with death, a common thematic pairing for poets of the Renaissance, such as Ronsard and Du Bellay, who, inspired by Petrarchan tradition, preferred a more pessimistic portrayal of love in opposition to the Platonic ideal of divine love.

52.   Winn notes that the image of the "cruel serpent," a symbol of seduction and destruction, juxtaposed to the image of Eros, who appears here with all his classic attributes (arrows, wings, and blindfold), announces the opposition on which the sonnet is constructed (*amor carnalis* vs. *amor spiritualis*) and the entirely Christian orientation of the last two strophes.

53.   This line was reorganized and converted from passive voice to active voice in English in an effort to offer an interpretation of the verse, which is not completely clear in the original. Apprehension in sixteenth-century French connotes a sense of alarm or anguish more than it signifies understanding or comprehension. However, in light of the stanza that follows, it appears that Coignard wanted to convey the mental paralysis that occurs in a mind poisoned by jealousy. The line could be translated as "the fear of which [that is, the fear of the thousand ignobilities] is frantically grasped," but this is an indistinct rendering of the French and does not contribute to the overarching theme of the first two stanzas.

54.   Celebrated on September 14, this day commemorates the return of the cross to Jerusalem in the seventh century. Chosroes II, king of Persia, had stolen the cross, after taking over Jerusalem and massacring the Christians. The Roman emperor Heraclius pursued him until the oldest son of Chosroes gave it back to him thirteen years later. Heraclius first placed the relic in Constantinople and then took it back to Jerusalem (Winn).

55.   Coignard echoes the *Vexilla Regis prodeunt,* a hymn composed by Venantius Fortunatus near the end of the sixth century and sung at vespers on the Sunday of the Passion to celebrate the mystery of the Cross (Winn).

56.   "Dulce lignum" is an expression that comes from the *Crux fidelis,* which is also sung on Good Friday (Winn).

57.   Coignard's "shadow of the cross" is a modification of the Biblical imagery found in Ps 57:1, a prayer for deliverance in which the psalmist seeks refuge under the wings of the Lord God. See also Ps 36:7, 63:8, 91:4.

58.   Celebrated on May 3, the day of the Invention of the Cross is the day on which Saint Helen, the mother of the Emperor Constantine, supposedly discovered the true Cross of Christ two hundred years after the Resurrection and ordered that the day be celebrated every year (Winn).

59.   Cf. *Vexilla Regis prodeunt:* "Arbor decora et fulgida, Ornata Regis purpura" (Winn).

60.   Cf. *Vexilla Regis:* "Qua vita mortem pertulit, Et morte vitam protulit" (Winn).

61.   Reminiscent of prayers to the Virgin Mary such as "Inviolata, integra et casta es, Maria" and "Felix coeli porta," which are sung occasionally at the Benediction of the Holy Communion and in other diverse circumstances (Winn).

62. Cf. Mt 25:1–13. Also reminiscent of Mk 13:33–37 and Luke 12:35–38.

63. The north wind in Greek mythology.

64. Winn notes that this poem on the return to God through repentance takes up the theme of storms and shipwrecks at sea, which is common to many religious poets of the end of the century. This theme is typically contrasted with the theme of the purifying water of tears and the outpouring of praise for the merciful God.

65. The anaphora in this sonnet calls to mind sonnet 2 of Louise Labé's *Oeuvres complètes*, ed. François Rigolot (Paris: Flammarion, 1986), 122, a comparison that has been made by Jeanine Moulin (*Anthologie de la poésie féminine* [Paris: Seghers, 1966]), 155; and Hugette Kaiser (*Gabrielle de Coignard, poétesse dévote* [Ph.D. diss., Emory University, 1975]), 32. The complete poems of Louise Labé will appear in this series.

66. Cf. Eph 5:2.

67. Cf. Jn 3:29. There is also a distant echo of Rv 21:2.

68. A literal translation would be "where the greatest marvel *perched* himself." Although the verb "to perch" does work in combination with Coignard's metaphorical "tree," it seemed an awkward word choice in English. The verb "to sacrifice" clarifies the meaning of the original. The four gospel references to the crucifixion are Mt 27:35, Mk 15:24, Lk 23:33, and John 19:23.

69. One of the rare allusions to the wars of religion (1562–98). See also sonnet 28.

70. Kaiser found a reference to such an epidemic in the annals of the city of Toulouse from the month of August 1580. According to Winn, there is an earlier reference in Pierre de l'Estoile's *Journal de Henri III, 1574—1580* (*Mémoires-journaux*, vol. 1, 361–62) to the epidemic that appeared in Paris in June of 1580. Coignard interprets it here as a curse sent by God.

71. The lack of contrition on the part of French Catholics, that would be made apparent through penitential weeping, prevents them from seeing their own persecution by the Protestants.

72. In these lines, Fizet notes, the author is expressing her anguish with regard to fleeting time; she does not have enough time to accomplish her resolutions. The conflict between her worldly life, with all its daily duties, and the contemplative life is evident. The preferred poetic response at the time, the *carpe diem* motif, does not figure among Coignard's meditations. According to Moulin, women poets did not turn to the notion of *carpe diem* as frequently as their male contemporaries (*Anthologie de la poésie féminine* [Paris: Seghers, 1966] 13–14). See also Cathy Yandell, *Carpe Corpus: Time and Gender in Early Modern France* (Newark: University of Delaware Press, 2000).

73. On external penitence and the mortification of the flesh, see Ignatius de Loyola's *Spiritual Exercises.*

74. Cf. Heb 12:12–14.

75. Cf. Ps 86:2.

76. Cf. Mt 10:38, 16:24; Lk 14:27. See also F. de Sales, *Introduction to a Devout Life*, part 3, chap. 37 (New York: Catholic Book Publishing Co., 1946), 310–11 (Winn).

77. The first two stanzas contain a distant echo of the prophecy Jesus Christ gave to his disciples at the Mount of Olives. Cf. Mt 24:3–44, Mk 13:3–37, Luke 21:5–36.

78.   Cf. Mt 10:22, 24:13; Mk 13:13; and Jn 16:22.

79.   The notion of "perfect" love develops considerably in the New Testament, especially in the gospel of Saint John (Winn). Cf. Jn 3:16, 15:13; 1 Cor 13:4–13; 1 Jn 4: 8–12.

80.   Cf. 2 Tm 1:13. Fizet notes that this triad of charity, love, and hope recalls that of faith, love, and hope, which is a frequent theme in the New Testament. 1 Cor 13:13 could have also been a possible model for this passage.

81.   On the theme of mystical marriage, see Sg 2:16, 6:3; 2 Cor 11:2; and Rv 19:7–8, 21:9.

82.   Cf. Mt 5:12 and Heb 10:35.

83.   A possible source for this rather obscure and unusual Biblical notion might be the Book of Joshua. Cf. Jos 6:17, 7:10–13, et seq.

84.   Lines 3–4 contain an allusion to Mt 6:19–21. See also Jn 18:36.

85.   Cf. Mt 10:22.

86.   A possible, albeit distant, allusion to Mt 3:11–12, which is about baptism with the Holy Spirit and fire.

87.   Coignard often uses the Biblical imagery of fire as a purifying force. Cf. Zec 13:9, Mal 3:2, 1 Cor 3:13, 1 Pt 1:7. See also sonnets 82, 84, and 87.

88.   Here Coignard is celebrating the day of her patron saint; the date today is March 24, but it was September 29 during the Renaissance. Fizet argues that the latter seems probable if put in the context of the following sonnet, which is dedicated to Saint Jerome, who is commemorated on September 30.

89.   Cf. Lk 1:26–38, where the archangel who prophesies the birth of God is named Gabriel. Luke 2:9–14 also describes the Annunciation but by an unnamed angel.

90.   Cf. Tb 6–12. Raphael, one of the seven archangels who present the prayers of the saints, accompanied the young Tobit in his travels and revealed to him the cure for his father's blindness.

91.   This day is celebrated on September 30.

92.   Cf. sonnet 32, final tercet.

93.   After having reproached himself in a dream for preferring pagan literature to Christian literature, Saint Jerome lived for five years as a hermit in the Syrian desert, where he learned Hebrew. A number of his letters plead in favor of asceticism (Winn).

94.   See Eugene Rice, *Saint Jerome in the Renaissance* (Baltimore: Johns Hopkins University Press, 1985), esp. chaps. 1–2 (Winn).

95.   The first stanza of this poem, a prayer to the Mother of Mercy, recalls the *Salve, Regina, Mater misericordiae*, a hymn sung from Trinity Sunday to Advent (Winn).

96.   Metaphors that evoke those found in the *Salve Regina*: "in hac lacrymarum valle" (Winn).

97.   Cf. Ps 59:3–4.

98.   For Winn, using the name of the goddess of fertility to designate wheat has no function beyond poetic ornament.

99.   According to Winn, among others, this image is most likely borrowed from

Louis of Granada. See *Le vray chemin* (fol. 273 a). Cf. also Prv 1:4, 2:10–11, 8:12, and 11:22.

100.   Cf. Ps 119:37.

101.   Military imagery is frequently found in the work of Coignard's contemporary Jean-Baptiste Chassignet (Winn). Cf. *Le mespris de la vie et consolation contre la mort*, sonnets 231, 351, 432, ed. A. Müller (Geneva: Droz, 1953).

102.   Cf. Ex 13:21, 14:19–20; Is 42:16, 49:10, 58:8.

103.   This type of emotional contradiction, caused by the absence or rejection of the beloved, is often described in love poetry of the Petrarchan tradition (Winn). Cf. Scève, *La Délie de Maurice Scève et ses cinquante emblèmes ou les noces secrètes de la poésie et du signe*, ed. Paul Ardouin (Paris: Librairie A.-G. Nizet, 1982), 434; Ronsard, *Le premier livre des amours*, nos. 12 and 43, vol. 1 of *Oeuvres Complètes*, ed. Gustave Cohen (Paris: Gallimard, 1950), 7, 20, et seq.

104.   Saint Peter's Day is celebrated June 29.

105.   Peter (Pierre) was also the name of Gabrielle de Coignard's husband.

106.   Lk 10:38–42.

107.   Fizet suggests that the conclusion to the sonnet reveals Coignard's ambivalence concerning her duties of mother and housewife on the one hand and a life devoted to religious meditation on the other and affirms the paradox inherent in the Scriptures concerning the role of women.

108.   Following the examples of the patristic commentators and Calvin (*Harmonie des Evangiles*), Fizet suggests that Coignard considers the piety of the two sisters as equal. At this point, instead of working against each other, the *praxis* (good works) and the *theoria* (faith, prayer) seem to complete each other, as both are necessary in the quest for salvation.

109.   Fizet notes that the juxtaposition of "active" and "contemplative" in lines 9–10 reinforces the theme in the preceding poem. However, Coignard insists more explicitly here that these two modes of life be brought together, underlining the struggle she experiences in trying to create harmony between body and soul. It was already evident in the sixteenth century that the "perfect" woman was supposed to fuse within herself two fundamentally incompatible roles.

110.   This day is celebrated on July 22.

111.   It is to Mary Magdalene that Christ resurrected appears first. Cf. Jn 20:11–18.

112.   Cf. Lk 7:37–38.

113.   For Biblical passages concerning Mary Magdalene's presence at the crucifixion, see Mt 27:55, Mk 15:40, Luke 23:49 (although she is not mentioned by name), and Jn 19:25.

114.   Cf. Lk 7:36–48.

115.   According to the tradition known to Coignard in the sixteenth century, after the Ascension of Christ, Mary Magdalene left Jerusalem and went to Provence, accompanied by Maximin and other Disciples of Christ. There exist three pilgrimage sites, one of which is at the feet of the mountains of the Vaucluse (Winn).

116.   For Coignard, Mary Magdalene is the sinner who repented, the *peccatrix* whose function is to reveal to the faithful "the mystery of conversion" (*conversio*) (Winn).

117.   "Hide your face from my sins" (Ps 50:9).

118.   Cf. Ps 22:14.

119.   Cf. Ps 6:6.

120.   From the verse "Let me hear joy and gladness; let the bones that you have crushed rejoice" (Ps 50:8).

121.   King David, reputed author of the Book of Psalms, by which Coignard was considerably inspired, as is evident by her frequent recourse to the Psalms for a great deal of the imagery she uses throughout the sonnets. See the introduction, note 81.

122.   Fizet notes that the majority of the sonnets in the collection reveal a conception of life as a pilgrimage.

123.   Coignard experienced some difficult years with the successive deaths of her father (January 1569), her mother (February 1571), her husband (in 1573), and her uncle Aymond Coignard in the same period.

124.   Allusion to the cup of suffering, cf. Mt 26:39, Mk 14:36, Lk 22:42, Jn 18:11.

125.   Coignard is referring to the disciples James and John, cf. Mt 20:22–23 and Mk 10:35–40.

126.   Cf. Jn 6:54.

127.   Cf. Rv 8–11.

128.   Cf. Rv 1:14.

129.   An allusion to the trumpet of the seventh angel who announces the Kingdom of God. Cf. Rv 11:15. Cf. also Mt 24:29–31, 1 Cor. 15:52, 1 Thes 4:16.

130.   Cf. Rv 20:12.

131.   Cf. Ex 15:7, Mt 3:12.

132.   Cf. Gn 2:7, 18:27, Ps 103:14.

133.   Cf. Jb 21:18, Ps 1:5, 83:13.

134.   This poem introduces a group of ten sonnets devoted to Christmas celebrations.

135.   Cf. Ps 104:24, Prv 3:19–20.

136.   Cf. Ps 18:10, 104:3.

137.   Cf. Mt 2:11, Lk 2:16.

138.   Cf. Is 42:7, 61:1; Lk 4:18–19.

139.   Cf. Ps 49:15, 86:13; Zec 9:11; Rv 1:18.

140.   Fizet notes that this sonnet contains reflections on the liturgy of the mass for Christmas Day and is largely based on the hymn *Jesu, Redemptor omnium.*

141.   This day is celebrated on December 26.

142.   Cf. Acts 7:55–59.

143.   She is referring to the Cathédral Saint-Etienne in Toulouse, which dates back to the thirteenth century. Pierre Salies found in the register of baptisms of Saint-

Etienne the names of Coignard's daughters. Cf. "Gabrielle de Coignard: Poétesse toulousaine du XVIe siècle," *Archistra* 79 (March–April 1987): 38 (Winn).

144.   Celebrated on December 27.

145.   Cf. Jn 13:23; 21:7, 20.

146.   Cf. Jn 19:26–27.

147.   Cf. Rv 1:9.

148.   Cf. Rv 1:102.

149.   Lam 3:24; Ps 16: 5, 73:25–26, 119:57; Prv 3:26.

150.   Jesus as a spouse of the soul is a common metaphor in sacred texts, most often in writings by female saints and mystics. For the author, the Lord becomes the substitute for her dead husband (Winn).

151.   An allusion to the words of the Canaanite woman through which Jesus knew her faith. See Mt 15:22–28.

152.   Cf. Is 40:11; Ez. 34:11–24; Jn 10:11–16; Rv 7:17.

153.   Sg 1:3.

154.   The celebration of the Circumcision (January 1) is the eighth day of the nativity. Cf. Lk 2:21.

155.   Cf. Sg 8:6.

156.   As Winn points out, the reminiscences of the *Psalms* are too numerous in these stanzas to specify. Cf. Ps 18:1–2, 33:20, et seq.

157.   Mt 2:1–2, 9–11. Celebrated on January 6, the purpose of Epiphany is to reveal the mystery of the Incarnation.

158.   Recalls Mt 2:11 and the second stanza of the hymn *Crudelis Herodes Deum* of the vespers (Winn).

159.   The three symbolic gifts of the Magi.

160.   Cf. Ps 51:17.

161.   Beginning in the fourth century, this liturgical celebration commemorates the Presentation of Jesus to the Temple in Jerusalem (Winn).

162.   Lk 2:22–23. Mary's presentation of Jesus is the symbol of the unreserved oblation that every Christian must make of his soul to God (Winn).

163.   Lk 2:29–32. According to Winn, this stanza comes from the second strophe of the song of Saint Simeon known by the title "Nunc dimittis": "Quia viderunt oculi mei salutare tuum . . . "

164.   Cf. Lk 2:35.

165.   Cf. Prv 3:34; Lk 2:34.

166.   "Against you, you alone, have I sinned" (Ps 51:4).

167.   Cf. Ps 10; Sir. 10:12–13. Pride is the first of the seven cardinal sins.

168.   An allusion to the Protestant refusal of the Crucifix.

169.   Ps 86:15, 103:8, 116:5, 118:1–2.

170.   Cf. Jer 29:11.

171.   Lines 1–6, cf. Mt 27:45; Mk 15:33; Lk 23:44. According to Fizet, this sonnet was composed for Good Friday.

172.   Cf. Is 53:5; 1 Pt 2:24.

173.   "Father, forgive them; for they do not know what they are doing" (Lk 23:34). This poem, like the preceding one, represents the scene of the crucifixion, and in this particular case some of the last words of Christ on the Cross.

174.   Mt 27:29; Mk 15:17.

175.   Mt 27:30; Mk 15:18–20; Lk 23:35.

176.   "All you who" from the verse: "Is it nothing to you, all you who pass by? Look and see if there is any sorrow like my sorrow, which was brought upon me, which the Lord inflicted on the day of his fierce anger" (Lam 1:12).

177.   Cf. 1 Tm 2:6; Mt 20:28.

178.   I.e., the night of Good Friday.

179.   An allusion to the night before Good Friday, when Jesus was praying in the garden and his disciples could not stay awake. See Mt 26:36–46; Mk 14:32–42; Lk 22:40–46.

180.   Fizet points out that the hair shirt establishes a thematic link with the penitential periods preceding the holy week.

181.   Cf. Mt 27:51–54.

182.   Cf. Louis of Granada, "Troisiesme traitté lequel contient une briefve reigle de la vie Chrestienne et traitte particulierement des remedes plus principaux contre le peché," in *Le vray chemin*, fol. 465a et passim. Granada advocates severe treatment of the body in order to tame the passions of the flesh.

183.   Fizet notes that this sonnet evokes the visual image of a procession of penitents. During the reign of Henri III, there were great efforts to encourage and strengthen the faith of Catholics. Out of these efforts grew a considerable number of penitent brotherhoods. According to Winn, starting in 1583, there were three in Toulouse, one of which was the *confrérie des Penitents bleus*, founded in 1576 with the support of Cardinal d'Armagnac (cf. sonnet 107).

184.   Cf. 2 Tm 4:8; Jas 1:12.

185.   In order to produce the spiritual experience in the way that Ignatius of Loyola understood it, the devotee, as Winn explains, must *choose* and *desire* that alone, the only thing that leads to the end. Contemplation of the Scriptures serves then to provoke the desire to follow and suffer with Christ. It is this desire of solidarity with Christ, of this "conformity with divine will" (Granada, *Le vray chemin*, fol. 185a) that is treated in the first two stanzas.

186.   Cf. Jn 10:11; Heb 13:20; 1 Pt 5:4.

187.   This expression, repeated in line 13, recalls the Sermon on the Mount, notably the eight Beatitudes; cf. Mt 5:8.

188.   There are numerous verses in the Psalms that are about divine guidance. Cf. Ps 16:7, 25:9, 48:14, 73:24.

189.   Reminiscent of Ps 31:10–11, 38:4–8.

190.   For other representations of nature in Coignard's poetry, see sonnets 92, 111, and 126.

191.   Cf. Ps 68:5, 146:9.

192.   Cf. Ps 116:8; Is 35:10; Rv 7:17, 21:4.

193.   Winn maintains that this sonnet is constructed on the opposition between the person who lives in sin (alluded to through the image of the shackles, cf. Heb 2:15) and is thus exposed to divine wrath, which is symbolized by the "sharp thistles" of the second line (cf. Gn 3:18), and the shepherd, that is, the one who has found the Lord and delights in the grace of the merciful God.

194.   Cf. Ps 23:1–3, 95:7.

195.   Cf. Ps 23:4.

196.   Winn remarks that Coignard repeatedly accuses herself of the sin of *acidia*, which the church considered a serious offense. This condition, which she qualifies here as laziness (cf. also sonnets 13 and 75), is defined elsewhere as boredom, a discouragement that extinguishes the desire to serve God (cf. sonnets 5 and 34) and the will to live (cf. sonnet 52). It also manifests itself as a disgust for religious exercises, a spiritual torpor, and a lack of zeal, fervor, or love (cf. sonnets 4, 36, 87, and 90).

197.   Fizet notes that the irony of this effort to dissimulate, which manifests itself here in the desire to remain stoic vis-à-vis the pains of age and sickness, and which is founded on religious faith, is also one of the traps and the basis of many reproaches made about women throughout the centuries: dissimulation is a "typically feminine" characteristic, whereas silence is one of the virtues imposed on women by convention.

198.   Adaptation of Is 29:16 and 45:9 and Jer 18:6.

199.   Cf. 1 Chr 28:9; Ps 139:4.

200.   Cf. Ps 78:39; Mt 26:41.

201.   November 2.

202.   According to Winn, the author draws her inspiration here from the "Prayer for the Dead," generally addressed to the Virgin Mary.

203.   Saint Michael, protector of the church, captain of the celestial armies, intercessor and bearer of prayers to God.

204.   Cf. sonnet 77, lines 3–4 and note 185.

205.   For Fizet, this sonnet brings to mind the Psalms of David. The psalmist, concerned he will be abandoned in old age, feels persecuted by his enemies and prays that God will grant him some rest (cf. Ps 71:9–10). In Coignard's case, one cannot speculate about the experiences on which the sonnet might be based. In opposing this sonnet with sonnet 69, one can see the contradiction that plagues the poet: devotional composition (a weapon against sin, a target and victim of its enemies, and an instrument of faith) does not necessarily favor what it seems to promise: harmonious communion with God through personal and creative meditation (as declared in sonnet 14).

206.   Fizet argues that Coignard's failure to carry out these promises made from time

to time to put an end to this occupation of writing demonstrates the injustice on which the opinions of certain critics are based (cf. the introduction). It is not to amuse herself or to distract herself that she writes, but the fact that she can resist all kinds of obstacles put in her path is proof of a compulsion to write similar to the one that one recognizes without hesitation in the works of many "great" male poets of the period.

207.   Cf. Ps 18:27; Mt 23:12; Lk 14:11, 18:14.

208.   See sonnet 24, note 63.

209.   Cf. sonnet 82, line 11.

210.   While the first stanza alludes to the civil wars of the period, the second stanza addresses an entirely different issue and could be linked, Winn suggests, with Old Testament divine wrath (cf. Rv 8:5). Winn maintains, however, that most likely the author is making allusion here to a comet sighted in 1577, discovered by Tycho Brahe, whose observations on the comet of November 13, 1577, and on comets in general are recorded in a treatise published in 1588, *Tychonis Brahe Dani de mundi: aetherei recentioribus phaenomenis liber secundus qui est de illustri stella caudata ab elapso fere triente anni 1577, usq; in finen Ianuariji sequentis conspecta.* See Donald K. Yeomans, *Comets: A Chronological History of Observation, Science, Myth, and Folklore* (New York: Wiley Science Eds., 1991), 33–42.

211.   Cf. Ps 51:17.

212.   Cf. Lk 5:17, 6:19.

213.   Cf. Prv 13:24.

214.   Cf. Mt 24:12.

215.   For the final tercet, cf. Ps 105:1–2, 108:1–4. Fizet notes that the assurance with which Coignard affirms in this final stanza the future readers of her poems eclipses the desire expressed in sonnet 14 to enclose her verse. In light of this sonnet 90, the earlier sonnet may be rather a conventional expression of prudence and modesty in the face of the accomplishment of the "great" classical poets and, by allusion, of the Pléiade—appropriate sentiments for a woman of the period and even more so for a Christian woman.

216.   Cf. Ps 104:5–10.

217.   According to Winn, in the Bible, the city is often a symbol of pride, violence, and corruption. Cf. Ps 55:10–12.

218.   A paraphrase of Ps 148.

219.   Cf. Ps 97:11.

220.   Winn notes the fusion of Biblical imagery (cf. Ps 38:2) with that of the arrows (implied by the French nouns "traicts" and "coups") and bittersweet poison so characteristic of the Platonic tradition.

221.   Fizet maintains that this poem is the synthesis of the reflections appearing from time to time on the subject of the dichotomy between soul and flesh, mind, and body. See "The heavy chariot of depraved flesh" (sonnet 13), "this mortal chariot" (sonnet 38), "this carnal skin" (sonnet 76), "its carnal burden" (sonnet 81), and "the cloister of this body" (sonnet 129) for a few examples of the metaphors and attributes

associated with the flesh in Coignard's poetry. Nowhere do these examples exceed, however, the force of the expression of the first two verses of this sonnet, where the choice of words strongly suggests the association of the body with hell.

222.   Coignard is addressing herself to the flesh here.

223.   The "one" here is referring to the soul ("ame"), which is a feminine noun in French.

224.   Inspired by the Graeco-Roman pastorale and especially by the works of Virgil, Theocritus, and Horace, the elegy of the rustic life had numerous variations during the sixteenth century (Winn). For other pastoral evocations, see sonnets 79, 92, 111, and 126.

225.   Cf. 1 Sm 15:22.

226.   Cf. Ps 23:4; Prv 3:26.

227.   Leitmotif in the Psalms. Cf. Ps 40:4, 55:23, 56:4.

228.   Lines 9–11, cf. Mt 5:10–12.

229.   Cf. Ps 123:1–2.

230.   Saint Thomas's Day is celebrated December 21. According to Winn, it was the apostle Thomas who baptized husbands and wives and instructed them in faith.

231.   Decided at the beginning of 1570 (cf. P. Salies, "Gabrielle de Coignard: Poétesse toulousaine du XVIe siècle," 38), Coignard's marriage would have been celebrated December 21, 1570.

232.   Cf. Lk 23:35–37.

233.   Night is personified in this sonnet and is feminine in gender in French.

234.   The pairing of the mother and the night in this poem is revealing, as Fizet and Berriot-Salvadore have both noted. The night is portrayed as a place of refuge and of maternal protection—a parallel that suggests a certain feminine sensibility. See sonnet 10, notes 31 and 32.

235.   Cf. Lk 23:48–49.

236.   An allusion to Mt 11:28.

237.   Analgesic and opiate drugs arriving from Asia Minor and Egypt (Winn).

238.   The practice of bloodletting was still considered effective during the Renaissance.

239.   See Mk 16:19, Lk 24:51, and Acts 1:9–11. The Ascension marks the end of Christ's life on earth, when He ascended into heaven forty days after the resurrection.

240.   Cf. Acts. 1:9–11 for the last three stanzas.

241.   Widows of certain social status, like Coignard, often had numerous possibilities to remarry. Some women preferred, however, to remain widows (in accordance with ecclesiastical doctrine), a choice that often was not supported by the family, who was motivated by political and economic interests (Fizet). See Claudia Opitz, *Fauenalltag im Mittelalter* (Wienheim und Basel: Beltz, 1985), and "Life in the Late Middle Ages," in *A History of Women in the West*, vol. 2, *Silence of the Middle Ages*, trans. Deborah Lucas Schneider, ed. Christiane Klapisch-Zuber, gen. eds. Georges Duby and Michelle Perrot (Cambridge, Mass.: Harvard University Press, 1992), chap. 9, pp. 267–317.

242.   The refusal to remarry is justified on the one hand, Winn argues, by what Saint Augustine called *sacramentum*—the indissolvability of matrimonial union—and on the other hand, by the pursuit of virtue, which by certain standards stands in opposition to the state of marriage.

243.   "True pleasures"—contrary to "deceitful pleasures"—for Coignard would be the liberating communion with God (Fizet).

244.   Radegonde (519–87) was queen of France. Revolted by the crimes committed by her husband, Clotaire I, son of Clovis, who had unjustly condemned his brother to death, Radegonde fled to Saint-Médard, then to Tours, where she became a nun, and then to Poitiers, where she founded the monastery of Sainte-Croix (Winn).

245.   A city in France.

246.   Fizet notes that the color "azure" in this first tercet must allude to one of the multiple aristocratic brotherhoods of penitents that were founded at the time of the resumption of the civil wars in Toulouse, most likely the *Pénitents Bleus*.

247.   Apollo, i.e., the "Sun."

248.   Coignard is most likely referring here to Monsieur Emond, who is also the author of the "Seven sermons . . . Against the Seven Deadly Sins, for the Seven States of the City of Toulouse, Before the Seven Bodies of the Apostles at Saint Sernin" (Winn).

249.   Cf. Jas 5:16.

250.   Cf. Mt 8:20.

251.   Cf. Mk 15:24; Lk 23:34; Jn 19:23–24.

252.   Cf. Matt 27:48; Mk 15:36; Lk 23:36; Jn 19:28–29.

253.   Jesus was put into the tomb of Joseph of Arimathea, since, as a poor man considered a criminal, He did not have a right to His own (Fizet). Cf. Lk 23:50–53; Jn 19:38–42.

254.   The liturgy of the Assumption (which is celebrated on August 15) is the inspiration for the images in this sonnet.

255.   Icarus attempted to escape from Crete on wings made by his father Daedalus. Icarus flew so high that the sun melted the wax that attached the wings to his body, causing him to fall to his death in the sea. Cf. Ovid *Metamorphoses* 8.182–239, trans. A.D. Melville, ed. E.J. Kenney (Oxford: Oxford University Press, 1986), 176–78.

256.   Cf. Prv 16:5, 21:4.

257.   Sonnets 112 to 118 are all linked by a common theme of the last words of Christ on the Cross, which make up part of the liturgy for Good Friday. "Pater dimitte illis" is from the beginning of the verse "Father forgive them; for they do not know what they are doing" (Lk 23:34).

258.   Coignard gives here her interpretation of the well-known passage from Genesis 4:8–16. Winn maintains that the analogy developed in the second quatrain between the murder of Abel by his brother and that of Christ by the Jews shows the indivisibility of the Old and New Testaments and highlights the redemptive mission of Christ, who figures here as the new Abel appeasing divine wrath forever.

259.   Cf. Lk 23:34.

260.   From the verse "Truly I tell you, today you will be with me in Paradise" (Lk 23:43).

261. Cf. Mt 27:38, 44; Mk 15:27; Lk 23:39—42.

262. Cf. Jn 8:12, 9:5.

263. Cf. Ps 147:3; Is 53:5.

264. Lk 23:43.

265. "Woman, here is your son" (Jn 19:26).

266. Jn 19:25—27.

267. "My God, my God, why have you forsaken me" (Mt 27:46; Mk 15:34).

268. Leitmotif in the Psalms. Cf. Ps 146:7—9, for example.

269. Cf. Phlm 2:6—8.

270. Is 63:3.

271. "I am thirsty" (Jn 19:28). See also Ps 22:15, 69:21.

272. Cf. Jos 24:7.

273. Cf. Ex 17:6; Ps 114:8.

274. Cf. Ex 14:22; Ps 66:6.

275. Cf. Mt 26:27—30.

276. "It is finished" (Jn 19:30).

277. Cf. Rv 5:1, 6—8.

278. Cf. Rv 21:9.

279. Cf. Jn 15:4—10.

280. According to Fizet, this sonnet summarizes the ensemble of the seven poems on the last seven words of Christ. Thus, the first verse refers back to sonnet 112, the fourth to sonnet 114, and the sixth to sonnet 113, whereas the other lines (with the exception of 9 and 10) speak of sacrifice in more general terms.

281. "Father, into your hands I commend my spirit" (Lk 23:46).

282. Lk 23:43.

283. Cf. Mt 27:35; Mk 15:24; Lk 23:34; Jn 19:23—24. See also Ps 22:18.

284. Lk 23:46.

285. Cf. Lk 4:18. See also Is 42:6—7.

286. The medical world of the sixteenth century believed that it was the humors—the six organic fluids of the human body—that influenced one's well-being. Such a belief explains the recourse to bloodletting in sonnet 103 (Fizet).

287. This is the second allusion Coignard makes to her daughters in this collection. The first reference is in sonnet 11, line 2.

288. Cf. 1 Cor 6:2; Rv 7:4—8, 21:12.

289. For the last two stanzas (lines 10—14), cf. Rv 7:9—10.

290. Winn explains that in the French bestiaries of this period, the salamander figures frequently in the part that treats the four elements. It represents fire. It is also the emblem of Francis I, the symbol of power and of the invincibility of the man who is under God's protection (cf. Dn 3:8—30). Cf. Aristotle, *Historia animalium* line 552b 16 (Trans. D'Arcy Wentworth Thompson. Oxford: Oxford University Press, 1910).

291. "Deceptive" (or "false" if translated literally) because of the chameleon's ability to change its appearance and its associations with dissimulation.

292. Cf. Ex 17:6.

293. Fizet comments here that for Coignard, life itself is a cruel exile from both her husband and God.

294. Athena, the goddess of wisdom and warfare, was a master in the art of weaving.

295. Cf. Theocritus, "The Distaff," idyll 28 in *The Idylls of Theocritus: A Verse Translation*, trans. Thelma Sargent (New York: W. W. Norton & Co., 1982), 115–16; Ronsard, "La quenoille," in *Le second livre des Amours*, vol. 1 of *Oeuvres Complètes* (Paris: Gallimard, 1950), 168; Catherine des Roches "A ma quenoille," in *Les Oeuvres*, ed. Anne Larsen (Geneva: Droz, 1993), 292.

296. In this sonnet, and in sonnet 123, it is clear, as Fizet also remarks, that the distaff is a metaphor for the poet's pen.

297. According to Ovid's *Metamorphoses* 2.6.1–145, Arachne, counted among the best weavers in Asia Minor, surpassed Athena's skills, provoking the anger of the goddess because of the talent she demonstrated in a contest that Athena had organized in order to expose the deficiencies and errors of mortals. Having been punished, Arachne hanged herself and was transformed, out of pity, into a spider by the goddess and not, as Coignard tells it, by Jupiter (Fizet).

298. This sonnet, as well as the preceding one, has received much critical attention, not only because of the importance of the distaff in women's literature of the Renaissance, but also because Coignard modifies the original story. As Winn explains, Coignard silences the contrition of Pallas and attributes to Jupiter, and not to the goddess as in the original legend, the metamorphosis of the ingenious spinner into a spider (lines 130–46), underlining in this way the support granted by God to those who serve Him (an idea developed in the last strophe). While the legend insists on the pride of the young girl who dares to proclaim herself the equal of the weaver of Olympia (lines 6–43)—an attitude that merits punishment in the sacred texts that Coignard claims to adhere to in her world (cf. Prv 16:5)—Coignard accentuates the humility and the virtue of Arachne that she contrasts with the wicked desire of those who are "great." The identification with Arachne (who is portrayed here as the innocent victim) and also with the Psalmist who invokes Yahweh in order to be avenged for his persecutors leads one to think that Coignard alludes here to her own production; cf. sonnet 127. See Paula Sommers, "Gendered Distaffs: Gabrielle de Coignard's Revision of Classical Tradition," *Classical and Modern Literature* 18, no. 13 (spring 1998), 203–10; "Female Subjectivity and the Distaff: Louise Labé, Catherine des Roches, and Gabrielle de Coignard," *Explorations in Renaissance Culture* 25 (1999): 139–50.

299. Cf. Prv 3:34; Jas 4:10; 1 Pt 5:5–6.

300. On this notion of will, see sonnets 77, 85, and 128.

301. Cf. Ps 46:1, 62:7, 91:2, 94:22, 144:2.

302. Celebrated on November 11.

303. 1 Tm 6:15; Rv 17:14, 19:16.

304. Saint Martin (326–97), having shared his coat with a destitute man (the night

after which he was converted when Christ appeared to him wearing the half of the coat he had given), was known above all for his kindness toward and protection of the poor.

305.   This expression of disappointment could refer to a number of events. Winn suggests that it might be an allusion to a frustrated desire for a brilliant career, cf. sonnets 42, 86, and 123. Fizet considers this stanza a suggestion that the author seems to have participated in a more worldly life than she professes to at the moment she is writing her sonnets.

306.   For lines 12 and 13, cf. Ps 119:135. For line 12, cf. also Ps 25:4, 86:11, 119:33–36. For line 13, cf. Ps 27:9, 31:16, 67:1, 69:17.

307.   Cf. Ps 19:9–11.

308.   Pierre de Ronsard died on December 27, 1585. Coignard composed this poem shortly before her own death.

309.   Apollo, god of the sun, music, and poetry, was also evoked, Fizet notes, by Ronsard in his *Derniers Vers*, composed on his deathbed and published posthumously in 1586. The comparison of the "prince of poets" with the Greek god is obvious.

310.   Mount Parnassus is dedicated to Apollo and the Muses.

311.   Cf. Jb 19:26; 1 Cor. 13:12.

SERIES EDITORS'
BIBLIOGRAPHY

Note—Items listed in the volume editor's bibliography are not repeated here.

PRIMARY SOURCES

Alberti, Leon Battista. *The Family in Renaissance Florence.* Translated by Renée Neu Watkins. Columbia, S.C.: University of South Carolina Press, 1969.

Arenal, Electa, and Stacey Schlau, eds. *Untold Sisters: Hispanic Nuns in Their Own Works.* Translated by Amanda Powell. Albuquerque, N.M.: University of New Mexico Press, 1989.

Astell, Mary. *The First English Feminist: Reflections on Marriage and Other Writings.* Edited and with an introduction by Bridget Hill. New York: St. Martin's Press, 1986.

Atherton, Margaret, ed. *Women Philosophers of the Early Modern Period.* Indianapolis, In.: Hackett Publishing Co., 1994.

Aughterson, Kate, ed. *Renaissance Woman: Constructions of Femininity in England: A Source Book.* London and New York: Routledge, 1995.

Barbaro, Francesco. *On Wifely Duties.* Translated by Benjamin Kohl. In *The Earthly Republic,* edited by Benjamin Kohl and R.G. Witt, 179–228. Philadelphia: University of Pennsylvania Press, 1978.

Behn, Aphra. *The Works of Aphra Behn.* 7 vols. Edited by Janet Todd. Columbus, Ohio: Ohio State University Press, 1992–96.

Boccaccio, Giovanni. *Famous Women.* Edited and translated by Virginia Brown. The I Tatti Renaissance Library. Cambridge, Mass.: Harvard University Press, 2001.

———. *Corbaccio or the Labyrinth of Love.* Translated by Anthony K. Cassell. 2d rev. ed. Binghamton, N.Y.: Medieval and Renaissance Texts and Studies, 1993.

Cerasano, S. P., and Marion Wynne-Davies, eds. *Readings in Renaissance Women's Drama: Criticism, History, and Performance 1594–1998.* London and New York: Routledge, 1998.

Christine de Pizan. *The Treasure of the City of Ladies.* Translated by Sarah Lawson. New York: Viking Penguin, 1985. Also translated and with an introduction by Charity Cannon Willard. Edited and with an introduction by Madeleine P. Cosman. New York: Persea Books, 1989.

Clarke, Danielle, ed. *Isabella Whitney, Mary Sidney and Aemilia Lanyer: Renaissance Women Poets.* New York: Penguin Books, 2000.

Crawford, Patricia, and Laura Gowing, eds. *Women's Worlds in Seventeenth-Century England: A Source Book.* London and New York: Routledge, 2000.

Daybell, James, ed. *Early Modern Women's Letter Writing, 1450–1700.* Houndmills, England, and New York: Palgrave, 2001.

Elizabeth I: Collected Works. Edited by Leah S. Marcus, Janel Mueller, and Mary Beth Rose. Chicago: University of Chicago Press, 2000.

Female and Male Voices in Early Modern England: An Anthology of Renaissance Writing. Edited by Betty S. Travitsky and Anne Lake Prescott. New York: Columbia University Press, 2000.

Ferguson, Moira, ed. *First Feminists: British Women Writers 1578–1799.* Bloomington, Ind.: Indiana University Press, 1985.

Galilei, Maria Celeste. *Sister Maria Celeste's Letters to her father, Galileo.* Edited and translated by Rinaldina Russell. Lincoln, Neb., and New York: Writers Club Press, 2000.

Gethner, Perry, ed. *The Lunatic Lover and Other Plays by French Women of the 17ᵗʰ and 18ᵗʰ Centuries.* Portsmouth, N.H.: Heinemann, 1994.

Glückel of Hameln (1646–1724). *The Memoirs of Glückel of Hameln.* Translated by Marvin Lowenthal. New introduction by Robert Rosen. New York: Schocken Books, 1977.

Humanist Educational Treatises. Edited and translated by Craig W. Kallendorf. The I Tatti Renaissance Library. Cambridge, Mass.: Harvard University Press, 2002.

Joscelin, Elizabeth. *The Mothers Legacy to Her Unborn Childe.* Edited by Jean leDrew Metcalfe. Toronto: University of Toronto Press, 2000.

Kaminsky, Amy Katz, ed. *Water Lilies, Flores del agua: An Anthology of Spanish Women Writers from the Fifteenth Through the Nineteenth Century.* Minneapolis, Minn.: University of Minnesota Press, 1996.

Kempe, Margery. *The Book of Margery Kempe.* Translated and edited by Lynn Staley. A Norton Critical Edition. New York: W.W. Norton, 2001.

Kors, Alan C., and Edward Peters, eds. *Witchcraft in Europe, 400–1700: A Documentary History.* Philadelphia: University of Pennsylvania Press, 2000.

Krämer, Heinrich, and Jacob Sprenger. *Malleus Maleficarum* (ca. 1487). Translated by Montague Summers. London: Pushkin Press, 1928. Reprint, New York: Dover, 1971.

Marguerite d'Angoulême, queen of Navarre. *The Heptameron.* Translated by P. A. Chilton. New York: Viking Penguin, 1984.

Mary of Agreda. *The Divine Life of the Most Holy Virgin.* Abridgment of *The Mystical City of God.* Abridged by Fr. Bonaventure Amedeo de Caesarea, M.C. Translated from the French by Abbé Joseph A. Boullan. Rockford, Ill.: Tan Books, 1997.

Myers, Kathleen A., and Amanda Powell, eds. *A Wild Country out in the Garden: The Spiritual Journals of a Colonial Mexican Nun.* Bloomington, Ind.: Indiana University Press, 1999.

Russell, Rinaldina, ed. *Sister Maria Celeste's Letters to Her Father, Galileo.* San Jose and New York: Writers Club Press, 2000.

Weyer, Johann. *Witches, Devils, and Doctors in the Renaissance: Johann Weyer, De praestigiis daemonum.* Edited by George Mora with Benjamin G. Kohl, Erik Midelfort, and

Helen Bacon. Translated by John Shea. Binghamton, N.Y.: Medieval and Renaissance Texts and Studies, 1991.

Wilson, Katharina M., ed. *Medieval Women Writers.* Athens, Ga.: University of Georgia Press, 1984.

Wilson, Katharina M., and Frank J. Warnke, eds. *Women Writers of the Seventeenth Century.* Athens, Ga.: University of Georgia Press, 1989.

Wollstonecraft, Mary. *A Vindication of the Rights of Men and a Vindication of the Rights of Women.* Edited by Sylvana Tomaselli. Cambridge: Cambridge University Press, 1995. Also *The Vindications of the Rights of Men, The Rights of Women.* Edited by D. L. Macdonald and Kathleen Scherf. Peterborough, Ontario, Canada: Broadview Press, 1997.

Women Critics, 1660–1820: An Anthology. Edited by the Folger Collective on Early Women Critics. Bloomington, Ind.: Indiana University Press, 1995.

Women Writers in English, 1350–1850: 15 volumes published through 1999 (projected 30-volume series suspended). Oxford: Oxford University Press.

Wroth, Lady Mary. *The Countess of Montgomery's Urania.* Edited by Josephine A. Roberts. Tempe, Ariz.: MRTS, 1995, 1999.

———. *Lady Mary Wroth's 'Love's Victory': The Penshurst Manuscript.* Edited by Michael G. Brennan. London: The Roxburghe Club, 1988.

———. *The Poems of Lady Mary Wroth.* Edited by Josephine A. Roberts. Baton Rouge: Louisiana State University Press, 1983.

de Zayas, Maria. *The Disenchantments of Love.* Translated by H. Patsy Boyer. Albany, N.Y.: State University of New York Press, 1997.

———. *The Enchantments of Love: Amorous and Exemplary Novels.* Translated by H. Patsy Boyer. Berkeley: University of California Press, 1990.

SECONDARY SOURCES

Ahlgren, Gillian. *Teresa of Avila and the Politics of Sanctity.* Ithaca: Cornell University Press, 1996.

Akkerman, Tjitske, and Siep Sturman, eds. *Feminist Thought in European History, 1400–2000.* London and New York: Routledge, 1997.

Backer, Anne Liot Backer. *Precious Women.* New York: Basic Books, 1974.

Barash, Carol. *English Women's Poetry, 1649–1714: Politics, Community, and Linguistic Authority.* New York and Oxford: Oxford University Press, 1996.

Battigelli, Anna. *Margaret Cavendish and the Exiles of the Mind.* Lexington, Ky: University of Kentucky Press, 1998.

Beasley, Faith. *Revising Memory: Women's Fiction and Memoirs in Seventeenth-Century France.* New Brunswick: Rutgers University Press, 1990.

Bilinkoff, Jodi. *The Avila of Saint Teresa: Religious Reform in a Sixteenth-Century City.* Ithaca: Cornell University Press, 1989.

Bissell, R. Ward. *Artemisia Gentileschi and the Authority of Art.* University Park, Penn.: Pennsylvania State University Press, 2000.

Blain, Virginia, Isobel Grundy, and Patricia Clements, eds. *The Feminist Companion to Literature in English: Women Writers from the Middle Ages to the Present.* New Haven: Yale University Press, 1990.

Bloch, R. Howard. *Medieval Misogyny and the Invention of Western Romantic Love.* Chicago: University of Chicago Press, 1991.

Bornstein, Daniel, and Roberto Rusconi, eds. *Women and Religion in Medieval and Renaissance Italy.* Translated by Margery J. Schneider. Chicago: University of Chicago Press, 1996.

Brant, Clare, and Diane Purkiss, eds. *Women, Texts and Histories, 1575–1760.* London and New York: Routledge, 1992.

Briggs, Robin. *Witches and Neighbours: The Social and Cultural Context of European Witchcraft.* New York: HarperCollins, 1995. Reprint, New York: Viking Penguin, 1996.

Brink, Jean R., ed. *Female Scholars: A Tradition of Learned Women before 1800.* Montréal: Eden Press Women's Publications, 1980.

Brown, Judith C. *Immodest Acts: The Life of a Lesbian Nun in Renaissance Italy.* New York: Oxford University Press, 1986.

Bynum, Carolyn Walker. *Holy Feast and Holy Fast: The Religious Significance of Food to Medieval Women.* Berkeley: University of California Press, 1987.

Cervigni, Dino S., ed. *Women Mystic Writers. Annali d'Italianistica* 13 (1995) (entire issue).

Cervigni, Dino S., and Rebecca West, eds. *Women's Voices in Italian Literature. Annali d'Italianistica* 7 (1989) (entire issue).

Charlton, Kenneth. *Women, Religion and Education in Early Modern England.* London and New York: Routledge, 1999.

Chojnacka, Monica. *Working Women in Early Modern Venice.* Baltimore: Johns Hopkins University Press, 2001.

Chojnacki, Stanley. *Women and Men in Renaissance Venice: Twelve Essays on Patrician Society.* Baltimore: Johns Hopkins University Press, 2000.

Cholakian, Patricia Francis. *Rape and Writing in the Heptameron of Marguerite de Navarre.* Carbondale and Edwardsville, Ill.: Southern Illinois University Press, 1991.

———. *Women and the Politics of Self-Representation in Seventeenth-Century France.* Newark: University of Delaware Press, 2000.

Clogan, Paul Maruice, ed. *Medievali et Humanistica: Literacy and the Lay Reader.* Lanham, Md.: Rowman and Littlefield, 2000.

Crabb, Ann. *The Strozzi of Florence: Widowhood and Family Solidarity in the Renaissance.* Ann Arbor: University of Michigan Press, 2000.

Cruz, Anne J., and Mary Elizabeth Perry, eds. *Culture and Control in Counter-Reformation Spain.* Minneapolis: University of Minnesota Press, 1992.

Davis, Natalie Zemon. *Women on the Margins: Three Seventeenth-Century Lives.* Cambridge, Mass.: Harvard University Press, 1995.

Davis, Natalie Zemon, and Arlette Farge, eds. *Renaissance and Enlightenment Paradoxes.* Vol. 3 of *A History of Women in the West.* Cambridge, Mass.: Harvard University Press, 1993.

DeJean, Joan. *Ancients against Moderns: Culture Wars and the Making of a Fin de Siècle.* Chicago: University of Chicago Press, 1997.

———. *Tender Geographies: Women and the Origins of the Novel in France.* New York: Columbia University Press, 1991.

Dixon, Laurinda S. *Perilous Chastity: Women and Illness in Pre-Enlightenment Art and Medicine.* Ithaca: Cornell Universitiy Press, 1995.

Dolan, Frances, E. *Whores of Babylon: Catholicism, Gender and Seventeenth-Century Print Culture.* Ithaca: Cornell University Press, 1999.

Donovan, Josephine. *Women and the Rise of the Novel, 1405–1726.* New York: St. Martin's Press, 1999.

De Erauso, Catalina. *Lieutenant Nun: Memoir of a Basque Transvestite in the New World.* Translated by Michele Ttepto and Gabriel Stepto, with a foreword by Marjorie Garber. Boston: Beacon Press, 1995.

Erickson, Amy Louise. *Women and Property in Early Modern England.* London and New York: Routledge, 1993.

Ezell, Margaret J. M. *The Patriarch's Wife: Literary Evidence and the History of the Family.* Chapel Hill, N.C.: University of North Carolina Press, 1987.

———. *Social Authorship and the Advent of Print.* Baltimore: Johns Hopkins University Press, 1999.

———. *Writing Women's Literary History.* Baltimore: Johns Hopkins University Press, 1993.

Fletcher, Anthony. *Gender, Sex and Subordination in England 1500–1800.* New Haven: Yale University Press, 1995.

Frye, Susan, and Karen Robertson, eds. *Maids and Mistresses, Cousins and Queens: Women's Alliances in Early Modern England.* Oxford: Oxford University Press, 1999.

Gallagher, Catherine. *Nobody's Story: The Vanishing Acts of Women Writers in the Marketplace, 1670–1820.* Berkeley: University of California Press, 1994.

Garrard, Mary D. *Artemisia Gentileschi: The Image of the Female Hero in Italian Baroque Art.* Princeton: Princeton University Press, 1989.

Gelbart, Nina Rattner. *The King's Midwife: A History and Mystery of Madame du Coudray.* Berkeley: University of California Press, 1998.

Goldberg, Jonathan. *Desiring Women Writing: English Renaissance Examples.* Stanford: Stanford University Press, 1997.

Goldsmith, Elizabeth C. *Exclusive Conversations: The Art of Interaction in Seventeenth-Century France.* Philadelphia: University of Pennsylvania Press, 1988.

———, ed. *Writing the Female Voice.* Boston: Northeastern University Press, 1989.

Goldsmith, Elizabeth C., and Dena Goodman, eds. *Going Public: Women and Publishing in Early Modern France.* Ithaca, N.Y.: Cornell University Press, 1995.

Greer, Margaret Rich. *Maria de Zayas Tells Baroque Tales of Love and the Cruelty of Men.* University Park, Penn.: Pennsylvania State University Press, 2000.

Hackett, Helen. *Women and Romance Fiction in the English Renaissance.* Cambridge: Cambridge University Press, 2000.

Hall, Kim F. *Things of Darkness: Economies of Race and Gender in Early Modern England.* Ithaca, N.Y.: Cornell University Press, 1995.

Hampton, Timothy. *Literature and the Nation in the Sixteenth Century: Inventing Renaissance France.* Ithaca, N.Y.: Cornell University Press, 2001.

Hardwick, Julie. *The Practice of Patriarchy: Gender and the Politics of Household Authority in Early Modern France.* University Park, Penn.: Pennsylvania State University Press, 1998.

Harth, Erica. *Ideology and Culture in Seventeenth-Century France.* Ithaca, N.Y.: Cornell University Press, 1983.

———. *Cartesian Women. Versions and Subversions of Rational Discourse in the Old Regime.* Ithaca, N.Y.: Cornell University Press, 1992.

Haselkorn, Anne M., and Betty Travitsky, eds. *The Renaissance Englishwoman in Print: Counterbalancing the Canon.* Amherst: University of Massachusetts Press, 1990.

Herlihy, David. "Did Women Have a Renaissance? A Reconsideration." *Medievalia et Humanistica*, NS 13 (1985): 1–22.

Hill, Bridget. *The Republican Virago: The Life and Times of Catharine Macaulay, Historian.* New York: Oxford University Press, 1992.

Hobby, Elaine. *Virtue of Necessity: English Women's Writing 1646–1688.* London: Virago Press, 1988.

Horowitz, Maryanne Cline. "Aristotle and Women." *Journal of the History of Biology* 9 (1976): 183–213.

Hufton, Olwen H. *The Prospect before Her: A History of Women in Western Europe, 1: 1500–1800.* New York: HarperCollins, 1996.

Hunt, Lynn, ed. *The Invention of Pornography: Obscenity and the Origins of Modernity, 1500–1800.* New York: Zone Books, 1996.

Hutner, Heidi, ed. *Rereading Aphra Behn: History, Theory, and Criticism.* Charlottesville, Va.: University Press of Virginia, 1993.

Hutson, Lorna, ed. *Feminism and Renaissance Studies.* New York: Oxford University Press, 1999.

James, Susan E. *Kateryn Parr: The Making of a Queen.* Aldershot and Brookfield: Ashgate Publishing Co., 1999.

Jankowski, Theodora A. *Women in Power in the Early Modern Drama.* Urbana, Ill.: University of Illinois Press, 1992.

Jansen, Katherine Ludwig. *The Making of the Magdalen: Preaching and Popular Devotion in the Later Middle Ages.* Princeton: Princeton University Press, 2000.

Jed, Stephanie H. *Chaste Thinking: The Rape of Lucretia and the Birth of Humanism.* Bloomington, Ind.: Indiana University Press, 1989.

Kagan, Richard L. *Lucrecia's Dreams: Politics and Prophecy in Sixteenth-Century Spain.* Berkeley: University of California Press, 1990.

Kelly, Joan. "Early Feminist Theory and the *Querelle des Femmes.*'" In *Women, History, and Theory: The Essays of Joan Kelly.* Chicago: University of Chicago Press, 1984.

King, Carole. *Renaissance Women Patrons: Wives and Widows in Italy, c. 1300–1550.* New York and Manchester: Manchester University Press (distributed in the United States by St. Martin's Press), 1998.

King, Margaret L. *Women of the Renaissance.* Foreword by Catharine R. Stimpson. Chicago: University of Chicago Press, 1991.

Klapisch-Zuber, Christiane, ed. *Silences of the Middle Ages.* Vol. 2 of *A History of Women in the West.* Cambridge, Mass.: Harvard University Press, 1992.

Krontiris, Tina. *Oppositional Voices: Women as Writers and Translators of Literature in the English Renaissance.* London and New York: Routledge, 1992.

Kuehn, Thomas. *Law, Family, and Women: Toward a Legal Anthropology of Renaissance Italy.* Chicago: University of Chicago Press, 1991.

Kunze, Bonnelyn Young. *Margaret Fell and the Rise of Quakerism.* Stanford: Stanford University Press, 1994.

Levin, Carole, and Jeanie Watson, eds. *Ambiguous Realities: Women in the Middle Ages and Renaissance.* Detroit: Wayne State University Press, 1987.

Levin, Carole, et al. *Extraordinary Women of the Medieval and Renaissance World: A Biographical Dictionary.* Westport, Conn.: Greenwood Press, 2000.

Lindsey, Karen. *Divorced Beheaded Survived: A Feminist Reinterpretation of the Wives of Henry VIII.* Reading, Mass.: Addison-Wesley Publishing Co., 1995.

Lochrie, Karma. *Margery Kempe and Translations of the Flesh*. Philadelphia: University of Pennsylvania Press, 1992.

Lougee, Carolyn C. *Le Paradis des Femmes: Women, Salons, and Social Stratification in Seventeenth-Century France*. Princeton: Princeton University Press, 1976.

Love, Harold. *The Culture and Commerce of Texts: Scribal Publication in Seventeenth-Century England*. Amherst, Mass.: University of Massachusetts Press, 1993.

MacCarthy, Bridget G. *The Female Pen: Women Writers and Novelists 1621–1818*. Preface by Janet Todd. New York: New York University Press, 1994. (Originally published by Cork University Press, 1946–47).

Maclean, Ian. *Woman Triumphant: Feminism in French Literature, 1610–1652*. Oxford: Clarendon Press, 1977.

Matter, E. Ann, and John Coakley, eds. *Creative Women in Medieval and Early Modern Italy*. Philadelphia: University of Pennsylvania Press, 1994.

McLeod, Glenda. *Virtue and Venom: Catalogs of Women from Antiquity to the Renaissance*. Ann Arbor: University of Michigan Press, 1991.

Meek, Christine, ed. *Women in Renaissance and Early Modern Europe*. Dublin-Portland: Four Courts Press, 2000.

Mendelson, Sara, and Patricia Crawford. *Women in Early Modern England, 1550–1720*. Oxford: Clarendon Press, 1998.

Merrim, Stephanie. *Early Modern Women's Writing and Sor Juana Inés de la Cruz*. Nashville, Tenn.: Vanderbilt University Press, 1999.

Messbarger, Rebecca. *The Century of Women: The Representations of Women in Eighteenth-Century Italian Public Discourse*. Toronto: University of Toronto Press, 2002.

Miller, Nancy K. *The Heroine's Text: Readings in the French and English Novel, 1722–1782*. New York: Columbia University Press, 1980.

Miller, Naomi J. *Changing the Subject: Mary Wroth and Figurations of Gender in Early Modern England*. Lexington, Ky.: University Press of Kentucky, 1996.

Miller, Naomi J., and Gary Waller, eds. *Reading Mary Wroth: Representing Alternatives in Early Modern England*. Knoxville, Tenn.: University of Tennessee Press, 1991.

Newman, Karen. *Fashioning Femininity and English Renaissance Drama*. Chicago and London: University of Chicago Press, 1991.

Ozment, Steven. *The Bürgermeister's Daughter: Scandal in a Sixteenth-Century German Town*. New York: St. Martin's Press, 1995.

Pacheco, Anita, ed. *Early [English] Women Writers: 1600–1720*. New York and London: Longman, 1998.

Panizza, Letizia, ed. *Women in Italian Renaissance Culture and Society*. Oxford: European Humanities Research Centre, 2000.

Panizza, Letizia, and Sharon Wood, eds. *A History of Women's Writing in Italy*. Cambridge: Cambridge University Press, 2000.

Pantel, Pauline Schmitt, ed. *From Ancient Goddesses to Christian Saints*. Vol. 1 of *A History of Women in the West*. Cambridge, Mass.: Harvard University Press, 1992.

Perry, Mary Elizabeth. *Crime and Society in Early Modern Seville*. Hanover, N.H.: University Press of New England, 1980.

———. *Gender and Disorder in Early Modern Seville*. Princeton: Princeton University Press, 1990.

Petroff, Elizabeth Alvilda, ed. *Medieval Women's Visionary Literature*. New York: Oxford University Press, 1986.

Perry, Ruth. *The Celebrated Mary Astell: An Early English Feminist.* Chicago: University of Chicago Press, 1986.

Rabil, Albert. *Laura Cereta: Quattrocento Humanist.* Binghamton, N.Y.: MRTS, 1981.

Rapley, Elizabeth. *A Social History of the Cloister: Daily Life in the Teaching Monasteries of the Old Regime.* Montreal: McGill-Queen's University Press, 2001.

Raven, James, Helen Small, and Naomi Tadmor, eds. *The Practice and Representation of Reading in England.* Cambridge: University Press, 1996.

Reardon, Colleen. *Holy Concord within Sacred Walls: Nuns and Music in Siena, 1575–1700.* Oxford: Oxford University Press, 2001.

Reiss, Sheryl E., and David G. Wilkins, ed. *Beyond Isabella: Secular Women Patrons of Art in Renaissance Italy.* Kirksville, Mo.: Truman State University Press, 2001.

Rheubottom, David. *Age, Marriage, and Politics in Fifteenth-Century Ragusa.* Oxford: Oxford University Press, 2000.

Richardson, Brian. *Printing, Writers and Readers in Renaissance Italy.* Cambridge: Cambridge University Press, 1999.

Riddle, John M. *Contraception and Abortion from the Ancient World to the Renaissance.* Cambridge, Mass.: Harvard University Press, 1992.

———. *Eve's Herbs: A History of Contraception and Abortion in the West.* Cambridge, Mass.: Harvard University Press, 1997.

Rose, Mary Beth. *The Expense of Spirit: Love and Sexuality in English Renaissance Drama.* Ithaca, N.Y.: Cornell University Press, 1988.

———. *Gender and Heroism in Early Modern English Literature.* Chicago: University of Chicago Press, 2002.

Rosenthal, Margaret F. *The Honest Courtesan: Veronica Franco, Citizen and Writer in Sixteenth-Century Venice.* Foreword by Catharine R. Stimpson. Chicago: University of Chicago Press, 1992.

Sackville-West, Vita. *Daughter of France: The Life of La Grande Mademoiselle.* Garden City, N.Y.: Doubleday, 1959.

Schiebinger, Londa. *The Mind Has No Sex?: Women in the Origins of Modern Science.* Cambridge, Mass.: Harvard University Press, 1991.

———. *Nature's Body: Gender in the Making of Modern Science.* Boston: Beacon Press, 1993.

Schutte, Anne Jacobson, Thomas Kuehn, and Silvana Seidel Menchi, eds. *Time, Space, and Women's Lives in Early Modern Europe.* Kirksville, Mo.: Truman State University Press, 2001.

Shannon, Laurie. *Sovereign Amity: Figures of Friendship in Shakespearean Contexts.* Chicago: University of Chicago Press, 2002.

Shemek, Deanna. *Ladies Errant: Wayward Women and Social Order in Early Modern Italy.* Durham, N.C.: Duke University Press, 1998.

Sobel, Dava. *Galileo's Daughter: A Historical Memoir of Science, Faith, and Love.* New York: Penguin Books, 2000.

Spencer, Jane. *The Rise of the Woman Novelist: From Aphra Behn to Jane Austen.* Oxford: Basil Blackwell, 1986.

Spender, Dale. *Mothers of the Novel: 100 Good Women Writers before Jane Austen.* London and New York: Routledge, 1986.

Sperling, Jutta Gisela. *Convents and the Body Politic in Late Renaissance Venice.* Foreword by Catharine R. Stimpson. Chicago: University of Chicago Press, 1999.

Steinbrügge, Lieselotte. *The Moral Sex: Woman's Nature in the French Enlightenment.* Translated by Pamela E. Selwyn. New York: Oxford University Press, 1995.

Stephens, Sonya, ed. *A History of Women's Writing in France.* Cambridge: Cambridge University Press, 2000.

Stuard, Susan M. "The Dominion of Gender: Women's Fortunes in the High Middle Ages." In *Becoming Visible: Women in European History,* edited by Renate Bridenthal, Claudia Koonz, and Susan M. Stuard. 3d ed. Boston: Houghton Mifflin, 1998.

Summit, Jennifer. *Lost Property: The Woman Writer and English Literary History, 1380–1589.* Chicago: University of Chicago Press, 2000.

Surtz, Ronald E. *The Guitar of God: Gender, Power, and Authority in the Visionary World of Mother Juana de la Cruz (1481–1534).* Philadelphia: University of Pennsylvania Press, 1991.

———. *Writing Women in Late Medieval and Early Modern Spain.* Philadelphia: University of Pennsylvania Press, 1995.

Teague, Frances. *Bathsua Makin, Woman of Learning.* Lewisburg, Penn.: Bucknell University Press, 1999.

Todd, Janet. *The Secret Life of Aphra Behn.* London, New York, and Sydney: Pandora, 2000.

———. *The Sign of Angelica: Women, Writing and Fiction, 1660–1800.* New York: Columbia University Press, 1989.

Van Dijk, Susan, Lia van Gemert, and Sheila Ottway, eds. *Writing the History of Women's Writing: Toward an International Approach.* Proceedings of the Colloquium, Amsterdam, 9–11 September. Amsterdam: Royal Netherlands Academy of Arts and Sciences, 2001.

Waithe, Mary Ellen, ed. *A History of Women Philosophers.* 3 vols. Dordrecht: Martinus Nijhoff, 1987.

Wall, Wendy. *The Imprint of Gender: Authorship and Publication in the English Renaissance.* Ithaca, N.Y.: Cornell University Press, 1993.

Walsh, William T. *St. Teresa of Avila: A Biography.* Rockford, Ill.: TAN Books and Publications, 1987.

Warner, Marina. *Alone of All Her Sex: The Myth and Cult of the Virgin Mary.* New York: Knopf, 1976.

Warnicke, Retha M. *The Marrying of Anne of Cleves: Royal Protocol in Tudor England.* Cambridge: Cambridge University Press, 2000.

Watt, Diane. *Secretaries of God: Women Prophets in Late Medieval and Early Modern England.* Cambridge: D. S. Brewer, 1997.

Weber, Alison. *Teresa of Avila and the Rhetoric of Femininity.* Princeton: Princeton University Press, 1990.

Welles, Marcia L. *Persephone's Girdle: Narratives of Rape in Seventeenth-Century Spanish Literature.* Nashville, Tenn.: Vanderbilt University Press, 2000.

Whitehead, Barbara J., ed. *Women's Education in Early Modern Europe: A History, 1500–1800.* New York and London: Garland Publishing Co., 1999.

———. *Working Women in Renaissance Germany.* New Brunswick, N.J.: Rutgers University Press, 1986.

Willard, Charity Cannon. *Christine de Pizan: Her Life and Works.* New York: Persea Books, 1984.

Wilson, Katharina, ed. *An Encyclopedia of Continental Women Writers*. New York: Garland, 1991.

Woodbridge, Linda. *Women and the English Renaissance: Literature and the Nature of Womankind, 1540–1620*. Urbana, Ill.: University of Illinois Press, 1984.

Woods, Susanne. *Lanyer: A Renaissance Woman Poet*. New York: Oxford University Press, 1999.

Woods, Susanne, and Margaret P. Hannay, eds. *Teaching Tudor and Stuart Women Writers*. New York: Modern Language Association, 2000.

INDEX